Born in Yorkshire, Mike James has lived in West Sussex since 1960. He joined the army from school and later, the Merchant Navy, as a deckhand. Coming ashore, he worked for twenty-five years in civil aviation and twenty more as a train driver, before retiring. Mike James is a pseudonym.

JUST BE CAREFUL
WHEN YOU FLY, PETER

X

PAUL

For D and M and ground staff everywhere.

Mike James

_____

MAYFLY

AUSTIN MACAULEY PUBLISHERS™

LONDON • CAMBRIDGE • NEW YORK • SHARJAH

A CIP catalogue record for this title is available from the British Library.

ISBN 9781035812363 (Paperback)
ISBN 9781035812370 (ePub e-book)

www.austinmacauley.com

First Published 2024
Austin Macauley Publishers Ltd®
1 Canada Square
Canary Wharf
London
E14 5AA

My thanks to LR for his insufferable encouragement, without which this book would no doubt remain no more than a slacker's failed project.

Table of Contents

"For most gulls, it is not flying that matters, but eating."
Richard Bach, Jonathan Livingston Seagull

Prologue

Rain. Persistent. Drizzling. A cold the day could not shake off. There were times, plenty of them, when everything went according to plan. Today wasn't shaping up to be one of them, or so I thought. Turned out I was wrong. But for now, gazing out at the curtain of rain sweeping across the apron, it was a vision of Gino's renowned pork chop, rather than flying, that presented itself, evermore persistently, to my famished senses. Continued resistance was clearly futile: it was time for lunch.

Early autumn 1966. We had been dawdling in the Ramp office all morning waiting for the weather to clear. It hadn't and my ride, *Hotel Alpha,* the company's twin-engine Piper Apache, a recent addition to the fleet intended for crew taxi work and private charters, languished out there on the ramp, drooping like a stood-up date, the rain ricocheting from its olive drab paintwork.

Still relatively new to the airline business and working on the ground staff of the slightly shabby airline Spanavia, the novelty of work that was enjoyable enough to make it worth getting up for, had not yet worn off. Nevertheless, on that wet autumn morning, I was desperate to avoid the drive involved in a routine visit to Woodside, our maintenance airfield, an hour or so's drive away to the west. Actually, I was routinely anxious to avoid going anywhere in my travesty of a car, if it could possibly be avoided. An abomination that featured the aesthetics of a loaf of bread, the ride comfort of a cement mixer and represented much of what was wrong with the British motor industry. It was the sort of car that might get you from A to B, but if your destination was C, probably not. So, when Jimmy, *HA*'s skipper, offered me a lift, my hesitation in accepting was about equal to the life expectancy of a flashbulb at the BAFTAs.

That I'd hesitated even momentarily sprang from the uncomfortable recollection of my last ride with him. It had been in the company of Sid Bardwell, Jimmy's instructor for his conversion course on the Apache. Sid, in his normal capacity as line captain, was a sight to behold and hardly one to inspire great confidence. His uniform looked like he'd worn it to fight a bear, the collars of his invariably-grey shirts curled like brandy snaps and his shoes would disgrace a gravedigger. On his right cheekbone, a livid purple scar testified to a motorcycle accident in his youth, and beneath its ever-present five o'clock shadow, his complexion was the texture and colour of a bowl of workhouse porridge. However, it was the spasms that really caught the attention; every minute or so his face would contort in the direction of the scar, and this would be accompanied by a writhing muscle spasm that passed Mexican-wave fashion across his shoulders. This affliction was particularly unfortunate as, ever the conscientious one, Sid had been in the practise of visiting the cabin during flights to chat to the passengers. That was until Fineman, the chief pilot, with exceedingly gentle diplomacy, asked him to please confine his contact with the customers to the public address, as his appearance was scaring the hell out of them.

But Sid was a fine pilot and the moment he sat at the controls of an aeroplane, he was at home, his afflictions evaporated and he became every inch the assured airman.

There had been four of us on that earlier flight, Jimmy and Sid up front, me and Brian, a positioning first officer, in the rear seats. What hadn't been made clear to us in the back was that this was to be a training flight, so there would be some "manoeuvres" on the way. These proved to be routine—except for the last one. First, Sid hauled *HA* up seven thousand feet, through scattered cloud, into clear air somewhere over Boscombe Down. Here, we skimmed low across a blanket of altostratus, so low that our prop tips whipped smoking strands from it; while above us, cirrocumulus dotted the deepening blue towards the boundary of the troposphere. Having "slipped the surly bonds" we found ourselves briefly in John McGee country. Sadly, his dance had proved a short one, as ours was to be today—albeit narrowly less tragically.

Now, Sid revealed his intention to demonstrate the Apache's admirable ability to recover from something he called 'an asymmetric power-on spin.' This involved enjoining Jimmy to place his hands in his lap and to keep them there. Sid then throttled back the port engine. The aircraft's starboard wing immediately reared up, the nose pitched down and the aircraft began a vicious spin to the left, tightened by the power being delivered from the right engine. In the back, we were still sorting out our disorientation when Jimmy, giving in to an atavistic desire for survival, grabbed the controls to initiate recovery.

It was a natural enough reflex, and one I wholeheartedly shared, but Sid was having none of it. We climbed back up to seven thousand feet and the procedure was repeated, only Jimmy was ordered *on no account* to intervene. This time the spin was allowed to develop fully: *HA* winged over and plunged back towards the clouds in a sickeningly-tight spiral, a disorientating grey mist descending before my eyes. Then, as Sid controlled the spin and just as I began to regain my senses, he initiated recovery, the effect of which was nearly as bad as the spin had been. Emerging just below the cloud base, having arrested the aircraft's rotation, he began to haul *AH* out of the dive, the G-force crushing us instantly down in our seats and back into semi-consciousness. Then, as we levelled out, sentience returning, a flash of silver to port caught my eye. For an instant, I registered the image of an RAF Lightening with the masked face of its pilot turned towards us. Then it was gone, rocketing silently past on a reciprocal course, a few scant feet from our wingtip. A second or so later the sound hit us. The Apache bucked in the slipstream and a distinct smell of kerosene pervaded the cabin, as we sat open-mouthed and silent.

Sid said, 'Oops.'

There would be nothing like that on today's trip however, a sedate cruise was promised.

Jimmy had given up a job in the Cairngorms after his crop-dusting Piper Pawnee suffered a scary low-altitude engine failure. Vowing never to fly single-engine aircraft ever again, he had joined our outfit, flying the twin-engine Apache, in the hope of eventual promotion to the big stuff. That day, he and his co-pilot Chris, a teacher who flew part-time with us, were to take *AH* on a round trip to Woodside and there would be a seat for me. But the weather was lousy: warm front conditions overhead had drawn the cloud base down to 400 feet and left it there while it went for a cup of tea.

As Jimmy knew only too well, this was instrument flying weather. But he was reluctant to fly in cloud today—no doubt a hangover from his barnstorming, crop-dusting days. After all, you don't get much cloud at the height of a field of barley. But a couple of hours later, with no sign of a break in the overcast, I finally gave in to my ravening appetite and, after asking Jimmy to call me on the canteen telephone should the weather clear and they decide to go, I legged it out it into the rain to what was to prove the most important lunch of my life.

Captain Lightfoot

In Ops, I am sitting in Bernie's office getting a lugubrious optical going-over. To his left, Jed is flying wingman, doing the questions. Bernie, or Captain Lightfoot as he likes to be addressed when important visitors are in the building, used to fly, but a dodgy ticker cost him his ticket. So now he only uses the captain title to add gravitas to his business meetings. He is HCA's operations manager, and Jed his assistant. They're cronies from the outfit's beginnings back in Manchester; they share the same flat vowel sounds and gruff mateyness. Today, despite a CV that looks like a Job Centre training aid for difficult-to-place sociopaths, I have managed to wangle an interview for one of the operations duty officer vacancies. At this point the jury's still out, though I see from his expression that Bernie is already metaphorically fingering the black cap.

I have been out of the ops game for some time, slogging away of late on the nightshift of an airline catering company. I love it like you'd love finding a smudge on your chest X-ray, which is a distinct possibility given the working conditions. Just one of the job's legion disadvantages is that every morning a dozen trucks back up to the loading dock, their filthy diesel engines pumping carcinogens in to the frosty air as we wrestle to load the catering carts. Add to that the utter tedium of the job and you also have the level of my engagement with it. I am not above losing my *sangfroid* in a tight spot, but a dropped tray of mille-feuille or a short-shipped box of plastic cutlery really doesn't trigger it. They've probably noticed that. Basically, I just want out; to get back behind a desk with all the comforts of a warm office and air that hasn't been flossed through a dozen twelve-cylinder diesel engines before I get to breath it. At the very least, HCA represents a golden opportunity for several more years of useful life and possibly the resumption of what in my lighter-headed moments I like to call my career. It is now more than twenty-five years since that rainy day in the ramp office, so I probably have a great future behind me.

Jed is relaxed, sitting back, giving his paunch room to breathe, scratching at the stubble he cultivates to disguise that weak chin. He's asking most of the questions. It's easy stuff, not much above the level of, which end of the aeroplane do the pilots sit in? What letter does Quebec represent in the phonetic alphabet? He's probably thinking it's pretty close to lunchtime—his borborygmi sound like a tube train with failed brakes—so he just wants to get this done. It's Bernie who cuts in, sharpening the relevance of the questioning.

'What do you know about CAP371?'

'Er…' seems like a good place to begin.

'The crew duty regulations?'

'Ah…' CAP371 is the document number for the Civil Aviation Authority's rules on crew duty hours. I didn't recognise that number, but since he's already told me what it represents, I manage to waffle on about what I do know about the regulations. But just when I begin to think I've blagged that one, Bernie drops his head, hunches his shoulders, his expression morphing into something Churchillian, the rheumy eyes regarding me with scant enthusiasm from beneath a furrowed brow.

'What can you tell me about TAFs and METARs?'

I resist the temptation to make some daft remark about Welshmen, electing instead to bumble through an explanation of the difference between a Terminal Area Forecast and a Meteorological Weather Report. Judging by Bernie's look of mild surprise, I'm in the ballpark with that one. But he's not done yet. Jed is scribbling notes now. I don't like the look of that, it's beginning to seem a bit professional, something I've never been that comfortable with. I'm more inclined to a jazz-orientated, improvisational approach to aviation—not something that has always appealed as much to my previous employers. I'm right to be worried, for now Bernie leans his elbows on the desk to deliver the killer question.

'Flight planning, how much of that have you done?'

Aargh, my *bête très noir*. Though, as it happens, I have done a bit, a while ago now and quite badly as I recall, though nobody actually died—as far as I know. I just hate flight planning; I bemoan its arcane routings, loath its incomprehensible ICAO addresses, detest its recalcitrant flight levels and bewail its cryptic waypoints. I hate it like the McDonalds hate the Campbells, like Tom hates Jerry…you get the picture.

Bernie cuts through the floundering answer I've embarked upon: 'We use the Phoenix automated planning system.' *'Do we? Christ on a bike, that's a break. I know how to press buttons.'* 'You would be trained on its use, of course.' *'Another result. This is getting better.'*

No, it's not. Suddenly, the *coup de gras*: 'IF…' (I note the heavy emphasis. It's generally a bad sign when people address you in capital letters) '…we were to offer you a position, what references can you supply?'

Oh shite. It's not that there's anything particularly terrible about the many jobs I've done—it's just that, taken together and written down, the overall effect is terrible; the rap sheet of a failed Walter Mitty. At least there has been no actual criminality, unlike the shift manager at my current workplace; the one who'd picked me up on my missed entry in the flight programme and patronised me to death with a lecture on the importance of attention to detail; only for it to be discovered, shortly thereafter, that he was paying a little too much attention to whole sides of beef, which were mysteriously levitating out through the back door into his mate's van. One had to admit to a certain quiet *schadenfreude* when he was taken away for a serving of porridge to compliment the beef.

But there is no time for further conjecture; to employ a flying metaphor, Bernie's eyebrows are past V1, approaching rotation, in the silence following his question. Quickly cobbling together a web of disingenuity and promises to supply the required at a later date, I divert attention from references by asking about pay and conditions. It works; Bernie sketches out the details and the interview shambles to a close with him promising to let me know the result in a few days. Dishearteningly, there are other applicants to be seen. Anybody with a decent haircut and a couple of hours' recent flight watch experience is going to look better than me. But, nothing ventured, etc.

A couple of days later, the letter arrives: 'Dear Mr James, I am pleased to inform you that, blah blah blah…' Well thrash me granny with a five iron if I didn't get it. How? I'm not quite sure, but I don't care. I do get a nasty twinge halfway down the next paragraph when I stumble upon the bit about the offer being "subject to satisfactory references". However, if I have one attribute in spades, it is imagination, and I have all the imagination I need to imagine three decent references with semi-legible signatures, from defunct airlines. They won't of course be complete works of fiction but, like a Daily Mail headline, there will be a grain of unrecognisably-distorted truth buried somewhere in each one of them.

There followed a couple of weeks of refresher training and shadowing too tedious to recount, until the morning finally arrived when I took the duty officer's chair alone and unsupported for the first time in…nope, don't remember…the King of Ops for the next twelve hours. A quiet day ensued, where everything went according to schedule, or close to it. It was a mercifully quiet start but one rarely to be repeated, at least not during the high season of charter work, the summer months.

Pilots may strut their stuff at the very top of the aviation heap, where captains are virtual demigods, masters of all they convey. But no airline is run from a cockpit. That business, the day-to-day administration, is overseen from an operations room. Here large Perspex flight watch boards (now replaced by computer monitors and flat screens), display the day's programme. Each flight's times—schedule departure, actual departure, estimated arrival and actual arrival—are monitored and the figures entered on the board, along with load details and other aircraft information. The room is furnished with teleprinters (computer terminals now), air and ground radios, telephones and lots of paper— even today, forests of paper. Depending on the size of the airline, an ops room may be staffed by just one person, or dozens of staff. But, in ultimate charge of the whole of day's business, is the operations duty officer. He or she must monitor everything that every other department—passenger-handling, engineering, crewing, catering, the list is endless—does, to fulfil the ops duty officer's raison d'être, to keep the show going, no matter what.

It's basically stress on toast, with a frustration garnish and a side order of aggro, with seconds if you want it.

So, I had arrived—did I but know it—in the best and nearly the last job of my ramshackle career in aviation. What made HCA unique was the camaraderie that pervaded the company. In Ops, it was undoubtedly the influence of Bernie, and more so Jed, which set the informal, not to say louche tone and fostered that camaraderie. It was also the first company I had worked for where everybody, from Harry Tailor the managing director down to "Trotsky" our oik Nav Department clerk, was known by his or her first name, or nickname, a fact that appealed to my bolshy egalitarianism. We also had a good crowd of experienced pilots and cabin crew, already quite a cohesive bunch since many of them were drawn from a former pioneering airline I had worked with when I'd first started in aviation.

Starting

That start, twenty-five years earlier, had been triggered by an advertisement in the local paper, informing readers that the airline Spanavia was recruiting ship's papers clerks for the summer season at Racebridge, its main operating base. Since this was only five miles distant and I was unemployed, it sounded interesting, if a bit puzzlingly nautical. I was also broke, so the to-me handsome seventy-five quid a month the job offered was a clinching incentive. I knew little about aviation (there are those who would claim I still don't), beyond the fact that aircraft had wings and generally flew pointy end first. But I was encouraged by the advertisement's assurance that, though previous experience was useful, it was not a prerequisite: training would be given.

The letter I received in response to mine stated that Henry Penfold, the Traffic Superintendent, would be pleased to interview me for one of the vacancies. And one week later, so it proved, he really was literally pleased to see me. This was because, as I soon learned, the comfortably-rounded Henry Penfold, with his cropped fair hair, fresh complexion, gleaming eye and ever-ready smile, was a genial Toby Jug of a man. I was welcomed with a grin, a warm handshake and an injunction to grab a chair, delivered in a northern accent I was never quite able to locate geographically. In those days a thin, partially-fabricated CV was no bar to employment and Mr P (as he was ever-after addressed by me), passed quickly over this minor obstacle and on to a description of the duties expected of a ship's papers clerk.

This was what I learnt. Aircraft, being long and thin (I knew that bit already, actually), are highly susceptible to changes in their centre of gravity—normally somewhere near the middle of the wings—when loads are applied to either end. The job of the ship's papers clerk was to fill out a loadsheet, before each flight, which detailed not only the weight of everything on the aircraft, right down to the water in the toilet, but also showed how the weight of the payload was to be distributed down the length of the aircraft; this to ensure that it did not exceed the aircraft's limitations on weight or its trim range. This last part was worked out with a drop-line graph; starting at the top of the graph (the aircraft's basic index), each weight shown in the horizontal columns below effected the direction, incrementally, fore or aft, of a carefully-drawn line. Until, at the bottom of the graph, the aircraft's final trim would be arrived at, confined between two shaded sections which indicated the fore and aft no-go areas, (the literal paradigm of the "safe envelope.") Sometimes a form of slide rule would be used instead of a trimsheet. Nowadays, computers make short work of such tedious calculations.

There were many other forms—customs declarations, duty-free forms, passenger and cargo manifests, airwaybills, lots more—all of which comprised the ship's papers. The load and trim sheets (sometimes combined in one form) had to be signed by both the clerk who'd complied them and the captain, and all the other paperwork had to be in order before any flight departed. This was basically what the job entailed. Though much of this stuff was essentially bureaucratic crap, the compilation of loadsheets was a responsible task which, as I was eventually to find out, could have serious consequences if not executed diligently.

There was much else to learn but, though there would be a couple of weeks' classroom training before joining the twelve-hour shift system, very much more would be learned on the job. It was just the way it was done; you picked it up reasonably quickly, or maybe they wouldn't want you back next season. Only a select few were kept on as permanent staff at the end of their first summer. In any case, there were a limited number of permanent jobs and it might take two or three seasons to get one, even if you were competent. The same rule applied to the check-in staff, mostly female, working up in the terminal.

Eddy "Scaz" Butcher, who was from the "Pool" and spoke with a marked accent, took six of us for the brief *ab initio* training course. A faintly piratical figure, he was on the short side, satanically-bearded, with tufts of jet-black hair sprouting mad-professor-like above his ears, whilst on top he was shinily bald. His movement and speech were light and quick, both routinely masked by the smoke from his incessant Old Holborn roll ups. He was pleasant and easy-going and his classes were largely stress-free. So, it was easy to forgive him for "back-squadding" three of us for a further week on the spurious grounds that we might benefit from the extra tuition, when in fact, as he admitted later, we were quite competent. It was just that he fancied another week off shift.

The season was already gathering momentum and we often found our class shifted out of the busy Ramp Office, where we were just in the way, banished as often as not to an empty aircraft on one of the distant parks out towards the runway. My least favourite of these winged classrooms was the DC3 more commonly known as the Dakota or "Dak"; a tailwheel aircraft whose floor when on the ground sloped steeply up towards the flightdeck. It was an odd sensation to stand in the aisle with no reference to the horizon, leaning effortlessly forward at a near-forty-five degrees, with your feet together. But I found sitting at this angle, straining against the backward pull of gravity whilst working on our practise loadsheets, particularly uncomfortable and faintly nauseating.

The course was soon over, Scaz running us through the very basics of the business, before cobbling together a final exam and allocating us—semi-useless neophytes that we were—in ones and twos, to our shifts. I got the preternaturally even-tempered Jerry Hart's shift, which came with the ebullient young Alan Brightman, also doing ship's papers. In his second season and an aviation wonk since he was old enough to heft his spotter's binoculars, he was vastly knowledgeable about the business. Piers Doleman, tall, lean, phlegmatic, with a refined accent and a dry, understated wit that could be cutting at times, was a ramp dispatcher. At thirty-five and the second oldest on the shift after Jerry, when he wasn't chasing departures out on the ramp, occupied himself with the breeding of pigs on his isolated smallholding. Val, was the Movement Controller, quite as tall as Piers and possessed of an equally dry sense of humour, though there was also warmth beneath her worldliness. A couple of temporary recruits like myself made up our number and together we launched ourselves on the season, bonding quickly as we tackled the demands of crowded summer daily programmes or "mayflies", as they were universally known.

The mayfly was published on the evening prior to the day to which it applied and was a most important document. Consisting of one or two A4 pages, our working day revolved around the information it contained: each flight's destination, aircraft type and registration, whether it was passenger or freight (including expected loads), its scheduled time of departure (STD) and any special instructions. In short, the mayfly ruled our lives. It foretold the quiet times when our duties would be pleasant, and it presaged the unwelcome, when it might be better if your bad back were to come on. So, it would be natural to suppose that the greatest care would be taken over its compilation. That's what you might think. Every airline issued its own mayfly; some were reliable, some not so. But one in particular became notorious for being not only consistently inaccurate but frequently laughable: ours. It was one of the line's most glaring examples of parsimony (Spanavia was already a byword for cheapskatery), that it had employed a young, inexperienced school-leaver—who must have regularly bunked geography—to compile our mayflies, judging by the nonsense she produced. She knew nothing about aviation, her spelling was abysmal and the 24-hour clock was quite beyond her. But for what the line paid her, she worked very hard indeed. So, while the Grey Ones at HQ in EC2 counted the coppers they had saved, possibly by the light of a tallow dip, the airport was trying to make sense of our ridiculous flying programme. There was a DC3 for example, supposedly operating a round trip to Clairmont Ferrand. Not only was it empty both ways, but it arrived back one hour before it was due to depart. Strange and previously unknown aircraft types began to make their appearance: the BAC 707, the De Haviland Comic and the Ilyushin 1-11. There were some odd times too. Who knew what 01630 was supposed to be, let alone 2500hrs? Then there was the spelling and that geography, hilarious at times: Toulon became "Toolong" and, having never heard of the place, but possibly being more familiar with the work of Walt Disney, the capital of the Sudan was rendered as "Cartoon". The only reliably accurate feature of her mayflies was to be found in the top right-hand corner of each page—the date. Usually.

Before long, the company had to acknowledge its mistake; a more experienced hand was drafted in to instruct and assist our harassed novice and the mayfly soon began to make sense again. For a while, we had been a laughing stock. But, since Big Brother (the glossy outfit that was Racebridge's main tenant) had always treated our operation with the benign contempt of a long-suffering haughty neighbour, we were largely untouched by this latest episode.

More inclined to think in broad strokes rather than in tiresome detail, I quickly discovered that dispatching flights out on the apron, which I took every opportunity to do, was more to my taste than sitting in the Ramp compiling documentation. I had to stick with the desk job for now, but I determined to get myself out on to the tarmac, dispatching, just as soon as the thing could be wangled.

Some of the training could be quite perfunctory, there being little time and limited staff to conduct it. This certainly applied to one girl, new to the check-in staff (they were known as receptionists.) Arriving on stand to await an aircraft being towed over from the park for a flight, my gaze was met by an extraordinary sight. When aircraft were ready, it was normal practise to release passengers to the gate from the departure lounge, where they would be held to await boarding. Unfortunately, the rookie receptionist hadn't quite grasped the brief. On arrival at the gate prematurely and not seeing an aircraft, but spotting a set of steps, she had led her passengers out onto the apron and marched them up the steps, halting them at the top, just short of the twenty-foot drop to the ground, to await the aircraft. The logistical impossibility of taxiing an aeroplane on to a set of steps clearly had not come to cloud her breezy optimism. A couple of dozen nonplussed passengers hovered uncomfortably on the steps, whilst behind them a queue of twice that number snaked across the apron from the gate. With the receptionist grasping the handrails at the top, stoically preventing any of her charges from pushing past her to plunge into the abyss, and traffic below diverting round the crocodile strung out across the tarmac, they waited; a frozen tableau of pale passengers, rocking dangerously on the steps (the steadying jacks had not been deployed), as onlookers and wasters gathered to enjoy the spectacle.

Steps themselves were often at the centre of little dramas. On one occasion, rushing from the flight deck, having just got the loadsheet signed while everybody else on the aeroplane and the ground drummed their fingers, waiting for my signal to close up, I had launched myself at the door, only to find that some zealot had already removed the steps. Scrabbling frantically at the doorframe, I just managed to prevent myself plunging to the ground. Others in a similar position had not been so fortunate; if there were no actual deaths, there were certainly instances of broken limbs. On another occasion, not only were the steps removed but, by the time I'd made it to the rear passenger door, it had been closed and the aircraft was taxiing. I was then faced with the prospect of either a round trip to Dusseldorf, leaving the shift shorthanded, or getting off somehow. The latter was problematical, as the skipper pointed out when I arrived breathlessly back in the flight deck. He had GMC (Ground Movement Control) clearance to the holding point just short of runway and, as the flight was already late, he was not going to stop until he got there. Nor was he prepared to wait when he arrived there for steps to be trundled all the way out, even if Ground Movement Control were to allow such a thing—which was unlikely. There was only one solution: following the flight engineer back to the rear door, we opened it, deployed the escape rope from its stowage in the door and then, tucking my hat into my jacket and with the signed loadsheet clenched between my teeth, I swung out Tarzan-style on the rope into the battering slipstream of the engines.

It was not a pretty decent; almost immediately my thrashing feet tangled in the VHF aerials on the underside of the fuselage just below the door. Struggling to get free of them I bent one, before continuing shambolically to the ground, en route collecting rope burns to my hands, before landing bum-first in an undignified heap, where I let out a yelp and the loadsheet blew away across the airport. The final indignity, as I started on the long limping walk back to the office, was to be hustled on my way by a gritty blast of prop wash from the departing flight.

The crews of the many country's airlines we handled demonstrated a range of national characteristics, and it was as well to be at least aware of the differences. For instance, Spanish charter airlines seemed to operate nicely-painted aircraft that were discretely falling to bits beneath their pretty makeup. A shortcoming that was to some extent compensated for by the beautiful, black-eyed stewardesses they employed. Up on the flightdeck there would be a quite bewildering number of crew beyond the customary three, wearing enough refulgent braid to justify the aviator shades they'd all be wearing. Requesting fuel figures from them would produce something akin to the anarchy of parliamentary debate, with just a suggestion of *coup d'état*, before the figures, scribbled on a slip of paper, were held aloft above the scrum. By contrast, the Spanish schedule airlines operated efficiently, with modern well-maintained aircraft. Scandinavian crews could be lumped together under the label "polite and efficient" and rarely seemed to have any technical problems. Most skippers would sign a blank return loadsheet when they arrived and show no further interest in it, even when it was completed. "Iss goot" seemed to be their favourite phrase. You could tell a Swedish skipper there was a two-hour ATC delay, that his passengers were involved in a drunken fight in the departure lounge and that HM Customs had discovered a bale of suspiciously herbal tobacco in the hold, and you'd get, 'OK, ya, iss goot.' Rumanians were efficient but distant, said little, but were lethally generous with the plum brandy. The Italians were fine, with the possible exception of Luca Bonasera, Racebridge's Alitalia rep. Not a bad bloke, but one who's passionate and volatile nature would often get the better of him. The slightest hitch during the turn round of his flight would result in an explosion of chicken feathers, accompanied by much gesticulation and heated words in rapid-fire Neapolitan, during which we would just get on with the job. After departure, he would quickly calm down, becoming again his affable self—until the next time.

For some unaccountable reason, the Israeli Air Force, regular visitors to Racebridge with a C130 Hercules aircraft, were always reluctant to pay their handling charge and would go to some lengths to ensure they didn't. One strategy they often employed was to wait for the dispatcher to return to the office to pick up their invoice, then quickly request start up and taxi clearance and be gone before any funds could be extracted from them. One day, tiring of this shabby deception, Jerry forestalled the tactic by phoning Ground Movement Control and requesting they withhold the C130's taxi clearance until their tab was cleared. As it was my flight, I was then given the invoice and the unenviable task of extracting the money. Out on the cargo park, I discovered that the 'Herc' had engines running and appeared ready to leave. I drew up off the port wing so that the skipper could see me, waved the invoice at him and waited for him to throttle back. He did nothing of the sort, but simply sat there staring impassively at me as the forward door slowly opened and the air stairs deployed. Now, the distance between the forward door and the prop line on a C130 it seemed to me, was about equal to the distance I could throw a horse, with a chariot attached. And he was gunning the engines, just daring me to run the gauntlet. In the end, I had no choice but to either give up and admit defeat, or clamp my hands over my ears and sprint past the screaming turboprops to the door. I chose the latter and stood deafened and shaking on the flightdeck while the crew made an opera out of searching pockets and bags to scrape up enough cash to pay the bill. From the production they turned it into, you'd have thought I was stealing their kids' pockets money. With the fee finally counted into my hand with exaggerated punctiliousness, I was then required to re-run the gauntlet back to the van as the Herc strained against its brakes, threatening to mince me for my temerity.

Back in the office I told Jerry I didn't want to do that again. He said 'OK.'

I said 'Pardon?'

It was well-known that the underpowered Sud Aviation Caravelle needed lashings of throttle, when fully loaded, to overcome its inertia and encourage it to start taxiing. This was amply demonstrated on one particular evening.

The French outfit operating the aircraft had a regular handling contract with us and, as was the custom at that time, the aircraft was parked parallel to the boarding gate in the pier—right outside our office this evening. The turnaround was complete; there were seventy-odd passengers on board and a heavy fuel load. With the doors closed, Alan, who'd been dispatching it, sprinted into the office to get out of the cold and, as the Caravelle's appallingly noisy Rolls Royce

Avons spooled up, we stood together waiting for the aircraft to move. The anti-collision beacons began their sweep, nav lights lit; the ground crew disconnected the ground power unit's umbilical, pulled the chocks away, stepped clear of the wing and gave the arm-raised, thumb-up all-clear signal to the cockpit. The Avons' roar ascended to a scream. The aircraft rocked, but stayed put. The flight would not be officially off our hands until the wheels turned. They weren't turning. More power was applied. The noise was shattering, but at last the wheels began to turn.

'Off chocks,' called Alan to Val in Movement Control.

The aircraft lumbered forward a few yards then swung away towards the taxiway. As we stood idly watching, we became aware of a strange noise, reminiscent of waves crashing on a beach and growing in volume beneath the racket of the Avons. Alan and I looked at each other with 'Eh…?' expressions on our faces, until Val, almost diving out of the glazed cubical of Movement Control, alerted us to our peril.

As the Caravelle swung, using an enormous amount of power, the jet efflux was taking out, in succession, the office windows in the base of the pier. Starting with Engineering, it swept on to Navigation, then Operations, then Movement Control. We were next. Just in time, we dropped behind the protective bulk of the office counter as our own windows imploded and a blizzard of glass fragments, borne in on a kerosene-scented sirocco, raked the office.

Oblivious to the devastation it had reeked, the aircraft rolled away towards the runway in blissful ignorance, as Alan and I straightened in stunned silence amid a snowstorm of descending paperwork, to watch it depart. *Merci et au revoir*, mate. Within 24 hours Racebridge's parking arrangements were changed: thereafter, aircraft were required to park nose in on the stands: a classic example if ever the was one of shutting the stable door *après le* bleedin' *cheval a boulonné.*

The Movement Control cubicle—simply a glass-partitioned box in the office, which looked out onto the ramp—was in a somewhat exposed position, as Val was to discover on another occasion. The cabs of the beaten-up Morris pickups we used as ramp transport were rarely cleaned and often littered with junk. On one occasion, this proved particularly hazardous. When one of the lads, hurrying back to park outside the office, took his foot off the accelerator, the vehicle's forward lurch dislodged a Coke bottle from under his seat, which rolled neatly to a stop under the brake pedal. As he approached the office, he stepped on the brake—and nothing happened. The van hit the kerb, mounted it, vaulted the sunken path and hit Movement Control office window—where Val was seated—fair and square. The glass shattered as the van's wheels baulked against the sill, arresting its forward movement, the bonnet lurching to a halt in a cascade of pulverised glass a foot from Val's shins. With massive *sangfroid,* she eyed the ashen face behind the steering wheel, announcing: 'Derek, on chocks' and mimed making a note in her movement log.

The company had been operating a series of flights between Berlin—where we had temporarily based an aircraft and crews—and Palma. One summer evening, on the return trip to Berlin, the aircraft had developed a technical problem, necessitating a diversion to Racebridge, as there were only limited technical facilities available to us in Berlin. The intention was that the passengers and crew would transfer to another aircraft to continue their journey home.

The plan was a simple one: a nice clean tarmac transfer. The inbound aircraft would be parked alongside *November Papa* its replacement and the passengers would walk across the tarmac between the two. All that was required was a note to HM Customs requesting permission to swap the duty-free bar over, ditto the catering and baggage, produce a new loadsheet and that would be it.

Only, no, it wouldn't.

Once on stand, the crew split up; three flightdeck and two stewardesses went ahead to get *NP* ready, while the remaining three cabin crew stayed behind with the passengers. Nobody wanted this extra flight, not the loaders or the caterers or us in Traffic or Engineering, and least of all not the crew who just wanted to get back to Berlin. There is nothing quite like a common purpose to bring normally fractious departments together and within an hour the weary passengers were aboard their new ride.

On the flight deck the first officer was calling for start-up clearance, while on the ground the driver of the tug fidgeted in his cab awaiting clearance to push the aircraft back into the taxiway. An engineer beneath the aircraft's nose, attached to it by the umbilical cord of his headset, stood ready to direct the proceedings. Doors were closed, the steps pulled off and, as the anti-collision lights began to rotate, one by one the engines whined into life.

After that, nothing. The aircraft just sat there, engines even at ground idle emitting an ear-splitting roar; beacons sweeping the darkness and everybody willing the bloody thing to start moving. Time passed. The engineer seated himself on the tow bar, crossed his legs, stuck his hands in his pockets and, with an absent look on his face, listened in to the conversation on the flight deck. Two minutes later he stood up and pulled his headset off in disgust. Almost immediately the engines began to wind down. Steps were rushed up to the forward door and as an engineer brushed past me, he voiced the obvious: 'Bastard snag.'

I followed him up to the flight deck, where a short conference took place. The technical problem was abstruse and, for the time being at least, a show-stopper. It had yet to be decided what to do with the passengers whilst it was fixed. More engineers crowded onto the flightdeck, none of them communicative and nobody prepared to estimate how long the delay might be. So, it fell to me to make the final decision. I decided that disembarking the passengers and sending them up to the relative comfort of the departure lounge was the best solution, given that they had already endured a diversion and a two-hour delay. The engineers didn't give a rat's arse what I did and the crew had no objections, so I radioed the office and we went with my decision.

There was another flight requiring my attention and whilst I was away dealing with it, a receptionist was sent down from Check-In to escort the passengers to the lounge. Ten minutes later my radio emitted a static fart, followed by the unmistakable Scouse tones of Jill in Movement Control: there was a problem in the pier, somebody was ill. I should get over there.

As I reached the top of the stairs to the pier, my heart sank as I spotted the receptionist crouching beside a recumbent figure. Wendy was not one of my favourite people; a neurotic, dopey blond who'd managed to burn me with a fag within moments of our paths first crossing. In a situation such as this one, she was the last person I would have chosen to share it with.

Deiter Wolf looked to be seventy, maybe more. He lay on his back, head pillowed on his wife's coat, sightless eyes half closed, his face lilac, his lips blue. Somebody had removed his false teeth and placed them on the floor beside him; a small necessary indignity. A big fair-haired man was applying cardiac massage, too gently. The fallen man's wife knelt beside him holding his hand. I had very little medical knowledge and almost no experience of what lay before me, nevertheless it was clear that Herr Wolf was beyond any help we could render. Shaken, I got on the radio to request an ambulance.

Wendy stopped me: 'It's on its way.'

I was struck by how cool and collected she was (because I wasn't) as she crouched beside the stricken Frau Wolf, laying a comforting arm across her shoulders and speaking quietly to her. We exchanged the briefest of glances, tacitly agreeing the diagnosis. I found that Wendy's calmness had a calming effect on me. I had misjudged her.

The sublingual nitro-glycerine administered by Herr Wolf's wife as the pain hit, patently hadn't worked. We stood back while the ambulance men went through the motions; and when the fruitless rituals of resuscitation had been satisfied, Wendy stayed with the widow whilst I went back to organising the turnaround.

But on reaching the Ramp office another shock awaited me—*November Papa* was serviceable after all and ready for re-boarding. As I got on with the business of the turnaround, registering out of the corner of my eye the little group precessing to the ambulance with the loaded gurney—Wendy still in attendance on the wife—it dawned on me that I had sent a tired old man with a bad heart up a long flight of stairs and a long walk to the terminal, for no reason at all. I couldn't have known of course, but had I waited just a little longer to make the decision, he might have stayed in his seat and at least made it home. *Es tut mir leid, Herr Wolf.*

It had been a long day, but the work was almost done. I had one more aircraft to meet and my share of the day's movements would be complete. Standing at the window of the Ramp office I watched as the DC3—my DC3—taxied past, heading to stand.

From Movement Control Lynn called, 'Find out if he's night-stopping, I've got to book the hotel.'

Reaching its designated spot, the DC3 swung to the right to bring it parallel with the pier—and that was when everything went into slow motion, the way catastrophes do.

It was strangely graceful the way the left landing gear folded and the aircraft pitched down onto its port wing. Open-mouthed, I watched as the prop hit the ground, sheared off the hub and, still spinning, climbed over the top of the aircraft, opening it up like a tin opener, before dropping down on the other side to spin away down the taxiway, growing smaller as the blades rolled up until, its momentum finally exhausted, it fell over with a loud clang.

'Yep, he's decided to night-stop,' I yelled and sprinted for the stricken aircraft, which according to my information carried thirty passengers. Though I was nearest to the incident, others were converging on the scene. But before anybody could reach it, the aircraft's passenger door was flung open and a woman appeared. Without waiting for boarding steps, she hitched her skirt, kicked off her shoes, jumped the short distance to the ground and legged it into the pier, never to be seen again. She was the stewardess. She didn't look back once. A more complete abandonment of her duty it would be hard to imagine.

Lots of helping hands got the passengers off. Thankfully, there had been no sign of fire, nevertheless within a couple of minutes a brace of fire trucks had *hoo-hawed* over to stand by with foam. The aircraft's engines had been shut down immediately and the situation brought quickly under control. It was only when all the passengers were off, that the co-pilot made an appearance to inform us that his skipper was missing, having exited the aircraft on the tail end of the evacuation. He was eventually located in the met office, blindly studying weather charts, apparently in shock.

Only later did we learn what had happened to him. One of the features of the American Wright Cyclone engines that power the DC3, is that they rotate counter-clockwise. Thus, when *SL*'s left propeller parted company with its engine, it spun inwards towards the fuselage. Unfortunately, the props on a DC3 are aligned with the cockpit and it was not unknown for a shearing left prop to remove the legs of the pilot in the left-hand seat. This was what had so nearly happened in this case; the 350lb prop, spinning at whatever RPM, had cut through the side of the aircraft as though through tin foil. But as the scything blade descended towards the skipper's legs, its downward momentum had been arrested when the tip of the prop struck the solid mass of the cockpit's centre console, so that it delivered no more than the lightest flick across the pilot's knees, before whirring away on its travels. Apart from some Jackson Pollock-pattern bruising, the skipper's knees survived the incident rather well. As did the aircraft; the DC3, a famously rugged old bus, sat on the park until a new wing and prop could be fitted and the damage to her skin and undercarriage patched up, then she was flown away to her base, apparently little the worse for the experience. Whether the same could be said of the skipper, or indeed the fleeing stewardess, I have no information.

Aviation was a child that had foregone the pleasures of growing up, forced to premature maturity by war, commercial necessity and the sheer speed of technological advance. Because this was so, many of the pioneers of aviation were still active among us at that time. Perhaps not the first generation who had flown the rattling bi-planes and who's only qualifications were supreme confidence, sheer bravado and a silk scarf. But, certainly the second generation, who'd learnt not only how to fly newer and faster machines, but also, of necessity, how to fight in them. Thus, in any gathering of pilots, such as in the airlines, there was still to be found some of these characters.

Yet, there is no common definable factor to identify airmen, not even, astonishingly, a universal love of flying. To some it is no more than job, while to others it is a way of life. They might be good at it—very good sometimes—or just capable, or even, occasionally, incompetent. They are often good natured, but just as likely to be ill-tempered. They are fat, thin humorous, dour, engaging, banal. And, since we were obliged to work with them during the least favourite part of their day—while stuck on the ground with service personnel swarming all over their aircraft—it behoved us ramp dispatchers to deploy sly diplomacy, if not outright cunning, in the performance of our duty. For we were necessarily pushing for departure, without appearing in any way to hustle the crew—especially the flight deck. More especially, the captain.

Among what was an already-colourful group, the exuberant Danny "Boy" Stanton nevertheless stood out from the crowd. He was unpredictable, flamboyant, unquestionably laddish and daring—the latter quality not often welcomed in airline flying. But as was readily acknowledged by his peers, he was also a very fine pilot. At the age of only twenty-one, he had been the youngest captain in the UK. And for a while, this adventurer—for undoubtedly that he was—worked for us at Spanavia.

Boy was a little under average height, compactly built, fresh of face and bright of eye, a tangle of black hair framing his round face. He moved like a sportsman, which was what he might have devoted himself to, had not flying engaged his affections first. But it was a close-run thing, for his love of cricket was second only to his flying, and he would go to enormous lengths to avoid missing a match. Not infrequently he reported for duty still wearing items of whites beneath his hastily-donned uniform. On one occasion, having taken a viciously-delivered Yorker in the mouth, he boarded his flight, to the consternation of passengers and crew alike, with an untidy row of freshly-applied bloody stitches in his lip, and a gap formerly occupied by an upper right incisor. Nothing kept Boy from either flying or cricket. Nothing. He often managed, by some magical means, to turn a delay into an early arrival home—followed by a swift getaway to some county field to turn out with the eleven.

The very idea that anyone could think more of a game than they did of the company, would never have occurred to the troglodytes at Haxair's headquarters in EC2, forming company policy with all the flair of a brickie demolishing an outside dunny. So, Boy was a complete mystery to some of them. A feeling which was undoubtedly mutual.

He also possessed a mischievous sense of curiosity, which on occasion, could get him into trouble. Once, when the co-pilot of the DC3 he was flying recounted a tale of how another DC3 captain had proved that it was possible to open his side window in flight and to thrust out and maintain a clenched fist against the 170-knot slipstream, Boy, instantly rising to the unspoken challenge, slid open his window and thrust out his fist. Thereafter, a very straight-faced co-pilot completed the rest of the flight, while Boy nursed cracked knuckles, a twisted elbow and badly contused dignity.

There were quite strictly-enforced rules regarding the wearing of uniform in public places: hats had to be worn, jackets buttoned up, etc. But to Boy, personal comfort clearly came before appearance. On one occasion, as I met his flight during a heatwave, his appearance at the forward passenger door as he disembarked, made quite an impression. His hat firmly planted on his head, his jacket buttoned up, tie neatly Windsor-knotted, his flight bag in hand, he descended the steps to a chorus of guffaws, to march smartly away in orange underpants, sock suspenders and polished shoes.

The old saying goes that there are old pilots and there are bold pilots, but there are no old bold pilots. Boy gave the lie to this assertion. Skilled though he was, it was another attribute—luck, which seemingly he possessed in spades and tested frequently (more than once to the point of destruction), that delivered him to old age.

One afternoon, at the controls of a twin-engine Airspeed Ambassador, he took off from an airport in Germany with forty-six passengers and four crew. The Airspeed Ambassador was less than beautiful to behold with its boat-shaped fuselage, triple tail assembly and huge propellers, like a couple of Dutch windmills hung from the high wing. But she was a sturdy beast and most pilots liked the type. On this occasion, though the take-off had been normal, during the climb out the starboard engine, the number two engine, forgot its lines and went into a faltering impression of that famous breakfast cereal when the milk is added, only louder. For a while Monty the first officer juggled mixture, throttle and fuel levers, coaxed, chided and threatened. But the offending engine refused to mend its ways and as the oil pressure began to drop, Boy ordered it to be shut down. The throttle was closed, fuel was shut off and the prop feathered to reduce drag.

The Bristol Centaurus engine had been designed to power the huge (it was bigger than a 747) Bristol Brabazon project which, as is customary with British inventions, the Government had cancelled before it entered service. The Centaurus was a strong and reliable engine and with two of them the Ambassador had twice the amount of power she needed. So, though its loss was serious matter, it was not of undue concern to Boy. Resignedly, he called the tower, declared a "Pan-Pan" (an urgent situation, rather than a "Mayday" which signifies an emergency) and requested landing clearance. It was quickly granted and he began a gentle turn back towards the airport. Meanwhile, the two stewardesses began moving through the cabin, reassuring passengers and checking that their seatbelts were secure.

It was then that the port engine blew up, vomiting black smoke and components into the slipstream. The aircraft's nose immediately dipped towards the winter chequerboard of fields below. At the subsequent enquiry, it was established that the engines had failed for unrelated reasons. What was so incredible, given the engines' reliability, was that the malfunctions should have occurred simultaneously. But as he wrestled to maintain control, Boy couldn't have cared less what the reasons were; right then, staying alive had attained a certain pre-eminence in his thinking.

For some frantic seconds, the crew's ingrained training kept them preoccupied. Externally the engine appeared much the same as it had before the explosion sent the aircraft staggering across the sky. But it took no great effort of the imagination to guess that its internals had been arbitrarily rearranged and was now about as much use as a Meccano set without the spanners. Hands flew to throttle and mixture levers, the engine's fire extinguisher was triggered and the prop feathered. Boy had pulled out of the turn—which without power was contributing to the rapid loss of airspeed—and restored wings-level flight, albeit with the nose down to prevent a stall. While Monty began transmitting a dignified but doom-laden Mayday, the senior stewardess got rapid ditching instructions from Boy, flung over his shoulder as he scanned the terrain below.

'Strap 'em in tight, Jenny. Heads on folded arms, sharp objects out of pockets, you know the drill. Make it bloody fast too. Then get aft and brace up.'

Anxiously, he searched ahead looking for a suitable landing site, as the altimeter unwound remorselessly. Only a thousand feet to go now, Boy carefully balancing airspeed against height, keeping the descent as shallow as he dared, hoarding altitude.

A deadly silence had descended on the flight deck, broken only by the gentle susurration of the slipstream against the aircraft's skin. Airliners are not intended to glide and therefore do not accomplish it well. Without power, the Ambassador was just twenty tons or so of marginally aerodynamic junk, with not much more than eight-hundred feet to go before it began ploughing up the Fatherland. Boy dared not attempt to turn; the aircraft would stall. He must land straight ahead, more or less regardless of whatever lay in their path.

'Try starting number two again.' His voice sounded strangely loud in the silent cockpit.

Monty set to with a will, though with precious little hope of success. That engine, if not in quite the state of its brother, was nevertheless also a non-runner. As they un-feathered the big prop the Ambassador slewed to its drag, forcing Boy to increase the nose-down attitude further to maintain airspeed. The starter was meshed; the engine coughed and banged and spluttered uselessly, spewing blue smoke from the exhaust stubs. Boy barely noticed it, his attention being centred on a dull patch of green he has spied, out there in the middle distance. An unprepossessing bit of weed-choked pasture, it would just have to do.

He pointed to it. 'We're going in there. Pull your harnesses tight. Give me flaps one. Leave the undercarriage till I say.' Extended, its extra drag would be considerable; so it was best left retracted until the last minute.

The cripple wallowed down through five hundred feet, the port engine trailing a banner of white extinguisher fluid, the starboard blue exhaust smoke. The game was up this time and Boy knew it: 'If you know any prayers, put a good word in for me.'

Back in the cabin a horrified, frozen silence brooded over the passengers. In a way, it was worse for the stewardesses; they were required to display a reassuring calm neither of them felt. Air crashes were rare, but as they knew only too well, when they did occur, they were generally fatal.

In the flight deck Boy's attention was locked onto the rapidly approaching strip of drab greenery, looking ever-more unsuitable as they drew closer and its bumps and ridges became more pronounced. What was the old saying? *'Any landing you walked away from was a good one?'* Well, it was down to him to make it so. It didn't matter that much what happened to him, or Monty come to that, in the next few minutes. What mattered was the fifty others in his care. Ultimately, that's what pilots are paid for: to bring everybody home safely. Not for every other working day when it's merely assiduous routine, but just that one day when they are truly required to earn their pay.

For Boy, today was the day.

The ground, blurring to a muddy green stripe by the speed of their approach, rose to meet them and Boy opened his mouth to call for more flap and for the gear to be put down. But his words were drowned by an explosion of sound as the starboard engine suddenly roared, impossibly, back into life. Power surged through the aircraft, Boy stabbing in a boot-full of right rudder to counteract the asymmetric thrust, fighting to keep the aircraft in the air. A split-second decision—whether to close the throttle and continue the ditching, or risk continuing the flight with a single unreliable engine—he'd made instantly: they would fly themselves out.

Boy's luck held out once again. With the throttle of the one good engine wide open, the Ambassador began to claw its painful way back into the sky. They no longer looked at the engine gauges, there was no point, whatever their readings they would be ignored. They needed five minutes more from that engine—clanging now like a plumber's tool bag—to see them safely back to the runway. Then, if it chose, it could go to hell.

Five more minutes.

They got it. The Ambassador limped crabwise over the runway threshold and Boy dumped her down as the starboard engine gave of its last, lapsing into jingling silence during the landing roll.

For a few days thereafter, Boy wasn't quite his usual boisterous self. His luck was not a fathomless reservoir. It was finite, and his feet had touched bottom with a rude jolt. Perhaps he had just realised that. Be that as it may, he certainly didn't allow it to affect his future adventures, which were to see him gun-running in trouble spots such as the Congo; shipping armaments—some of it nuclear—for shadowy British and American "officials"; transporting heavy water for the Chinese; narrowly escaping being shot down by rebels as he flew government troops in the Sudan; and languishing in filthy jails as far apart as Venezuela and Nigeria.

But always there was cricket, that most English of pursuits, and for all I know, even now as an old man, he still walks out in whites, bat under arm, pulling on the gloves, to face his oldest and most implacable adversary.

Fog

In Ops it is 1801 Zulu, late December. Captain Jerry Powell strides into the office, politely doffing his cap and assuming his serial-killer's smile.

'Good evening, gentlemen.'

This title, just conceivably applicable to Gary the duty officer, is pushing it a bit in his young assistant Jeep's case. Even so, they both respond, Jeep a little distractedly as he is trying to figure out what is wrong with the overflight request to the Turkish Department of Civil Aviation that he has been trying to send since it was dumped in Ops by somebody from upstairs on their way to something more interesting. It takes Gary less than five seconds to discover and point out what the problem is—that Jeep has left out the whole of the address line. Quickly (at least for him) Jeep adds the missing line and hits the send button, a split second before Gary has time to point out that the clearance also bears the wrong flight number.

During this small diversion Jerry retires to the outer office to greet his crew. The anonymous backs, hunched over paperwork, turn as he greets them and with a perceptible but quickly disguised sinking of the spirits, he registers and greets in turn Brian, his garrulous flight engineer, and Trevor, a most unpopular first officer who is presently labouring over the fuel figures with the aid of a calculator the size of a roofing slate. Jerry may expect to have the uplift debated to four decimal places before he cuts the nonsense short and rounds it up to the nearest hundred pounds. With little inclination on this winter's evening to talk bollocks with Brian (there will be opportunity enough on the long grind down to Athens), Jerry grabs a fistful of met and retreats again to the Ops room.

'It looked a bit fuzzy on the way in. Have you got an actual?'

Gary, uncharacteristically caustic, glances out of the window and says: 'Well, there's a shower coming in. But that's just the nightshift.'

One floor below an Ops room now vibrant with laughter, a slinking figure with a face which Jed with bludgeoning humour has described as resembling

"Clement Freud's dog," enters at speed (he is two minutes late), carrying his trademark grubby Greenpeace bag, its Rainbow Warrior quote as always carried facing inwards lest the bearer should lose any more street cred than he already lacks.

It is I.

Just in front of me flight attendant Sue Luscombe ('stewardess' was so last decade and 'hostess' is definitely passé), emerges from the crew room, turns right, begins to climb the stairs. She is in civvies: stretch Lycra pants, a somewhat skimpy button through top (which isn't, for the top couple of buttons), and spike heels that look like she raided the props department of a production of Cabaret for them. A shade consciously tarty perhaps, but lethal to the unsuspecting libido. I follow her at a respectful distance as far as the first landing, wondering how it is that the owner of such a body can have a head as empty as Jed's parking space in a crisis. Nature compensating for its own shortcomings maybe.

I am intrigued. 'Where are you going Susan?'

She stops. Turns. She is two steps above me and I try, not entirely successfully, to avoid looking at her décolletage.

'The toilet.'

'Not right now. The kit—you can't be positioning in that.'

'Oh, party.'

'Right.' I pause a moment by the Ops room door to watch her climb the next flight.

'Penny for your thoughts?'

I turn, startled, to take a double whammy from Senior Flight Attendant Maggie Kennedy's electric blue eyeliner. Judging by the knowing look in her eye she would be wasting her money, clearly having arrived at her own conclusion.

I settle for 'Not worth it.' But the look in Maggie's eyes tells me that I am condemned out of hand, along with the rest of my beastly tribe. I find the cynicism of some cabin crew really quite shocking.

Thirty seconds later in the Ops room, Gary, eager to get away, says: 'OK, crew's all in for the Athens and *Golf Delta* is on 34—no closure yet. *X-Ray Mike* estimates at 2330. Chan says to call him on Portishead with the 2120 Racebridge actuals—forecast is crap tonight. *X-Ray November* is number two for the hanger for "A" check, estimating serviceable at 0700. But if that's a Big Al engineer's 0700, you'd better swap it with *XM* now for the Orlando. Two girls to call out for the morning, they're on the sheet. Envelope for Dickie when he checks in. Fog forecast from 2200 Zulu. Stanstead reckon they can handle but they want plenty of notice. Astra's got a flat battery. Don't forget that Phoenix has a scheduled outage from 2359 to 0400, so do your flight plans early. And the third floor are still in with some suits from Golding. That's it, I'm outta here.'

I say, 'Hang on, I'll get a pen.'

Jeep gets the overflight request away at the fourth attempt and strides over to the crewing window where our newest flight attendant, freshly transferred from Manchester and looking too young to be up this late, let alone flying, waits to collect the Athens bar float. I copy the following dialogue with one ear whilst listening to Gary tiredly repeating the hand-over with the other.

F/A: 'Er, I am not being funny but I just ran into this really weird guy downstairs in the hall. Where do I sign?'

Jeep: 'Just there. Did you? How do you mean weird?'

F/A: 'Well, he had this really really scruffy old suit on. And he talked Londonish, you know, like you. Sorry. And he didn't seem to know what he was doing. And he sort of asked me how I was. So, I asked him if he had a pass, and what did he want, and did he know this was private property? But he just sort of laughed. I think he was a bit drunk. He wished me Merry Christmas.'

Jeep: 'Did he have glasses? Going thin on top? sixtyish? Walks like he's just about to step in dog shite?'

F/A: 'Yes. Do you know him?'

Jeep: 'Mm, sounds like Harry, the managing director.'

A flurry of activity now. Dermot "Irish" (he's not Irish), Reid, Greg Porter and Tony Collins—my off-duty Ops colleagues—push through the door to collide with the impossibly young-looking and now rather whey-faced stewardess who is fleeing in the other direction, pursued by Jeep, who is trying to give her the bar float she has forgotten in the onset of an anxiety attack. This invites the inevitable laddish barracking from the trio of off-duty ops duty officers:

'Christ Jeep! Is that what you call foreplay?' and 'Run like buggery girl, he's a sod when he's roused.' and 'Oy Jeep, why don't you ask her if she'll take a cheque instead?' etc.

Jeep, with amazing dexterity, is just able to simultaneously dodge round Sledge, my assistant, who is puffing up the stairs with a wedge of NOTAMS (Notes to Airman: general information relevant to the route they are to fly) under his arm, and to offer them the finger, before disappearing from view round the bend of the staircase.

Before any of them can respond to this provocation they are all struck to silence by the sudden reappearance of F/A Luscombe, who descends amongst them from the floor above, on her way back to the crew room. As she approaches, imperceptibly she squares her shoulders, artfully elevating that which youth and fine genes renders quite unnecessary. But oh, as she reaches the bottom step of the landing, suddenly there is something wrong with her shoe, necessitating that she bend to fix it. The blouse gapes and as the French have it, *Il y a du monde au balcon* applies. Her work done, she straightens to grant them a silent 'Hello boys' with a lifted eyebrow before wafting past on a hint of Chanel. She's good. A pro. The ensuing stunned silence is broken only by Sledge's stertorous breathing as he reaches the landing, apparently without noticing the vision sliding hydraulically past him in the opposite direction.

Moments later the trio bursts into the Ops room, all mirth and schoolboy lust, there to kidnap a very willing Gary, and to depart on a chorus of laughter for the ground floor, having commandeered Jeep to chauffer them to the terminal. From there, the train will speed them to London for a Christmas thrash which—if it proceeds to the form of previous years—none of them will be able to remember anything of come morning: Greg Porter won't be able to find his underpants; Irish will have a tattoo, possibly on his buttocks and a date he can't remember making with an exotic dancer he can't remember meeting; Tony will be reminiscing alcoholically about a Boys From The Lough gig he went to in '85; and Gary Appleby will be just politely smashed. Or something like that. And when it's all over we shall have to decant them from the terminal into vans, distributing their sleeping forms in offices throughout the building, until morning brings them pain, regret, despair, and in one instance perhaps even a case of NSU.

By the time Jeep returns from the crew room, I have settled into the Captain Kirk chair reserved for controllers. Tony has, quite unaccountably, had this placed on a platform raised nine inches above the rest of the Ops room; whilst Sledge is seated at the ops console, which, equally unaccountably, is of massive construction considering it only has to support two monitors, an HF radio and a couple of telephones, and looks as if it might have been looted from a decommissioned Russian power station. Tony, who's design the Ops room is, seems to have modelled his work on the Albert Speer school of architecture.

Jeep appears a little breathless as he bursts through the door, but it is by no means certain that this is from the exertion of the stairs. 'Oy, did you see Luscombe just now, in bloody civvies?'

Sledge is pre-occupied with some paperwork and it falls to me to respond. Airily I reply, 'Can't say I noticed.'

'Yeah, right.' Grinning all over his face, he grabs his coat and car keys and heads for the door, diverting via my desk just long enough to lean over and say: 'You're more full of bollocks than Tom Jones' underpants, mate.' Before departing with, 'Anyway you prefer that Whassname from Dispatch, don'tcher?' flung over his shoulder.

I am out of my seat in an instant. 'That, Carter, is an outrageous lie and calumny, you seedy git, a slur on a fine woman and my reputation. If you ever repeat it, I shall have you rostered on nights for the next ten years—on Collins's shift. D'you hear?' Only his laughter receding down the stairs confirms that he has.

"Whassname," or Rachel, is the strikingly good-looking Amazonian from Flight Dispatch; intelligent, good company, a bit scruffy and quite without any overt trace of vanity. Her mass of black hair invariably looks as though she comes to work on a motorbike, her shoes are scuffed and there is always biro ink on her blouse and her fingers. Occasionally, in the small hours of the night, when the work is done, all is quiet and there is time to kill, she wanders out from Big Al's headquarters in search of coffee and conversation, sometimes to visit us here at Hangar F. That is all it is, but the rumour mill, if it were to be fed by Jeep, would have both our reputations sullied. I think I may still have a reputation, I'm just not sure it's one I'd want to keep. But being unjustly condemned for turpitude twice in the space of five minutes, is intolerable.

Turning, I find Sledge eyeing me with amused detachment. 'What are you gawping at boy? Why don't you get on to the Gocon (the abbreviation for Ground Movement Controller, the Ops supremo over at Big Brother, at what was our parent airline till it shrugged us off) and order the de-icer rig for the morning.'

Suppressing a smile, he reaches for the telephone and punches in the number.

OK, I admit it, I have this thing about the de-icers: Big Brother has just three of the things (despite the fact that in aviation terms they only cost a busker's hat-takings each) and once a year, when the airport is ankle deep in frost, somebody goes round to the exposed parking place where they have lain rusting since last winter, and tries to start them up. It is not a pretty sight. The main problem however, is that they have a fundamental design fault—they don't work below 32°F. But just to keep up appearances, and to satisfy pilots who don't seem to appreciate the aesthetics of ice on their aircraft, we have to go through the motions of spraying, and this entails waiting while the one working unit of the three services every other aircraft on the field before it comes to ours. Oh, they pretend there is a strict order of service based on scheduled departure time, but we know better.

2130 and I am distracted from my work by the animal noises Sledge has begun making whilst poring over the glossy magazine spread out on the desk in front of him. Anxious for an excuse to abandon the apparently insoluble problem of how to flight plan the morning's Orlando when the Phoenix flight planning system has a scheduled outage from 2359hrs—an hour before the North Atlantic Tracks are published—I leave my seat to sneak up behind him and look over his shoulder. My blood chills.

'Tasty ey?' Observes Sledge, licking his lips. 'Look at those curves.'

'But it's a gun.'

'TAAS, 0.357 Magnum Desert Eagle, actually.'

'I thought you were abusing yourself with one of Jed's perv mags from his desk drawer.'

'Gas, semi-automatic…'

'Yes, very nice…'

'152 mill barrel, 6 groove rifling…'

'Sledge…'

'Combat sights, 9-round box mag…'

'Er, Sledge lad.'

'…Steel frame of course. A few ounces heavier than the aluminium, better balance though.'

'Let me get you one of Jed's perv mags from his desk drawer.'

'Rimmed cartridge, bit unusual, revolver ammo really. And they even do it in fifty cal Action Express—heavy artillery. Luvvly.'

'Sledge! Pull yourself together, boy, you're drooling. Why don't you try for the de-icer rig again? There's a good lad.'

Nobody else will have Sledge on their shift. I mean, just because he's twenty-seven, doesn't have a girlfriend, still lives with his mum, and collects large calibre semi-automatic weapons, it doesn't necessarily mean he's a loose cannon, does it? No, he's alright really, even if he did give me that present once—two spent .45 calibre cartridge cases. I just wondered whom he had spent them on.

My reverie is broken by a cracklingly loud transmission from the VHF: 'HCA Ops, this is the Ceejet 521. Good evening.'

Sledge reads my look of discomfort, accurately predicts its cause, and turns to his keyboard. I grab the nearest telephone and start dialling with my spare hand whilst returning *X-ray Mike's* call with the other. 'Ceejet 521, HCA Ops. Good evening, Tim.'

XM's opening call is delivered by its first officer, who's friendly tones I recognise as that of Bernie Lightfoot's son: 'Estimating at 2215 with 373 plus 4 (infants). And I think they're going to have us in the hold. You got the latest actuals?'

Rapidly extemporising while Sledge's hurried request for the UK major actuals (which I may have omitted to order earlier when they were published) is being processed, I offer: 'They should be with us in a moment. Bit of a problem with the system tonight. Stand by.'

Suddenly Chan Morgan, 521's skipper is on, barking as he does when he hopes to get Ops running around like headless chickens just for his amusement; a harmless little trait he shares with one of our other captains, Guy "The Testosterone Kid" Vaillancourt.

'Come on, down there! Get it together! You will be interested to know that we have been given an RVR of fifty metres, which I am sure you are aware is way below our minima. At present reckoning I would say we have about ten minutes holding fuel before we divert. So, how is it looking there now? Where do you want us to go? Where are the UK actuals I requested earlier? Oh, and what contingencies have you arranged, like coaches for the passengers and crew transport? Because in a few minutes you could have a big problem on your hands.'

I can't help thinking that this last is a major misreading of the situation on Chan's part, since I am the one down here in the Parker Knoll with tea at my elbow; whereas he is up there, romping around the hold in the fog, at the controls of the oldest example of that aircraft in the world, and with less spare fuel than I've got in the old Citroen downstairs. So, who exactly has the big problem is at best a moot point. But I get his drift of course. It's a moral question really.

It is one of the strange paradoxes of life that marginally incompetent layabouts, such as I, find that something really bad often happens just when they are right in the middle of a major cosmetic repair job, and would much sooner have a bit of good luck to help things along. Now is one of those times, for just as the duty officer of our handling agent in Stanstead answers my call and Sledge passes me a bunch of actuals that look like God has decided Final Judgement will be tonight, Harry Tailor, the afore-mentioned MD and his second-in-command Don Moss, usher into the office two senior management suits from Golding (the big travel group that has expressed an interest in acquiring us), to show them what a professional outfit we are. My first line of defence is to wind the gain on the VHF all the way down to prevent them from hearing any further unguarded remarks from Chan.

In his most avuncular and gentle tone, Harry asks 'How's it going?'

Always a sensitive soul, he correctly interprets my strangled cry of greeting and vaguely flapping hand as, '*Not now for Chrissake—please,*' and deflects the suits smoothly away to Crewing. Whilst quietly pleading with Stanstead to accept our diversion if it becomes necessary (and getting a mouthful in return for not asking them earlier), I notice Don Moss out of the corner of my eye, bringing up the rear of the management crocodile. He is just itching to weigh in with the awkward questions, but Harry's presence prevents any such affront to the pecking order. He catches my expression and his face tightens—we understand each other. Yep, and another nice Pringle too. What is that? Puss yellow? It reads a good nine on the Vomit Index.

I slam the phone down, grab the met, and spotting the little green carrier wave indicator light flickering on the VHF, take a smart step backwards to shield it from Moss's view. He's got hours on a part-share bugsmasher somewhere and reckons he's got aviation sorted. Well I bloody-well haven't, so would he please sod off. I need him now like I need a bomb threat and a baggage ID.

I scan the met. We are crap. I look out of the window, the street lamp opposite is lightly haloed with mist; nothing much there, but the RVR is 50 metres. My meteorology is schoolboy stuff. (I took a proper met course once and I was with them all the way to the adiabatic lapse rate. But I must have made a left at "hygroscopic nuclei" when everybody else turned right. I'm more pine-cone anyway.) All I know is, when the short hairs on the back of my neck stand up, something is wrong. It's been a pretty mild day, clear sky now, temperature dropping like a stone, so there's a chunk of radiation fog out there. It's behind me on the other side of the hangar so I can't see it. And with no wind to speak of it could be sitting there on the runway all night. On the other hand, I tell Chan

'Stanstead', and right after that the ATC supervisor goes out onto the control tower catwalk, unties its string from the handrail, the little cloud floats away, it's 1000 metres for the rest of the night and everybody says 'Well what do you expect, bloody Mike James was on.'

Harry flits quietly by like a moth, the Golding guys in Indian file behind him. They smile at me and I take two warm, firm, handshakes with my free hand. Using the experience I have garnered from my years of study of the Human Condition, I judge that yes, HCA will be safe in their hands.

Well, you can't always be right.

The moment the door swishes to behind them, I launch myself at the volume knob of the VHF as Sledge puts the phone down from ATC. 'Supervisor says 521 is trying to call us on company.'

'Really. See about that de-icer rig, there's a good lad.'

I turn the volume up and get '...down there? We divert in two minutes', delivered really quite crisply. I can imagine Chan up there sitting in shirtsleeves, headset clamped over his prematurely-bald pate, muttering into the mike from the corner of his mouth, through clenched teeth. He has surprisingly clear diction considering this strange characteristic. I manage to prevaricate for quite a decent time really before Chan makes me actually say the words, 'divert to Stanstead.' After that it's downhill all the way. The next actual gives 500 metres at the touchdown point, but Chan is already off company frequency—even if I dared to suggest he turn around. Which is just as well because the hole closes almost immediately, right after British Midland get two 737s in, winning the Smug Bastards of The Night Award, hands down.

0630. I don't know what Sledge is doing with the centrefold of Guns & Ammo, but it's making him breathless again, so I get him to ask when we can expect the de-icer rig for *GD*. Now, in my Ladybird Eye Spy the Weather book, it says that fog tends to thicken just before dawn. Not this bloody morning it doesn't—by 0500 we have CAVOK (Ceiling and visibility ok, in other words a clear sky), and everybody and his entourage who waited down route for the weather to lift, is streaming into Racebridge—while we are in Stanstead number three in line for attention to a Short 360 and a Dak with a fuel leak. Perfect. I try to think what, or whom, I would rather be instead of the duty officer tonight. It's a toss-up between drummer with the Count Basie Band, or Sue Luscombe's shower taps. (I know, but steam brings on my sinuses, and the band would be regular work.)

'Well, boy? What's the bloody word on that rig?' I suppose I'm getting a bit ratty now.

Sledge clasps the phone to his chest. Do I hear faint laughter on the other end? 'He says we are number one for it, when they get it started. It doesn't like the cold mornings.'

I blurt out, 'Incompetent sods! Why don't they ge…' Glancing down at the flight plans on the desk in front of me, I have just discovered that I've inadvertently routed the Orlando right through the North Atlantic Tracks (Published twice daily and based on current winds, they dictate traffic routes in both directions between Europe and North America). But it's only when I pick them up to look more closely at the camel's back flight levels this has produced, that I notice Jerry's handover sheet on the desk beneath them, and I am reminded that I should have called out the two flight attendants an hour ago. It's a natural reaction to ask: 'Who relieves me this morning?'

Sledge swivels his chair round. 'Greg, I think.'

'Where are they all?' I delegated the transportation and distribution of the inebriated bodies of my fellow controllers to him, some hours ago.

'Dermot is in NAV, under Fanny's desk. Greg's is in Jed's office…'

'Has he still got underpants on?'

'…Yes, but they're not his, apparently. And the last time I saw Tony, he was wondering about in the hall downstairs trying to find his living room.'

I call both F/As and cajole them into reducing their report time. But since one of them is Samba Bailey and about as reliable as a rope bridge in an Indiana Jones movie, I'll be lucky if I get her at all. Things are not shaping up well this morning as I re-start the Orlando plans.

The telephones on our respective desks ring simultaneously. We answer them together. I get Steve, one of the nicer movement controllers over at Big Bro, and things take a turn for the better. The airport, Steve tells me, is chocker; all the flights that were held down route have converged here as the weather cleared and the place is now swamped. For the latest arrivals, it's a minimum hour thirty wait for the Honey Wagon (toilet bowser), two hours to get the catering off, and Check-In looks like Rourke's Drift. Suddenly I'm Top Gun, I'm Schwartzkopf, Jessie James, and as cool as John Belushi's Ray-Bans. *XM* is in Stanstead, number two now to the Short 360, transfer coaches for the passenger are already booked, and the catering is *en route.* Good or what? All I have to do now is make it look like I planned it that way.

But fame can be an elusive thing: *sic transit gloria*, and all that.

Sledge puts the phone down from Engineers. 'What do you want first, the good news or the bad?'

'Get on with it boy.' I say airily, already imagining the admiring looks and congratulatory remarks I shall be receiving for my cool solution of The Fog Business.

'Well, the good news is that we have definitely got the de-icer rig...'

'A small victory, but nevertheless a welcome one,' I observe expansively.

'...because it just rammed GD's port wing. Navigation light's had it, static dischargers gone and the tip of the aileron might be buckled. Engineers are rushed off their feet; they can't look at it for at least an hour.'

A pause.

'Er Sledge old chap, I think my bad back is coming on. Just take young Porter a cup of java and tell him everything's as per the board...'

I've had better episodes. But though it was a long time ago, the Iran thing wasn't one of them.

Chalice

During my second season in the Ramp, Mr P, in his customary jovial manner, asked me what I knew about lost luggage. I answered, truthfully, very little, but hazarded a guess that it was luggage that was lost. He seemed to think I had a grasp of the basics and invited me to either set up a lost luggage department to cope with company's growing mishandled baggage problem, or to bugger off at the end of the season as there were presently no other vacancies for permanent staff. Knowing virtually nothing about what the job entailed, but being more than familiar with the dole queue, I ripped his arm off. It got me a rat-hole cubicle between Mr P's office and the Ramp to serve as my office, a telephone, a desk, an unlimited supply of biros, two box files (one for "Lost", one for "Found"), and dozy Edward Barker, the object of a glaring bit of nepotism on the part of his uncle, the managing director.

Barker was slow, obdurate and crushingly dull. Whereas his uncle was unpredictable, authoritarian and slipperier than a conga eel in a bucket of yoghurt. Occasionally, when he tired of making paperclip daisy-chains or whatever he did up there at Head Office, he would pay a flying visit to the Ramp to hang around the office, looking over shoulders, making facile remarks and generally infringing everybody's airspace. He looked and behaved like a man who was desperate to make himself indispensable before anybody—say, the board of directors—discovered otherwise.

I thought we did remarkably well with the baggage thing, but by the end of the season it began to dawn on me—too late—that we had made a fatal tactical error: we had found the majority of the luggage, the season of mist and mellow fruitfulness was well advanced, and the flow of misplaced baggage had dried to a trickle. We held out as long as we could, losing and finding the same tan Revelation for days on end, until a deeply-suspicious Mr P decided an audit was due. Half a minute's perusal of our record book was enough for him to forensically establish that we were on a 'bloody doddle.' It was back to the Ramp for me. Barker however, continued to bask in the refulgence of the MD's nepotism. He not only took over the lost luggage role, but was moved into an empty office of his own two doors down from the Ramp, where he took great delight in my evident chagrin at the sight of him sprawling indolently at what should have been *my* desk, for the remainder of the winter.

Winter, and our business being largely charter, a quieter time for the line, with relatively little to do until the first intrepid holidaymakers began the yearly pilgrimage to Spain and all points beachward. Time enough then for recreational activities of various kinds, from the wholly innocent to the downright reprehensible. Skylarking was rife, card pools burgeoned on night shifts, and parties were so frequent that unofficial rosters were drawn up so that shifts could be split. Those who's "turn" it was would eschew uniform jackets and ties for mufti, and with cans and bottles secreted in rolled-up raincoats, disappear until dawn, if not for the rest of their shift. There were also trysts of a more intimate nature: affairs were begun, affairs were ended, some culminating in marriage, some in the reverse. There was more intrigue, passion and perfidy than a whole shelfful of airport bookshop fiction. Rumour, fuelled by idleness, ebbed and flowed; sometimes accurate, often not, usually unfair, occasionally damaging. Some listened, some spread it, a few did both, very few neither.

During quiet periods, training and routine check flights for the pilots offered us groundlings the opportunity to escape the monotony of the office to tag along. Many an afternoon found us over Southern England reclining—not always entirely at ease—in an otherwise deserted cabin, while those up front put the aircraft through a series of simulated emergencies, such as engine fires or hydraulic system failures. It was a case of the luck of the draw; you might spend hours making continuous approaches, landings and immediate take-offs ("bumps and goes" as they were known), with some fledgling first officer dumping the aircraft down one wheel at a time in a continuous series of shattering impacts. Or you might spend the whole time cruising serenely in winter sunshine, rumpled cumulus below, and above your head deep blue all the way to infinity. On my very first such trip, the first officer under training was the devastatingly handsome and charming, Hugo Blackwood who, with his chiselled features and shock of unruly golden locks, looked every inch the romantic lead movie star. Happily married to the equally beautiful Melissa, he seemed to spend a great deal of his time politely stepping over the swooning females that littered his path. That day, he was a little tardy in responding to the fact that the training captain had shut down the port engine to simulate its failure at the very instant the aircraft left the ground. For a breathless second, I watched the wingtip dip to actually brush the grass at the side of the runway before Hugo re-established control and climbed away. I had barely recovered my composure when, on the next landing, the left main gear hit a rabbit on the runway which exploded pinkly across the glass of my window. Had I had any, I might have added my lunch to my side of the glass.

But aircraft were not the only thing in the air, so was change and it was not many weeks before I was beckoned once more into Mr P's office. As I entered, my self-preservation beacon instantly triggered, for sat beside him was Jack Bradbury, Spanavia's fearsome operations manager, bristling quietly. His manner always put me in mind of a pan on the point of boiling over. And on the occasions when it did, which was not infrequently, it was best to be outside splashing distance of it. A pair of heavily-pouched blue eyes in a puffy, lined and florid face, adorned with a thick yellow moustache, surveyed me with basilisk intensity as I took the chair Mr P was indicating. I took it slowly, giving myself time to complete a rapid mental review of my recent transgressions to assess how deep the ordure I was descending into might be.

It turned out to be another job offer—and almost as unnerving as the prospect of a disciplinary. Bradbury took the lead. Cargo business was picking up and it had been decided that a dedicated loadmaster was needed to deal with it. The job would entail taking freight enquiries from the Commercial Department in London, working out the viability of loads (could it be physically accommodated in the chosen aircraft, that sort of thing), supervising loading, working out the trim, completing paperwork and, on occasions, travelling with the aircraft to oversee unloading and delivery. I would transfer from the Traffic Department to Operations, and answer directly to Bradbury.

The selection of a suitable person for this new post, I suspected, had been made in the company's characteristic "Oy-you-with-your-hands-in-your-pockets-come-here-and-do-this" fashion, the one that had worked out so well for it in its recruitment of its recently-redundant lost luggage officer. To most normal, reasonably-ambitious people, this would have seemed like a grand opportunity. I wasn't all that that normal and not really that ambitious, beyond wanting to stay employed long enough to get paid and blow it on something unworthy. Nevertheless, the job constituted an advancement and sounded interesting. Unfortunately, it also had something of the aspect of a poisoned chalice about it.

There is nothing new about loadmastering, the job has been around since aeroplanes and freight got together. Most airlines with cargo business included them as part of the crew. The problem was that Spanavia, being mainly a passenger carrier, had never needed one before. But times were changing; with cargo business on the rise and our expanding fleet more able to handle it, the time was right to put freight on a more professional footing. *'Professional?'* Right. Why me? Only recently I had been reproved for not answering the telephone professionally—and they wanted *me* to introduce loadmastering to the company? What were they thinking? I had but two years' experience in the business, little-better than 11-plus maths, the organisational skills of a biscuit (though the baggage-finding thing had worked out alright), had trouble getting out of bed in the morning and hated administration. Basically, I was a surf bum, only without the board…and the ability to surf…and the rat-tail hair…and the location…Okay, forget that analogy. And then it occurred to me—of course, why hadn't I thought of it before? The chances were that nobody else had wanted the job; others, quantumly better suited to the post, had been approached for the role and wisely shrunk from the prospect of working under Bradbury's beetling scrutiny. I didn't shrink, I went for it; grabbed the permanent contract, the marginal extra money, the travel, the opportunity to work alone, the implied confidence in me, even the expense account I had been warned on no account to use. Whatever, I grabbed it.

Woodside. During World War II, Mosquitoes and Typhoons and Spitfires had flown into combat from here. After the war, it had been handed over to civilian use and, though it was busy with a gliding club and an aircraft engineering company, ever since it had been gently decaying. Pineapple mayweed and giant cow parsley sprouted beside the runway and rabbits foraged beneath the wings of the abandoned aircraft that littered the place. This was Spanavia's engineering base. It had minimal facilities, not even runway lighting. (Recently we'd taken off at nightfall using the headlamps of an engineering van parked at the other end of the runway to mark the point by which, if we weren't airborne, we would become inseparable from the van.) Buildings were scattered loosely about the single-story control tower and the airfield was surrounded by trees, except for notches at each end of the runway's extended centre lines. It was a decidedly rural place where aviation was conducted against a background of birdsong and the hum of insects.

Bradbury had dispatched me there to take a weight and balance course, to learn the difference between mean aerodynamic chord and static mean chord (still shaky on that); to make sure I knew how to calculate floor loading and cargo restraint; to swat up on preparing APS sheets, the basic document issued for each aircraft on which its load and trim was based—and how to make tea for myself with the classroom's useless kettle.

Harry Tubbs, the line's RAF-trained engineering director, who would one day lead Spanavia, took me his only pupil for the week-long course. He was a patient, quiet man who must have had many more important calls on his time than to teach me such basic stuff as this. But if he had, he betrayed no impatience and by the end of the week, whatever I hadn't grasped could be ascribed to my opacity rather than to any deficiency in his teaching.

So, I launched on my new role from my old Lost Luggage rat-hole, with not much more than a telephone, a notepad and gritted teeth.

Not long after this, I rashly decided that forty greyhounds and half a dozen handlers would fit into the cabin of a DC3. It is possible that even Commercial, ever-ready to accept that a "no" from me actually meant "yes" or at least "maybe", suspected my judgement, because they asked me to go on the flight to ensure that all went well. Half the load was to be collected from Dublin, the other half from Belfast and the whole yapping assembly brought back to Racebridge for some big greyhound hoolie in London. I found that once more I would be flying with the aerobatically inclined Sid Bardwell, though mercifully there would be none of that this time.

I suppose if I'd thought about it while considering this load, I would have taken the boxes containing the beasts into greater account. But somehow, when I was given the initial enquiry, my mind conjured up a simple picture of forty, thin, racy doggies standing obediently in ten neat rows of four. The reality wasn't like that at all. On arrival at Dublin, I flung back the door to catch my first glimpse of the Emerald Isle and found most of it obscure by an enormous heap of wire mesh boxes, around which a herd of wall-eyed greyhounds and half a dozen handlers was milling. The latter soon set to work coaxing their charges into the boxes, while I kept a discrete distance, not a bit unnerved by the hungry-looking, yellow-fanged, temperamental parcels of solid muscle. One of the handlers, a cheerful ruddy-faced man with hands the size of dartboards, mistook my expression of indifference for one of nervous uncertainty and smiled encouragingly.

'Sure, aren't dey friendly little fellers, de lot of 'em? An' dayed not hort a floi.'

I supposed that was why some of them were muzzled, in case they gave somebody a licking. But to prove I was in fact an animal lover, I walked over to one of the cages and gently scratched the ear of its occupant with my biro. It ate it.

We reached Belfast by early afternoon and there on the grass beside the apron stood the other half of our cargo. Sid Bardwell stuck his head out of the flight deck, took one look at the chaos of dogs, boxes and handlers, said 'Right, leave it to you. If you want anything use the phone,' and withdrew to his sanctuary.

By the time the last box was loaded and the handlers strapped into their seats, the cabin looked like a particularly untidy race day at Romford Dog Track. The boxes formed a solid two-high wall, all the way to the flightdeck bulkhead. What little space remaining by the aft door was occupied by the handlers, behind which was the toilet, containing a further two dogs. Between the handlers and the toilet there was me, wondering why I hadn't thought of my own seating arrangements earlier. We took off in dirty weather doing its best to degenerate into filthy weather, turned east and headed for home. I was seated on one of the dog boxes with a greatcoat on top of it to make a cushion and a shield—the dog wasn't one of the muzzled ones. Rain thundered spasmodically on the fuselage and the Dak bucked and wallowed as she ground through thickening cloud. Somewhere over the Irish Sea the air began to grow noticeably colder. At length, even the handlers, who all seemed to possess flasks of some warming draught, noticed it too and asked if they could have some heat. Not sure that the old bus even had cabin heating, I fought my way to the interphone by the door and with the handset against my ear pressed the flightdeck call button. All this got me was a C above top C at about fifty decibels for my troubles. For the next five minutes, I continued to call the flightdeck, then gave up. The thing was useless; Sid remained ignorant of our plight. The handlers took it philosophically. They just turned up their collars and spent a little more time with their flasks. So that by the time we arrived, they were really quite "warm", having supplemented their flasks with a bottle of some golden elixir. And I was now wearing my greatcoat—and standing.

The following day, sitting in the rat-hole, I reviewed the performance of my first flight as loadmaster. All things considered, it hadn't been too bad. I may have slightly misjudged the size of the load, but what was a couple of dogs in the toilet, unless anybody wanted to go in there? After all, only a gang of well-lubricated Irishmen would want to do such a thing. And six seats for seven people? Well, that was just a silly little arithmetical error. As for the dud telephone, I could hardly be blamed for that, and Sid agreed with me—right after he got out through the flightdeck emergency exit, the cabin door having being completely blocked by the boxes. (Well yes, strictly speaking, that was illegal.) On reflection the two stray dogs on the taxiway might have been a problem, but the 1-11 stopped in time, so that was alright.

Taken altogether, not a bad trip. After all, one profits from experience, I told myself. And I would certainly do better next time—Jack Bradbury more or less insisted on that.

The loads enquiries dribbled in in a constant stream from Commercial in London, most of which posed no logistical problems. For those that did, I sought the advice of Ted Napper, the head loader. His vast experience allowed him to assess a load simply by first frowning at me dyspeptically, then glaring at the details I'd scribbled on a sheet of paper, resetting his hat on his head, then passing his verdict—along with some wind. He didn't trouble himself with such intricacies as floor loading, but left that to me, settling for giving out cryptic warnings such as, 'Looks quite compact' or 'Not very big for its weight, is it?' Though he always appeared grudging, his help was invaluable and I soon learned to trust the crusty old sod's wisdom.

Cargo came in all shapes, sizes and descriptions, from plastic portable bidets to gold bullion. The latter presented a curious aspect (the former too, come to think of it), when loaded. The aircraft would be completely empty except for two rows of house-brick-sized fibre boxes, ranged down the cabin floor with spreader boards beneath them to distribute their weight, each box containing a single bar of bullion. Yet the aircraft would take off to deliver the stuff to the Gnomes of Zurich at something like maximum take-off weight. In those days, a rather more casual approach was taken to airport security. To illustrate this, one of the loaders, in a reckless demonstration of bravado, put on a duffle coat and with some difficulty managed to secrete one gold bar in each of the coat's sturdy pockets. Then he staggered off the aircraft and out of the nearest gate leading landside. He then turned back and replaced the gold, just to show how easy it would be to swipe what in those days constituted ten grand's-worth (about £145,000 today). He needn't have come back, but he did.

The Irish are nearly as keen on their greyhounds as they are their horses and we would regularly ship the latter, to and from Dublin and Belfast, for bloodstock purposes and for the races. Horses were usually shipped in one of our venerable Bristol 170s, so that sometimes the more refined Arabian horseflesh we transported was worth rather more than the aircraft carrying them.

There had been the usual flurry of activity around the arrival of a new addition to our fleet and I had been unable to get anywhere near her for a couple days. But late in the afternoon of the third, I drove out to the cargo park to get acquainted and found the aircraft deserted at last. From the moment I saw her it struck me that she had a distinct personality, as she sat there quietly warming her battered flanks in the sunshine, the twin black rectangles of her windshields above the long nose staring back at me with the wisdom of a million miles.

Tango Charlie was a shabby-looking affront to aviation; a superannuated DC7 freighter, looking every bit her age—whatever that may have been—and the latest addition to Haxair's fleet. Her arrival had given the line its long reach back, having lost it with the retirement of its old Avro Yorks. (Lancasters converted to the civilian role.) The company famously didn't spring much for paint jobs, let alone for its cargo hacks. So, *TC* looked like she's been tarted up for a stock car race, her grimy bare metal enlivened by the addition of a livid green strip along the line of the cabin windows, surmounted amidships by the company's name, executed in a font of Balkan severity. The only other identifiable colour on the aircraft being the beige carbon streaks, veined with oil, which fanned out aft over the wings from each of her four engines. Down her flanks, in line with the props, were many dents inflicted by ice hurled from the blades of her propellers. Unsightly repairs had been affected here with aluminium patches rivetted over the original damaged skin. As I was to discover, in flight the leaky pressure seal on her forward freight door roared like a bull elephant in musth, and at take-off power the old girl left an eyeball-searing trail of oily blue smoke in her wake. Nevertheless, she maintained a shabby sort of dignity, a legacy of the clean lines the Douglas Aircraft Company had designed into the marque. Back in the fifties, as the height of her fashion, with movie stars and crooners pausing on her boarding steps for the cameras, she would have looked the business.

Now though, she was a tacky disgrace. No matter, I loved *Tango Charlie,* she was my favourite aeroplane of the fleet. This declaration of friendship may or may not have been accepted, but she offered dispensation to no one and was often cantankerous and downright unreliable. I was her loadmaster—an acutely inexperienced and inept loadmaster, perhaps—but nevertheless her loadmaster, and together we were about to embark on what I thought, incorrectly as it turned out, would be a quick trip to the Middle East.

Business, as far as it concerned me, had been slack of late and I was enjoying leisurely days and early finishes. But at precisely 1130 hrs one Thursday morning my lotus-eating was brought to an abrupt end.

Eric Fenner was on duty, so I was easing through Operations as unobtrusively as possibly, trying to merge with the paintwork, yet make the best possible speed for the door. The choice of lunch venue had been a difficult one: The Fox was nearest, but the quality of its provender marginal. It would be a ploughman's eaten at the semi-crouch in the crowded saloon to avoid a dart in the temple. Or a plate of chef's delicious pie at the more distant Brave Piper, taken in the garden beneath the shade of a Martini umbrella. No contest really. I was in the very act of placing my hand on the door handle, when Fenner performed one of his slow-motion leaps, seemingly out of nowhere.

Fenner was the senior operation's duty officer. Ex-RAF, fifty-ish, a strange, chain-smoking, twittery, bird-like little man with a toothbrush moustache and round startled eyes set in a thin face. His baggy suit hung on his skeletal frame like becalmed sails. His movements were reminiscent of a wounded bird trying to take off; his behaviour fussy, anxious and importuning. Worst of all, I was to some extent at his disposal and he had a nasty habit of disposing me.

It was imperative that eye contact be avoided. I made a feint towards him which caught him somewhat off-guard. A sweep to the left and the door would be mine. But Fenner wasn't to be so easily out manoeuvred; fleeing down the line of the low partition dividing Ops from the main office thoroughfare, he executed a tight right wheel at the end and came on at the gallop. If I had opened the door at this point, his momentum would have planted him in the back of it. Effective, but it lacked finesse, and in any case would have contravened the rules of engagement. Instead, I decided on a strategic withdrawal to Crewing, followed by a galloping retreat through Bradbury's outer office—still enemy territory—finally making good my escape via the exit in Flight Planning. So determined, I turned with Fenner at my heels, and in that instant the campaign was lost: Pete

Ashington from the Nav office having chosen that moment to enter from Crewing, he blocked my line of retreat, unwittingly completing a classic pincer movement.

With as much dignity as I could muster, I hauled my colours, hoping the terms of surrender would be merciful. Fenner gave me a big, malevolent, nicotine-stained, rabbit-toothed, despotic smile. No prisoners then, I thought miserably.

El Presidente said: 'How would you like a trip.' He wasn't asking.

So that was it: transportation. Probably for life. Harsh terms these. I asked him where, half expecting St Helena or Elbe.

'Teheran,' he said.

'Oh,' I said, wondering if he knew I wasn't all that keen on hot countries.

Iran

On board, there would be thirty in-calf, pedigree Friesian cows, which we were to transport from Brussels to Teheran, via a tech stop in Istanbul. The animals would be penned side by side—heads to port, tails to starboard—within a framework of scaffolding poles, the deck protected from their excretions by a covering of canvas sheets covered with straw. A narrow gangway on the port side would give access to the animals and to the rear of the aircraft. According to the paperwork, Katarina, a Swedish farm manager charged with the animals' welfare, would be joining us in Brussels to accompanying the cattle to their final destination. I was charged with the welfare of the aircraft's cabin and to this end, a few hours earlier, had stood blenching before Jack Bradbury as he signed over to me the humane killer and its cartridges.

Bradbury was not a man to be trifled with at the best of times. This was not the best of times. His normally florid face had taken on a pre-cerebrovascular puce, and his bristling yellow moustache looked like an angry little porcupine trying to climb up his nostrils. He clearly thought I was as incompetent as I thought I was. Possibly more so. Therefore, handing me a gun and putting me in charge of cabin safety must have seemed to him like handing Guy Fawkes a blazing torch and inviting him to inspect the cellars. The instructions for the weapon's use were brief, peremptory: if any animal escaped the pen, or threatened a cabin window with its horns (the aircraft was pressurised), I was required to press the muzzle of the weapon to the miscreant's forehead and squeeze off. I wondered if he knew how unlikely that was and just what a poltroon I was? Judging by his demeanour, it was odds-on he did.

Before departure there was one more job to be done, which for anyone else would be to run the gauntlet. It involved a visit to the freight office to collect the flight's cargo documentation, where ruled the fearsomely misanthropic Harry Banks. Somewhere in his fifties, red of face and choleric of nature, Harry was a loner. Though occasionally there would be an assistant working with him, he was nevertheless always essentially alone: he worked alone and he dined alone, he lived alone and he'd probably die alone, and doubtless that would be how he'd want it. He appeared to be someone who didn't need company (although there was the persistent rumour of a regular weekend liaison somewhere.) A man of obsessively regular habit, every day at ten minutes to one he would don the grey three-quarter length carcoat—the one he had been born in—and make his way to the canteen. There, with a copy of a broadsheet propped before him on the sauce bottles, he would sit alone, chewing through his lunch with an expression of mild revulsion on his face. At this time, he was incommunicado and only the fool or desperado would approach. Anybody with the trousers to try would earn his customary opening explosive 'Christ almighty!' followed by a growled instruction to get hence and to come to the office after 1400. At which point, the conversation would be over and nobody with an ounce of common sense would attempt continue it, not even if it was to tell him his office had wings.

The extraordinary thing was that, despite Harry's wintery ill-humour, he was quite unaccountably civil to me, even when I adopted the gross familiarity of using his Christian name, a special favour he returned. I can only imagine he thought I was somebody I wasn't. I certainly did my best to be that person—whoever he thought that was—whenever I visited his office, keeping my visits brief, my conversation friendly but business-like, and never questioning his instructions. This special relationship was a wonder to my colleagues and a source of some jealousy at the ease with which I was able to conduct business with the peppery Harry.

My visit today was no different from any previous, except that the documentation, which included much veterinary paperwork, was enormous. But one thing that could be relied on, was its accuracy. Harry was punctilious, there was never any error in his work, a fact that would have some significance for us down the line.

A prematurely dark early evening greeted us in Brussels, along with the first of many tribulations that would beset the trip: the cargo was not there. It should have been waiting for us when we arrived. We should have loaded up and departed for Istanbul hours ago. Instead, after a long impatient wait, the skipper Billy McNair had declared that we would night stop. So saying, the crew had departed for the hastily-arranged hotel accommodation our agent had found, leaving me alone on *TC* to await the arrival of the cattle.

A storm was brewing, a big one; the darkening sky was barricaded with cloud and, not far off to the East, a single towering anvil-headed cumulonimbus with fire in its hair held centre stage. The air trapped in the cabin was fetid, almost viscous. *TC* needed ventilating, and so did I. On the flightdeck, the little white light above the battery master switch glowed, indicating that *TC* was receiving power from the bellowing ground power unit on the tarmac beneath her nose. I would need that. Locating the hydraulic pump selector, the only switch on the engineer's crowded panel who's purpose I had been shown, I flicked it on. Back in the cabin, removing the locks from the forward freight door, I reached under a small flap in the fuselage wall to press and hold the switch in the 'up' position. A thump and an ascending whine and the hydraulic ram in the door frame began to extend, pushing the heavy door outwards and upwards. Seconds later, a rending twang reminded me, just too late, that I had forgotten to disconnect the ventilation conduit and electrical supply which crossed the freight door to feed air and lighting to the port side of the cabin. They were disconnected now.

With the door fully elevated and its bracing strut fitted, I surveyed the damage. I'd got off lightly; just an easily-fixable couple of bent pins in the electrical socket, that was all. With the door open the air moved more freely, but only a little more. The dry ramp on which we were parked was pale, dusty, almost white, so that when the first big raindrops plopped onto it the black disks of moisture stood out like spots on a dalmatian. Suddenly, away to the right, a billion volts or so spread a vein of fire down the sky, doubtless leaving a nasty scorch mark somewhere on Belgium, before an ear-splitting crack announced the arrival of the thunder, and shortly thereafter, the rain. It began as a rattle on the fuselage, then a drumming that quickly increased in volume to a continuous roar as the sky opened. Despite the ferocity of the storm, it was pleasant to sit in the warm dry cabin, gazing through the waterfall cascading from the lip of the raised door, at the lashing rain streaming off the props and bouncing a foot high from the wing. But the storm's force was soon spent, the rain dwindling to a persistent drizzle as the thunder rolled away northwards to where spectral lightening continued to flicker, silently now, amongst the heaped clouds. As darkness fell, Brussels became a sparkle of lights. Big jets blasted off into a now-starry sky. I waited. It was late when I finally gave up the vigil. Snapping the battery master switch off and plunging *TC* into darkness, I groped my way back to the double seats rigged opposite the freight door and curled up uncomfortably on one of them, trying either to get some sleep or put my back out, I can't remember which, but I seem to remember that the latter was the end result. It was not until 0200 that the agent came to inform me that the cattle would not now be arriving until the morning and to suggest I follow the crew to the hotel to grab a few hours rest.

It was not a great start.

With the afternoon sun marching window-shaped patches of light across the backs of our gently mooing cargo, we droned south-east at a steady 300 knots. At this stage, there was little for me to do but keep an eye on the cattle and carry oceans of tea to the flight deck. The skipper, Billy McNair was, like me, a tea-drinking Olympian, whom I would challenge often before we saw home again. Sharing the flying duties with him were the company's safety captain, the laconic bearded Antipodean, John Shepherd; first officer Brett Lockwood—possessor of the finest RAF-pattern "wizard prang" moustache I'd ever seen—and a brace of flight engineers, Paddy and Dave—the latter a handsome rogue who, a couple of years later, would find himself languishing in a North African slammer on smuggling charges. All of the crew were either instructing or being instructed on *TC's* operational particularities, which I had learned were legion. Katarina, the Swedish farm manager and cattle expert, and I completed the team.

Byzantium, Constantinople, Istanbul, the gateway to the East, it was sliding by beneath the port wing as *TC* turned onto final approach, and the two sleep-ridden laggards in the back were missing it all. But the fluctuating air pressure and the more urgent note of the engines brought us to full wakefulness and to the windows.

From up here, the city looked deceptively peaceful in the afternoon sunshine. From the jumble of architecture, tall fingers of minarets pierced the sky, roseate and white and topped with flashing gold. The waters of the Golden Horn, coppery with reflected sunlight and painful to the naked eye, discouraged all but the briefest acknowledgment of the Galata Bridge, at who's northern end the old European quarter of Pera tumbled down to the water's edge. While on the other side of the crowded harbour, the huge mosque of Suleiman the Magnificent (I didn't know that at the time), with its four minarets, dominated the old part of the city. And beyond it, the 200-foot Galata Tower showed that they knew how to do high-rise, only elegantly, way back in the fourteenth century.

The muezzins were calling the faithful as we taxied onto stand. As usual, the props had barely stopped turning before the flight crew were thinning out to the hotel, leaving Katarina and I to look after our charges. A wall of warm air greeted us as I raised the fore and aft cargo doors and Katarina, a slight figure in army-surplus combats and gold-rimmed spectacles, her hair scraped hard back into a bun, set about the unimaginably tedious and strenuous task of hand milking thirty gravid beasts. With those wrists, she could probably have strangled them all and saved herself the trouble of having to repeat the process, as she would be so obliged in the morning.

As the frothing buckets were handed out to the loaders for disposal, it became clear that avoidance of waste was the order of the day, the buckets being passed among the ground crew and the blood-heat contents quaffed on the spot. Later, Katarina and I, with the agent along to act as interpreter, rode perilously down to the Grand Bazaar in the back of a pickup, in search of hay to assuage the hunger of our cargo.

It took a rattling, jolting half hour to reach our destination, during which the pick-up traded tree-lined avenues for dusty roads, roads for squalid streets, finally spurning those for narrow lanes with patchy cobbles and long tracts of well-trodden earth. Here, the buildings leaned inwards so closely that one side of the thoroughfare lay in black shadow, while the buildings on the opposite side wore a geometric band of sunlight down to the level of the shuttered upper windows, before the buildings opposite cast them also into shadow. The only time these streets would get an even distribution of light would be at high noon.

At last, we pulled up before a pair of battered, paintless doors framing a black rectangle, within which a low-powered bulb wasn't making much progress. Katarina walked up to the doors and hallooed into the darkness. A villainous-looking old bloke with a big grizzled moustache and an avaricious glint in his eye, emerged to demand a king's ransom for ten bales of hay. Katarina bartered him down to something unreasonable and we loaded up. Picking straws out of our hair, we bade him farewell. He eyed us sourly, saying nothing as we drove away. He probably thought the stuff in our hair was rightly his too.

Much later, a guard having been set to watch over the cattle, we finally headed to the hotel to join the rest of the crew. Yes, there was the magnificence of the Blue Mosque; the quirkiness of the Basilica Cistern with its upside-down Medusa head; the splendour of the Topkapi Palace and the myriad other seductions Istanbul had to offer. More relevant to our immediate needs however, there was food and there were beds at the hotel, and both laid prior claims. The jewel in the navel of Byzantium had managed without us for going on 3,000 years, postponement of our visit *sine die* wasn't going to trouble it much.

With the cattle safely fed and watered, a cab sped us south from the city through a no-man's land of building sites and half-finished apartment blocks. Wide roads rolled away on either side, frequently to peter out into heaps of sand and gravel, guarded by bogged-down cement mixers and the bleached carcasses of abandoned trucks. A few ragged kids roamed the sites, stopping to stare as we swept past. The road curved left into a climbing gradient and gradually the buildings began to take on the aspect of near-completion. At the top of the slope, the taxi turned abruptly from the road, swept between a pair of white-columned gateposts and deposited us, at the end of a short drive, before the eight stories of dazzling white stone and green-tinted glass that was the hotel. Shrubs and flowers abounded, and just visible behind the building, a streak of the Marmara glittered in the late afternoon sunshine.

Inside, the air conditioning was just right. And the concierge's smile remained just right, even when a rancid-smelling duo presented itself to him: an affront to his otherwise-pristine lobby. No doubt this explained the rapidity with which our rooms were allocated and why a bellboy, who looked uncannily like Peter Lorrie and struggled with Katarina's massive suitcase, hustled us into the lift before we trod anything into the carpet. Depositing Katarina at her room, two doors down from mine, having arranged to call for her in half an hour to escort her down to dinner with the rest of the crew, I was left with the nakedly acquisitive Peter Lorrie at my door. A desperate search of my pockets produced only a mutilated fag packet, two bob English and a small tumbleweed of pocket-fluff. Awkward. I really had to see Billy about funds. Meantime, all I could offer Peter Lorrie was a broad smile, my repeated thanks and a rapidly-closing door on his distraught countenance.

Half an hour later, I walked down the hall and tapped on the wrong door. At least that's what it felt like when my knock was answered. It was that much-clichéd moment from the movies, where the dowdily-dressed heroin transforms herself into a vision of femininity. Gone were the androgynous combats, replaced by a simple black dress. Her hair, released from its prison-warder-pattern bun, fell about her shoulders to frame a lightly made-up oval face. Whereas, in my thrice-worn grey-white shirt and crumpled trousers, I looked like a remand prisoner who'd made a run for it. I managed some incoherent noises of appreciation and, staying a couple of steps behind her so as not to sully the image, we walked down to the bar to join the rest of the crew. They saw us. They parted. Katarina walked into their midst and they closed around her like the waters of the Red Sea closing around the pursuing Egyptians.

The following day there was just time to take a swim in the Marmara from the small beach behind the hotel; the water pool-table blue and as warm as milk. A brief moment of relaxation before we headed back to the airport.

Airborne again and heading east with a dash of south in it, the atmosphere in the aircraft had deteriorated considerably since yesterday: it reeked like a farmyard, the cattle slipping on the canvas floor covering, slimed now with their droppings. The penning was also in poor shape, sagging where the cattle had leant on it.

Back in her passenger-carrying days, *TC* would have offered her customers a certain level of comfort. These were no longer her glory days, not by a long chalk. To convert her to cargo configuration, every furnishing had been stripped out; seats, carpets, curtains, fittings, the lot, leaving the cabin an unadorned empty tube. The only reminder of her previous life the rows of reading lights, air louvres and call buttons on the panels above the windows on each side of the aircraft. The removal of all this sound-deadening material was not without consequence. The DC7 was equipped with four Wright Cyclones, the most powerful radial engines built in the USA at the time. With a combined thrust of over 13,000 horsepower, they levied a heavy price for their services: noise. Unrelenting, inescapable, exhausting noise, accompanied by rattling tides of vibration that ebbed and flowed between her wingtips and along the entire length of the fuselage. Cabin pressurisation rendered food, drink and cigarettes flavourless. There was nothing to do but doze fitfully on the two double seats rigged aft of the flightdeck door, or re-read two-day old newspapers.

In contrast to our discomfort, the cattle seemed to have accepted their strange new environment with equanimity, standing quietly—when they weren't slipping—in a head-drooping row. In fact, so great was their relaxation that Katarina became, I thought at first, unaccountably concerned and took to patrolling the gangway. The reason for her disquiet soon became apparent. It started with the number six in the line, who had become so snuggly wedged between the flanks of her sisters, that she took it into her head to lie down. Whereupon Five and Seven grasped the opportunity to take the weight off and planted their behinds on her.

This presaged the start of a dangerous trend.

Katarina quickly explained that if any animal laid down and couldn't regain its feet because its neighbours were leaning on it, given the conditions and its advanced pregnancy, the animal was likely to die where it lay. They had to be kept on their feet at all costs. So saying, she ducked under the penning and in amongst her charges.

Number Three chose this moment to add to our troubles by putting a hoof through the penning; she looked as though she were trying to make up her mind whether to join me in the gangway or simply retrieve her foot. Six was acting like she wanted to roll over and have someone tickle her tummy, and Five and Seven were resisting Katarina's gasping attempts to get them to give up their seat on Six. Then, as if we didn't have enough to deal with, from the other end of the line Thirty loosed off a terrible wailing moo, which Katarina interpreted as: 'I think I'm going to calve now.' Well, if she was, nature would just have to take its course, we had our work cut out already.

If Three got into the gangway there was the real danger of her running amok in the cabin, even putting a horn through a window. To prevent that I would have to shoot her—or more likely, cravenly hand the gun to Katarina to do it. Impelled by the appalling thought, I clapped on to Three's prodigal leg, bent close to her left ear and shouted some abuse down it. I got a face-full of ruminant-rich tongue and a white eye for my trouble, then she delicately extracted her leg from my grasp and withdrew it to its rightful place. Relieved, I went to Katarina's aid, grabbing hold of Six's halter while Katarina hauled on its tail. After much straining and cursing, we managed to get her back on her feet, despite Five and Seven, who did everything they could to obstruct our endeavours. By the time Katarina came to examine Thirty, the animal had quietened down considerably; the immediate danger of her giving birth having apparently passed.

We slumped dirty, tired and sweaty back into our seats, daring any beast to disturb us further. Katarina told me how Friesians had originally been imported into England from Holland at the turn of the century, and was just explaining how this shipment was the first in a five-year farming plan for Iran, when the engines took on a different note and the cabin tilted as we began our approach to Teheran's Mehrabad Airport. Up front, the flight crew were pushing a few piloty buttons and pulling one or two levers, quite oblivious of the heroic efforts we had made to save them.

Somewhat incautiously, we had relaxed in the belief that the hardest part of the job was over. But once on the ground, our anxiety quickly began to ratchet back up as the freight doors were opened and the oven-breath of afternoon washed in. The cattle didn't like it; they moved restlessly against the penning, lowing their dissatisfaction. Katarina was on the alert again. At her behest, a water bucket chain was quickly established with the ground crew, while the skipper made contact with a bloke in para-military uniform who had come to meet us and whom we supposed to be our agent.

Now, Billy was what you might call an anxious airman. As far as I could tell he was a good pilot (his landings were all greasers), with many flying hours logged on DC7s. But he was a worrier; ever suspicious of the weather, doubtful about serviceability, always on the lookout for trouble. Normally pleasant and affable, when stressed, his cherubic features were inclined to suffuse deep pink and he was liable to speak sharply and not always diplomatically.

He was anxious now.

It was hardly surprising. This was the first flight of an important Iranian government-sponsored farming programme, intended to introduce pedigree cattle to the country, and the company was salivating at the prospect of many more such flights. Everything needed to go well, but right now the first, very expensive consignment was sitting out here on the ramp frying, and nobody seemed to be doing anything to fix it. Where, for instance, were the livestock ramps? The trucks to transport the animals? The handlers? The consignees? The fuss everybody should be making to get the problem sorted out? These were questions he put to the paramilitary in a tone of some asperity, his pleasant Scot's burr thickening as his voice rose to an accusatory pitch and his index finger embarked on a series of belligerent air stabs in the direction of the agent's chest.

In a state of barely-suppressed outrage, the agent cut the diatribe short, demanded our cargo manifests and retired in high dudgeon—to return very shortly afterwards with back-up in the shape of a couple of grim-faced blokes in similarly marshal attire. With a shock, I had only just noticed that he was wearing a Sam Browne with a semi-automatic dangling from it, his hand resting absently on its butt. His pals at the foot of the steps were also carrying. It was ridiculous to imagine that he would draw the thing on us, nevertheless it encouraged rapid compliance when he demanded our passports. Billy made noises of protest but sensibly complied. Then, while Katarina was allowed to stay to minister to her charges, we were escorted from the aircraft.

The sun struck blindingly up at us from the ramp as we walked, the white concrete shimmering, exuding vision-distorting waves of heat that transformed aircraft and equipment into wobbling surrealist shapes. The baking ground scorched through the soles of our shoes and we began to shed jackets and ties as we walked towards the terminal. Stepping out of the glare into the building, the temperature plunged in the brutally-efficient air conditioning, sweat chilled on our brows and for the moment we were as blind as bats. Unnecessarily supplementing the air conditioning, were several of those fans to be seen in old Bogart movies. Hung from the ceiling on long metal poles, they rotated at a dignified fifteen RPM, serving no useful purpose whatsoever as far as I could see, except maybe as set dressing. It was a gloomy building; what light there was coming from a line of small windows set high in the walls just below the ceiling. The agent led us through the hall to deposit us in a small side room, closed the door firmly behind us and left us to stew. Through the slats of the drawn blinds all that was visible was a few yards of sun-baked ramp and a couple of parked vehicles. The office featured a desk, a couple of chairs, a telephone and a palpable air of hostility. Nobody spoke. We had got off on the wrong foot here: our aircraft was unwelcome, its cargo more so, we were unwelcome and Billy, who's temper may have carried him further than he intended, appeared to be top of the unwelcome-in-Teheran list. His anger had subsided and he sat quietly now, drawing on a cigarette and staring at the floor.

Fifteen minutes later High Dudgeon was back—only without the altitude. In fact, he displayed perplexity and embarrassment now in equal measure as he beckoned us to follow him, a request it was impossible to comply with since he insisted on holding the door for us. Then, scampering to the head of the column, he led us a short distance to what turned out to be a comfortably-furnished, well-stocked bar. Snapping his fingers at the white-jacketed barmen he dished out our passports.

'Please make yourselves comfortable. Order whatever you want, no charge. I will be as quick as I can.' A few clipped words to the barman and he was gone.

Whatever had caused the sudden change of heart, none of us could guess, nor did we care; we were soon comfortably seated around the bar, we had our passports back, iced drinks in our hands and we were no longer persona non grata. Shortly afterwards, Katarina arrived. The tight bun at the back of her head was coming apart, damp strands of it hanging lankly about her sweat-streaked face. Her glasses were dusty and there were bits of straw caught in her clothing.

'It's hot,' she said as we all shot guiltily to our feet. Taking her pick of the seven stools that were simultaneously offered, she sank the frosty glass of lager she was given and asked for more.

Eventually our man returned, offered Katarina a stiff military bow and turned to Billy. His hands writhed together as he sought the words to say what he had to say, which obviously wasn't going to be welcome to us. It appeared that he had discovered from our documentation that our business, and therefore our presence, was legitimate after all. (It was in any case inconceivable that Harry's paperwork could be wrong.) Nevertheless, there was the bad news.

'The animals are not consigned to Teheran—'

'But…' interjected Billy.

'…I know, Captain, your documentation states that this is so, but I am sorry, this is incorrect.' He held up an airway bill. 'The consignee named here does not reside in Teheran. His company has no office here. We have not been notified of your flight. No one requested permission to land livestock here, which would in any case have been refused. We have no equipment here to unload animals, and without the presence of the consignee it would not be permitted, anyway.' He shrugged. 'I am sorry sir.' There was no doubting his sincerity.

Reluctantly, Billy nodded his acceptance and everybody began venting their frustrations, until the agent coughed loudly to attract our attention.

'I suppose,' he began deferentially, 'you could take the cattle to the consignee.'

The way he said it, I thought he was going to give us directions by road: *start your aircraft and turn left out of the main gate.*

Usher asked, 'Where is the consignee?'

'Isfahan.'

Price looked at Stuart: 'Isfah-what?'

'Where?' asked Billy.

'Issssfahan' the agent repeated slowly. 'To the south' and he pointed like maybe he had a hand-bearing compass in his pocket.

Billy, again exercised, began listing all the reasons we should be disembarking our cargo here. This time the agent retained his composure, but remained firm: the animals would not be unloaded in Tehran, they must be taken to Isfahan. Further discussion was not invited. The *fait* was well and truly *accompli.*

A scramble for charts ensued. Isfahan was quickly located, 330 kilometres to the south, in the desert. It boasted a single runway, was surrounded by hills and lacked all but the most basic facilities. So basic in fact, that they did not include such luxuries as runway lights, let alone an instrument landing system. It did have a control tower and VHF telephony, though it wasn't entirely certain that there would be anybody in the tower when we arrived and, even so, would they have the radio switched on?

Further pessimistic conjecture was abandoned, for there was no time to lose. We had an hour and a half of daylight left to make Isfahan, or we'd be staying in Teheran till sun up—by which time we'd probably be shipping barbeque.

Katarina grabbed my arm and bundled me out of the bar: 'We have to do the milking, you know. They are in pain.'

I didn't get a chance to tell her I'd never milked anything in my life, except maybe my petty cash allowance. For all I knew, you grabbed the beast's tail and cranked until gold top gushed out of its ears. Out on the baking aeroplane, Katarina soon discovered that my ineptitude was quite unshakable and got on with the job alone. There was no time to milk the whole line, just the three or four urgent cases. The remainder would have to wait.

Though we had barely sufficient fuel for the trip, there was no time to uplift more (pilots always want more fuel). But, assured by the agent that Esso operated in Isfahan, it was not long before *TC* was climbing out of Tehran. A brief vision of minarets spiking the haze of the city wheeled beneath us as we turned south; a scene that quickly gave way to a drab palette of sand, dotted with scrub vegetation.

By now, the cabin looked and smelt like the proverbial Augean livery. The penning was straining audibly under the weight the animals were subjecting it to as they grew evermore restless in their cramped, slippery surroundings. The sudden changes of pitch they had to endure during take-off and landing, and the bumps and lurches they experienced in flight, unsettled them and there was much stamping and many a white eye to be seen. The situation was deteriorating rapidly now. They had already been on board for double the scheduled time and they desperately needed grass, water, fresh air and the freedom to move. They were in poor shape and we were soon struggling to maintain order as they tested the rickety penning and more and more of them attempted to lie down. At the end of the line with a little more room to spare, Thirty managed it, then rolled over on her side. Katarina took of her glasses, leaned on the penning and looked down sadly at the moaning animal. She crouched beside it and caressed its neck. It lifted its head in feeble response, then laid it down again. A glazed eye stared unblinkingly at the ceiling. I glanced at the black box beside my seat, then down at the still animal: I didn't think it would be needed. Katarina stood up, replaced her glasses and we went back to work on the rest of them.

We landed at twilight, straight in, no fancy approach patterns. Standing inside the flight deck door as we taxied in and stooping to look out of the cockpit windows, I spotted a small single-storey terminal building in the sweeping beams of the landing lights, its whitewashed walls bordered by neat flower beds. To its left, another low building atop which was displayed the familiar oval of the Esso sign, and to the left again stood the control tower. The rest was just sand and tarmac—though there were a couple of mysterious black shapes out in the gloom of no-man's land, between the terminal building and the runway. My curiosity was tweaked, but there was no time to indulge it now as *TC* lumbered to a halt in front of the terminal and we experienced the customary brief, crushing silence that follows the shutting down of engines.

As I had already learnt, flight crew do not like to hang about when a statutory minimum rest period is about to start, and the engines were still emitting erratic volleys of cooling ticks as Billy and Co fled to the hotel accommodation which had been arranged by Farrokh. A big man of much natural authority, Farrokh appeared to be in charge of everything. This left Katarina and I with the task of supervising the disembarkation of the cattle—except that, as far as we could make out, there was no way of accomplishing this. Farrokh's English was decidedly rudimentary, but since we had no answering grasp of Farsi, he was as it were the one-eyed king in the land of the blind. Thus, by much gesturing and repetition, he explained that there was no livestock equipment at Isfahan: no ramps, no scissors trucks, nothing. Now, since *TC's* floor was fifteen feet above the ground, this was a further setback to a trip that seemed to me to have fiasco written all over it—and having authored not a few of my own, I knew about fiascos.

But we reckoned without Farrokh's ingenuity and the determination of his gang. Improvisation was the operative system and enthusiasm its fuel: we could only stand back and admire it in action. First, a set of heavy passenger steps was placed on the back of a flatbed truck (I have no idea how they did that). Planks were then laid lengthways down the steps to form a ramp. This assemblage was then backed up to *TC's* open rear cargo door and the jacks on the steps used to align the top step with the door sill and to steady the truck. More planks were then positioned to form a second ramp at ninety degrees to the first, from the bed of the truck to the ground where the consignee's wagons awaited the cattle.

When all was secured, Katarina joined the gang at the rear freight door to supervise the offloading, starting off by working what seemed to me a miracle. Yelling and hauling on its halter, she bullied and coaxed Thirty until it rose from the dead and tottered to its feet, bellowing its displeasure in a disgraceful display of ingratitude. I watched with horrid fascination as it became the first beast to face the descent. Natural reluctance was evident, but no dallying was to be entertained: a rope had been passed across the animal's hindquarters, a loader taking hold of each end of it, while a third got a grip of the animal's halter. It was then frog-marched to the door, where the halter man let go, and sidestepped to get out of the way as the two men at the rear hauled forward on the rope. As the beast teetered reluctantly on the threshold, two more of the gang put their shoulders to its rump and pushed, hard. The cow stumbled out onto the steep incline of the ramp and, to avoiding somersaulting, sat down. It tobogganed rapidly down the planks—wearing an expression similar to that which you might expect your granny to wear on finding herself on a theme park death ride—to collide noisily with the back of the cab of the truck; the handler waiting there to receive it executing a neat matador-like *cemsl* to avoid being flattened. Though Katarina watched this spectacle through splayed fingers, the animal arrived unscathed, if a little stunned. It was quickly coaxed via the second smaller ramp to the ground and led off to the truck, before its induced temporary amenability wore off.

Having seen this routine repeated a couple of times and finding myself surplus to requirements, I took myself off to the cabin in search of the box of soft drinks we'd loaded in Istanbul. With a bottle of Fanta and an opener, I sat down in the open forward freight door, legs dangling, the still-warm wind off the desert drying the sweat on my face. It may have been tiredness or distraction (I had just spotted a huge inverted wasp floating in the top of the Fanta bottle and was musing on what the Coca Cola Company would make of Iran's addition of *corpus delicti* to its carbonated beverages), or I might have detected the uncomfortable motion of the floor earlier; an odd bobbing sensation. I was puzzled, an emotion quickly replaced by one of horror as realisation set in. Leaping to my feet I tried to attract the attention of the crowd down aft, but the light was poor where I stood, the gangway obstructed with people and the noise

72

level high. Desperately, I raced into the flight deck, stumbled down the forward steps and back under *TC*'s belly, noting as I did so the nose wheel bouncing lightly on the tarmac.

Error, it appeared, had crept in—again—and my beloved *TC* was about to sit on her tail. This would unquestionably end my career—and very possibly hers. I had omitted to fit the tail post, the stout metal rod which hung down under the tail—a common feature of nosewheel aircraft—to support it during loading and unloading, during which the aircraft might become unbalanced. Now, as I stood below the rear cargo door, gesticulating to the loaders like a tic tac man in a sudden change of odds, I dared not look at the narrowing gap between the aircraft's tail and the ground. Up there in the doorway I could see clearly the problem: a crowd of men and the cattle they had moved aft ready for disembarkation.

It was Farrokh who was first to correctly interpret my frantic signals. Immediately, he set about moving the cattle back to the front of the cabin, before coming down to join me as I retrieved the tail post from its stowage in the rear hold. However, we quickly discovered that despite having shifted the cattle forward, the gap between the tail and the ground was still smaller than the post. It is a peculiarity of tricycle undercarriage aircraft that, even when the centre of gravity has been restored (as was the case here), they often maintain their tail-heavy attitude until the engines are started, at which point the true centre of gravity asserts itself and the aircraft lurches forward, sometimes quite spectacularly. But *TC's* engines would not be started again before we departed, so further improvisation was indicated—Farrokh's speciality. It wasn't pretty, but it worked: he found a lump hammer and, attaching the post to the lug under the tail, hammered it as near vertical as made no difference.

With the cattle consigned at last to the waiting trucks, I bade Katarina—who was to travel on with her charges to their ultimate destination—goodbye and a metallic-blue ford bore her away in the van of a billowing dust cloud, while Farrokh summoned a cab to take me to the hotel. Before leaving, I asked that the aircraft be cleaned and that the sheets covering the floor be placed in the hold. For a moment, I thought I detected fleeting puzzlement on Farrokh's face, but he accepted the request without demur.

A newish powder-blue Chevy Impala with slippery plastic protective seat covers sped me through the streets. As we turned down a pleasant lamp-lit avenue and I recovered from my latest slalom across the back seat, I expressed mild surprise at finding so many young people at this late hour (it was nearly midnight), seated beneath the trees, apparently engrossed in study. The driver explained that they were students from the university, intent on study. The Groves of Academe made literal. One had to admire their scholarly dedication, a level of application not quite matched, I fancied, by their UK counterparts. Or maybe I just moved among like-minded under-achievers.

An anonymous door in a whitewashed wall led off the street into the hotel's walled compound. Shrubs lined the paths and a quadrangle was set with beds of poppies, irises and the deep yellow of Austrian briar. From somewhere nearby came the soothing scatter of an unseen fountain. Inside, I had a fleeting impression of polished mosaic floors and low comfy-looking sofas as I climbed the stairs to the first-floor quad surrounding a central garden, off which led the rooms. In my room, there was just time to peel off my by-now filthy uniform before a low bed, the size of a couple of grand pianos and shrouded in a mosquito net, claimed me. With the final reassuring thought that we would at last be heading home tomorrow, Morpheus gave me the shot. Sadly, the thought turned out to be not worth the electrons it was written on.

A muffled squeak of surprise woke me. I was just in time to catch a glimpse of a horrified chambermaid retreating from the appalling vision of me spread-eagled naked on the bed under the net (it had been a hot night), before the door slammed—the Do Not Disturb sign swinging accusingly from the inside handle in her wake. Unsure of local custom, I spent much of the morning wondering what retribution might be demanded for such an outrage. Angry blokes in dishdashas, wielding unnecessarily-sharp knives, featured quite a bit in my fevered imagination. But back out at the airport, other concerns quickly replaced the recurring vision I had of my ritual gralloching in the hotel garden.

It was when we trooped into the Esso office to order the fuel for our return journey that the first of the day's embuggerances—not counting the affronted maid thing—made its appearance. The scene went thus:

Billy: 'Good morning. We'd like some 115/145 octane Avgas, please.'

Polite Bloke In Open-Neck White Shirt, Seated At Desk: 'I'm sorry, sir, we don't stock that here. Only kerosene for the Viscounts.' And he pointed out of the window to where the amorphous shapes which had so intrigued me the night before had resolved, in the harsh light of day, into two Vickers Viscounts. Although, even at this distance, it was clear that neither of these particular examples would be troubling their element ever again. They were windowless with flat tyres and gaping hatches. The nearest one also appeared to have anhedral wings—not a feature of the original design—the droop indicating a broken main spar.

But there was no time for further conjecture, back here in the office Billy was reaching take-off power, along the lines of: 'Why the bleddy hail ded they sayned us here eff ye've nae fuel?'

It was hardly surprising that much of this was lost on the Esso rep, but he must have got the gist of it for he quickly offered a solution: tankers, with the correct fuel, could be dispatched from Mehrabad, a four-and-a-half-hour drive away to the north. Problem solved. However, our gremlin hadn't finished with us yet (it had barely got started.) It would take, the rep told us, twenty-four hours to arrange and to transport across the desert. Amongst the crew there was much shaking of heads and examining of shoes in silent frustration. Dave the engineer was an expectant father who had let it be known that 'The missus (was) about to drop'; Brett was sucking the end of his moustache and possibly wondering why he had ever left the RAF; and Billy was pink to the tips of his ears with dissatisfaction. The atmosphere was so tense that I was quite relieved when the question of payment for the fuel arose and I was dispatched to the aircraft to retrieve the fuel carnet (credit card), from the Perspex holder fixed to the inside of the flight deck door.

It was still only mid-morning but the ramp was already oven-hot. I had decided on a quick detour to reconnoitre the wrecked Viscounts, Jock having muttered darkly about the possible value of any avionic equipment that might have been left on board to rot. But I just wanted to satisfy my inveterate curiosity: think cats. I was half way across the intervening scrub between the parking ramp and the aircraft when the dark shapes—half a dozen of them—rose up in the penumbra beneath the starboard wing of the nearest wreck. I halted. One of the shapes moved out into the sunlight, a couple of the others closing up behind. Dogs: mean-looking, rangy, vulpine, yellow-eyed dogs. They were a rough bunch; lop-eared and mangy, with piano-key ribcages and high—presumably empty—bellies. The leader stood stock still, head drooping, watching me. I like dogs. I didn't like these dogs. Curiosity extinguished, I turned about and continued on my errand towards *TC*, surfing on her own shimmering mirror image on the baking concrete.

It was not only the suffocating sirocco released when I opened *TC's* door that sent me reeling, but the choking stench borne out upon it. Taking a deep breath and with a handkerchief over my nose and mouth, I stepped into the cabin. It had undoubtedly been cleaned, though the canvas sheets had not been placed in the hold as I had requested. Instead, they had been folded neatly and stacked amidships. But they had clearly been cleaned and could not account for the intensity of the stink, so I went in search of somebody. It turned out to be Farrokh (didn't he ever go home?) He came striding across from the terminal, smiling, to meet me and our conversation proceeded thus:

'Salam.'

'Er, yes…Shazam, Farrokh. I asked for the sheets to be put in the hold.'

'Yes, all sheets in hold.'

'No, they're in the cabin.'

'No, in hold, pliss.'

'No, don't think so.'

'Yes. Come, pliss.'

I followed him to the rear hold. He opened it and, smiling triumphantly, held out a hand in a "ta-dah" gesture. A moment's bafflement and then realisation. A simple misunderstanding had arisen over our respective pronunciation and therefore our interpretation of the word "sheets". This had resulted in the carful collection and packing of twenty-odd plastic fertiliser bags of dung from the cabin and their stowage in the stifling heat of the rear hold, where they quickly cooked down into neatly-packaged parcels of liquifying putridity. Little wonder the aircraft smelt worse than a line of rock-festival crappers. The misunderstanding was quickly and cheerfully cleared up, the bags donated to the terminal building flower beds. Leaving the *TC's* door open to air the cabin, I collected the carnet and headed back to the Esso office.

I handed the card to Billy. He handed it to the Rep. The rep took it, smiled, looked at the card, stopped smiling and handed it back. What emerged from the swearing and general agitation that followed was that the carnet was out of date; it was out of date and the company had no credit arrangement here. Much consternation and discussion followed, but what it boiled down to was that we should have to pay cash for any fuel, in advance. A whip round ensued. Including much of the funds the skipper held for expenses, such as accommodation and handling fees, it raised just enough to buy 1200 gallons of fuel and its transportation from Mehrabad. We would not be going anywhere near home on that, but it would get us to Beirut where, apparently, our credit was good.

With nothing else to do but await the tankers' arrival the next day, a somewhat subdued crew trailed back to the hotel. Even these seasoned airmen were beginning to feel a bit unloved. Nobody seemed to know about us, much less care. Our own company hadn't even bothered to supply us with a valid fuel carnet, let alone ensure that our cargo was expected at its destination. It was probably all down to a bit of slackness and an equal amount of bad luck. Not that it mattered; there was nothing to be done about it now but grit our teeth, wait for the fuel, then get ourselves home.

It was as well that we had not included the First Law of Sod—that whatever one wants most doesn't happen—in our calculations, for that latter and most important desire was, again, to be thwarted.

That afternoon Jock and I went downtown. Having made it across the blistering expanse of Shah Square, we strolled through the cool labyrinth of elegant arcades and decorated arches that comprise the Grand Bazaar. Reputed to be one of the finest in the Middle East, rugs, jewellery and kitchenware fought for supremacy of space with vegetable stalls, spice racks and clothing outlets. Despite its glazed roof, the bazaar was ill-lit. Most of the stalls appeared to be narrow yet of considerable depth, and each one had its own method of lighting. The more prosperous featured strings of bare electric bulbs suspended inside their stalls; others, hissing acetylene or paraffin lamps. Isfahan, I soon discovered, is renowned for its carpets and there were many stalls piled with them, beautiful, multi-coloured and intricately-patterned. Other stalls rang to the sound of silversmiths' hammers as craftsmen hunched over trays and vessels, engaged in delicate engraving. Elsewhere, there were wood-carvers, weavers producing vividly-coloured cotton textiles, venders offering fruit and tobacco and almonds.

Passing one stall, a pair of brass lamps caught my eye. The stallholder was on the case, instantly: 'You like this lamps? Twenty-five pounds English.'

It was a pleasant surprise to discover that so many Iranians we had met understood and spoke English so well. And in this instance, even seemed conversant with the current exchange rate.

Jock said, 'No, too much. Ten pounds.'

The stallholder parried: 'I give them for twenty pounds, for you.'

I'd have given him the original asking price, that's how good I was with money. Fortunately, I only had fifteen quid in my pocket. Anyway, Jock was looking after my interests quite well, so I kept my mouth shut.

'Not worth it,' he growled, rapping his knuckles on one of the lamps and looking generally knowledgeable on the subject of brassware.

The stallholder's, 'No, please, see. Very fine,' was lost on Stewart and he took my arm to lead me from the clutches of this apparently unscrupulous villain.

'Eighteen pounds. You take.' His tone demonstrating plainly that at this price he would be bankrupted. But as we melted into the crowd, a last despairing 'Fifteen pounds. Come, you take!' rang out behind us. Jock remained adamant; they were not worth it. We would find a better bargain elsewhere. I presumed he knew a great deal more about these things than I, so I let him lead me away, appreciative of the trouble he was taking on my behalf. But we saw no more lamps and returned empty-handed to the hotel.

In the cool half-light of the lounge, I found Billy taking refuge from the heat of the afternoon. The room was deserted, quiet but for the distant play of the fountain in the garden; the atmosphere just right for whiling away the long empty hours of our enforced stay. Tea was in plentiful supply and, judging by the accumulation of crockery on the low table in front of Billy, had already been taken full advantage of. The skipper was drawing on a cigarette, squinting thoughtfully through the smoke, an attitude most characteristic of him. With him in this apparently reflective mood, and given a little persuasion, I thought I should be able to get him yarning till dinnertime. And with fresh tea ordered, so it proved.

I fed him random questions and each time some parenthesis in his answer offered the opportunity for further questions, which would lead him to reveal another part of his past. He was a good storyteller; these were not aimless ramblings, nor did they seem like braggadocio. They were told simply, his own part often taking second place in the events he described. For instance, he waxed long and lyrical on his wartime instructor on Lancasters, who showed him not just how to fly, but how to survive in what was a notoriously short-lived profession. Yet he was reticent about his own part in the war. But eventually, it came out: thirty missions flown to complete his tour, but one of them discounted for some reason, requiring that he fly one more. And the inevitable; bounced by a German night-fighter on the way home, badly damaged and crashing on the approach to base, only Gallagher and two others surviving, he with back injuries that put him in hospital for five months. Thereafter posted—much to his disgust—to a glider squadron and given a rifle, which was a mystery to him and remained so. Preferring the option of returning from the fray—a luxury not afforded to glider pilots, who were expected to look after themselves once having landed—after a couple of missions, he managed to wangle a posting elsewhere and passed the remainder of the war quietly. Both his father and brother had been pilots, the latter not as fortunate as Gallaher, had not survived the war. Listening to him, I found myself revising my opinion of him: he was not the nervous flyer I had thought him to be, but one who had learnt diligence and caution to stay alive. It had worked then, and it worked now.

Much later, as we sat on, drinking tea and chatting, out of the corner of my eye I spotted Jock slipping furtively across the foyer and up the stairs—bearing *my* lamps. I filed it under "Youthful Lessons in Gullibility", annotated it "Learned" and decided to avoid shopping with Jock ever again.

That evening we sauntered out into a blood-red dusk and a taxi bore us away to a restaurant recommended to us by its driver, (no doubt a little baksheesh from its proprietor having influenced his choice). The journey took fifteen minutes, involving many turns, relieved by short fast runs down broad avenues, before we drew up outside a modern single-story building close to where the magnificent 17th century Khaju bridge crosses the waters of the Zayanderud River. Though the restaurant itself was set in what looked like a builder's yard, the interior was cosily lit, the light falling in carefully-arranged pools on crisp white linen and engraved silverware; the floor and walls adorned with beautiful Isfahan carpets. Wine and dishes of unleavened bread were brought to us, then we were abandoned for a couple of hours while an important trade delegation in the private banqueting room hogged all the facilities. We might have been lepers. An apologetic manager delivered more wine and promises of food soon, but it was not until after the delegation had departed that plates of shashlik (rice, beef, grilled vegetables), appeared, by which time most of the crew were so hammered the chef could have fried one of the carpets and served that.

As we ate, a four-piece band strolled through its western repertoire with its hands in its pockets. Towards the end of the evening, Billy asked if he could borrow the leader's accordion and sit in with the band. He was welcomed warmly and emboldened, I offered my drumming services. Despite the fact that I am a southpaw which necessitated switching the ancient Ludwig kit round, I too was welcomed. Billy turned out to be quite a proficient player, launching into fair rendition of *Blue Moon*, which he also sang. Strangely, unlike most people who lose their accent when singing, Billy kept his, regaling a bemused restaurant with something that came out as 'Bloo Mun.' By 0200 the place was empty, but we were still there, one of the waiters briefly abandoning chair-stacking to reinforce the rhythm section with hand-clapping, while the rest of the crew formed a tottering semi-circle round the bandstand, providing desultory vocal backing in more or less sympathetic diatonics, until the taxi arrived. It turned out to be a small, aged Fiat, who's driver gulped audibly as we advanced on him mob-handed. The skipper took the front seat as was only proper, three piled into the back with a further two on their laps, and Price stood between the front and back seats with his upper half projecting through the open sun roof, looking for all the world like a minor banana-republic dictator who couldn't afford a full motorcade.

By afternoon the next day, the tankers had arrived and, much sobered, we were back at the airport, eager to set off for Beirut, where we would be able to fill up with sufficient fuel to get us home. The stingy load the tankers had brought didn't take long to complete; the bottom of the funds barrel was scraped to the wood to pay our handling fees, and the crew set about bringing *TC* to life. I bade Farrokh "Khodafez" (goodbye), which I'd assiduously learnt at the hotel. But when he answered with what sounded like "sofa cosh", but on subsequent inquiry was probably safar khosh—"bon voyage", he might have been telling me his sandals were on fire.

With the engines rumbling one by one into smoky life, I strapped myself into the crew seat rigged down aft. Out of the window, a ground crewman pulled the chock clear of the port main gear. Beyond him, the Viscount wrecks baked in the sun. But just as I was wondering if the mangy dogs were still out there under that wing, the scene began to dissolve, with astonishing rapidity, into a creamy, yellowish opacity. As the engines ran down into silence, a rising wind could be heard—and felt as it began to buffet the aircraft. There was nothing to be done but wait as the sandstorm shot-blasted what was left of *TC's* scruffy paintwork. It was as if some malign entity was passing the time on its day off in persecution of our little band, just for the hell of it. All I knew was that if I didn't get a clean shirt soon, the collar of the one I was wearing was going to behead me.

Half an hour later the wind was gone, the sun was back on duty and we were airborne for Beirut, a tad over 800 nautical miles away. Almost due west with a bit of north in it, we were headed towards the distant violet smudge of the Zagros mountains, beyond who's barren peaks the waters of the Gulf lick Iran's dry lips. For a few moments, as we climbed out, Isfahan was revealed in plan, clearly visible the arrow-straight line of the Chahar Bagh, Shah Abbas's grand avenue, driven with ruthless precision through the heart of the city. Then it was gone and below, only the desert, a blinding, featureless expanse as we headed for the border of Iraq.

Sometime later, waking up from a catnap and with nothing better to do, I strolled forward to see if tea was required. But as I reached the forward crew seat by the flight deck door, Billy stopped me.

'Hang on a minute. We've a wee problem.'

I sat down beside him, containing my curiosity. Whatever the problem was, its solution required a chart and me to shut up while Billy pored over it. Moments later he strode into the flight deck, still carrying the chart. He was gone but a minute or two before *TC* banked smartly to port. Shortly thereafter, he re-emerged to give me the news. It seemed that our jinx was getting playful again: the sandstorm which had struck Isfahan had fled west, stealing a march on us, and was now threatening our destination. With not enough fuel to hold until the storm cleared, our only option was to divert. Though Kuwait at the north end of the Persian Gulf was a good deal closer, for some reason never explained to me (maybe it too had been affected by weather), Bahrain, nearly 250 miles further south, had been chosen as our alternate. It would be a close-run thing.

Unaware of just how close a run thing it actually was, I went back to my previous occupation—idle window-gazing, as the glittering waters of the Gulf rolled by beneath.

Billy, now at the controls, greased it on at RAF Muharraq, Bahrain (there was barely a ripple on my tea as we touched), following it with a smart-ish taxi to the parking ramp and an equally nimble engine shutdown. In the flight deck, I noted some rueful expressions and meaningful glances in the direction of the engineer's panel. It was Dave, still seated at it and tapping a fuel gauge with his index finger for emphasis, who enlightened me:

'I hope you packed your cozzie. Ten more minutes and you'd have needed it.'

By now, we were so poor that we could no longer afford handling fees. Out here, a sharply competitive system operated: the first handling agent to get steps up to the aircraft got the contract. To forestall this, we developed a system of our own. Stowed in the flight deck was a folding steel emergency ladder. Now, when we arrived anywhere, one of us would open the flight deck door while another rapidly deployed the ladder. Once in place, nobody could put steps on and we could choose only the bare minimum of ground support.

With the door latched back and our ladder deployed, we were greeted by a most welcome sight. For striding across the ramp with a broad smile came an RAF officer, immaculate—if a shade Blimpish—in tropical whites, shorts and all. He immediately put us at our ease. Whatever our status, sufficient fuel would be supplied on credit to get us to Beirut. Whilst it was being loaded, the crew checked the weather and filed a flight plan, before our new friend showed us to the restaurant; all arches and mosaic flooring. Actually, it was more like a canteen with architectural fringe benefits. Here, a somewhat surreal little scene was enacted. As the sun set, we sat at a table with a red gingham cloth, on which familiar English sauce bottles—Heinz and HP—were marshalled, together with a plastic cruet set, to be served egg and chips by a waiter wearing the traditional white *thawb*. Having set our dishes down, he collected a small mat, took himself to the doorway of the canteen, faced Mecca and knelt to his prayers, while we ate our very English corner café fare.

Replete and with *TC* refuelled, we were eager to press on as a stifling night fell on the island. Beirut lay over a thousand miles distant and we were anxious to conclude our odyssey of improvisation and get home. Sadly, there is more than enough space on a virtually empty DC7 to accommodate a jinx, even a huge, obdurate, clingy one such as had accompanied us from the beginning of the trip—and sure enough it was with us again, ready for more mischief, as we lifted off into the deepening velvet of a Gulf dusk, climbing northwest.

Beirut: the nexus between East and West, at that time still a go-to destination for the jet set, where Christians, Muslims, Druze and a couple of dozen other sects had managed to rub along together for centuries—albeit not always peaceably. Here, the handling agent was a real pro; our ladder was nowhere near deployment before a set of steps was pushing into the gap of the opening flight deck door, to claim handling rights over us. Damn, they were good. And at the top of the steps stood Eli Wallach, the Mexican guy from *The Good, the Bad and the Ugly*. Or rather, that was who he looked like. His name was Youssef, a tubby, effulgent, piratical character, who greeted Billy like an old friend—which apparently, he was—with a bear hug and some noisy cheek kissing.

Leaving Jock behind to tinker with the aircraft, the rest of us made our way to Youssef's office in the terminal: constructed almost entirely of glass, it contained a littered desk, two filing cabinets, half a dozen chairs, three telephones, a telex machine and a couple of desk fans, shaking their heads slowly in protest at their own inadequacy.

News from home awaited us. Much to Dave's pleasure and exasperation, in equal measure, he learned that he had become a father in his absence. Youssef, a Maronite unencumbered by prohibition, quickly produced a bottle of scotch to join us in wetting the baby's head. Between swigs, he picked up the telephone and set about the task of finding us hotel rooms, at one point covering the mouthpiece to ask if we wanted them: 'With or without…ah…company?' With Billy's answer firmly in the negative, he gave a shrug and got on with it.

Shortly afterwards Jock re-joined us and we turned to greet him with a glass, ready to share Dave's joyous news. But the grim set of his jaw and the amorphous black mass he carried in his hand stopped us dead in our tracks. Without uttering a word, he had become the spectre at the feast.

'Tail de-icer motor. It's toast,' was all he said before downing his scotch.

This meant nothing to me, it was flyer stuff. It fell to Brett to enlighten me. Located along the leading edges of *TC's* tail assembly and wings were strips of rubber which pulsated to break up the accretion of ice when those conditions prevailed. That much I knew already. But Brett pointed out that our route home lay over the Alps, where icing conditions certainly would prevail, and the offensively-smelling object Jock held up for our inspection was the motor which produced the pulsations. Without it 'We're buggered,' was how Brett put it.

Now, to me this did not seem like an insurmountable problem. In a transient attack of stupid, spawned no doubt from desperation to get home and burn my clothing in the garden, what I wondered was wrong with nipping off west down the Med at say, just above the height of the nearest obstruction (like Crete or one of those gin-palace yachts out of Cannes), and hanging a right at Gibraltar? I may have been a little unhinged at the time.

We were, in effect, AOG (Aircraft on Ground—the highest priority classification meaning that the aircraft was grounded awaiting spares or repair). Only, in this case we were going to fly anyway—just not home, not yet.

Youssef was on the phone, doing his thing; ringing round, calling in favours, cajoling, scrounging, all that stuff. This was his territory, his shtick. He had the part numbers; he had the contacts: he didn't need us. There was really nothing we could do but put ourselves in his hands. So, assured that he would be doing his best, we took ourselves off to the hotel, having arranged to report back to the airport after our minimum crew rest period of twelve hours. (At this time, the loadmaster wasn't included in crew duty hour limitations. In effect, this meant that I could work until I fell over on my face. The refreshed crew would then step over my recumbent form and go fly the aeroplane. This was almost literally the case on a couple of occasions).

At the hotel, having eaten, we trooped in the direction of the softly-played piano we'd heard whilst in the restaurant, to find ourselves in the lounge, confronted by what looked like an outtake from *Casablanca.* It was late evening; the place was deserted. Over by the French windows stood a concert grand and seated at it, ambling through a Gershwin tune, sat a middle-aged man in a white dinner jacket. Behind him, long white curtains billowed in the warm breeze from the open windows, through which a balcony could be glimpsed and beyond that a spangle of lights around the harbour.

He was a pleasant bloke, the pianist. English, he spoke wistfully of home as though he were trapped here, playing daily for the guests—and being largely ignored by them—through lunch, afternoon tea and dinner. We gave him a couple of requests to exercise his musical memory and he performed them well, with the occasional indiscipline in the timing that can afflict musicians who customarily play solo. We stayed for a while then bade him goodnight and headed off to bed, leaving him to play out his melancholy to the empty room.

Early afternoon the next day found us back at the airport, shoehorned into Youssef's little office. Clearly more crowded than our countable number would suggest, for the unwelcome guest, our gremlin, was right in there with us. In tones of injured professional pride, Youssef related how, in spite of his best efforts, he had been unable to source a replacement motor. This despite the fact that TMA was based right there operating DC6s, a close relation of the DC7, with some compatible parts. But money, light blackmail, even contact with some of his most distant cousins had failed to produce the goods.

He was down, but not quite out. Not yet.

He turned to Billy. He had, it seemed, a friend, excellent in matters of acquisition, who might be able to help. But there was a problem, he was not here. Billy said why not get him here? Youssef said it was because he was in Damascus, where some Douglas aeroplanes similar to ours were based and thus, it was to be hoped, spares. A profound silence ensued. The only alternative to the services of Youssef's resourceful friend, was to telex Engineering back at

Racebridge and then to wait while a spare was found and shipped down to us. This was not a real alternative for a near stir-crazy crew.

Everybody's thoughts must have been along the same lines, but nobody bothered to say anything—not any more. Instead, they retreated each behind his allotted task: charts blossomed across Youssef's desk, slide rules were consulted.

Damascus lay little more than fifty nautical miles to the south east, albeit in diametrically the opposite direction to home. There was however nothing for it but to accept our fate and get on with it. Youssef made the call to Damascus. Having satisfied the usual diplomatic niceties, we filed a flight plan, fuelled up and by early evening *TC* was aloft again, heading for the Syrian border.

Damascus: the "pearl of the east", *ash-Shām* to its citizens; famed for its gardens, its orchards, its hundreds of mosques; claimed to be the oldest continuously inhabited city in the world, and of course, the conversion site of St Paul. Right. Nice. Good. All we knew was that it was back to the emergency ladder strategy: we were broke, the aeroplane was broke (sic), we were critically short of fresh laundry, deeply fed up and just wanted to get home.

Somebody called Sayid—who looked a lot like Youssef and might have been him but for the 16-karat bridge work—eschewed our shaky ladder, choosing to reserve his welcome for us at its foot.

As I had discovered in just these few short days, out here most things were possible, but it took time and negotiation—and money, to arrive at mutually-acceptable terms. This was what was undertaken now, between Billy—the rest of the crew forming a Greek chorus behind him—and Sayid. Since I could contribute nothing of value to these proceedings, which were anyway tedious, I was excluded.

The devil, they say, makes work for idle hands—and my hands were idle. We were parked on a remote stand (so as not to lower the tone possibly) and not far away, on the other side of a chain-link fence, my eye had been caught by a new curiosity. Rummaging for my little instamatic camera, I strolled over to the fence where a neat row of Mig 21s in desert camouflage, their spiky nose air intakes painted a perky green, presented themselves to the viewfinder. And a split second later, so did a Syrian soldier with a semi-automatic rifle and an expression that did not read *entente cordial*. I smiled nervously. He didn't. Lowering the camera very slowly and deliberately so that he could see how much I *wasn't* taking a picture of his air force, I waved. He didn't. So, I backed up, rotated 180 degrees and ran away in slo-mo, hoping soldier boy wouldn't have to gun me down before he cracked a smile this afternoon.

Whatever agreement had been reached by the Ladder-foot Horse Trading Company, it had not apparently included an immediate solution to our technical problem. Instead, with our engineers under instructions to report back to the airport at dawn, we all headed downtown for yet another night stop.

Of the hotel itself I remember little, only that it was tucked into a narrow side street, its modest entrance atop a short flight of steps. What I do remember is the hall porter, or rather the bellhop—which in this case exactly described the young man who sprang from the foyer to greet our taxi. For his left leg was missing above the knee and he supported himself on a crutch, which, as I was to discover, was the least of its duties. Out of sensitivity for his handicap, we hung on to our bags. He was having none of that; in case we should be in any doubt as to his abilities, he took the steps, with three suitcases and the crutch, like his shoes were on fire. We quickly learned that this—the foyer and the frontage of the hotel— was his kingdom, which he ruled with benign authoritarianism. Though willing to tackle any job, it would be accomplished in his own way and determinedly unaided.

Later, having little money to fritter away in the bazaar or on other less reputable pursuits, most of the crew gathered in the hotel's small bar, where we discovered that it's only attraction—apart from the obvious one—was an old tape recording of a very drunk German stewardess singing a bawdy ballad. The lyrics were mostly in English and of startling crudity, punctuated by filthy jokes. The singing was poor and the recording worse, so I took myself off to the street. As I passed out of the hotel, I noticed a shoeshine boy seated beside the door, surrounded by the tools of his trade. Awkwardly refusing his services, I walked out into the street. The "boy" was about my age, obliged to squat there on the pavement in frayed trousers and dirty vest, ministering to the footwear of passers-by, while I strutted around in my uniform with its little bits of braid. My naive youthful egalitarianism was offended: he the shoeshine boy, and the ragged kids who had begged change from us in Istanbul, and the loaders drinking our cows' milk in Teheran, we were all equals. And yet patently, their situations dictated that they were not. I was revelling in my lofty disapproval, but slowly, as I walked, my native cynicism began to reassert itself: universal equality was utopian bunkum. It would never happen. Yes, life could be great—just as long as you weren't born poor, into the third world, or a war zone. Then it dawned on me, by refusing his services, because I was embarrassed or outraged or whatever else, wasn't I actively contributing to the shoeshine's oppression? Of course, I was.

Bugger it. I retraced my steps, hesitatingly enquired if the "boy" was still open for business and, finding that he was, took my seat on the box. As he slapped soapy water onto my shoes and started deftly scrubbing them with a couple of brushes, I asked if he spoke any English, enunciating clearly and gesticulating a bit to aid interpretation. As he dried my shoes with an old towel, he looked up and smiled.

'Yes, I speak English, or French if you'd prefer.'

After that we fell into conversation. I learnt that he was attending university and that "this" (here he tapped my shoe), earnt him extra money. In six months, he would have his degree. Then he would be starting work at the airport. Without qualifications in English and maths, he told me, 'It would be impossible to work there…'

He broke off and stared at me. I hadn't meant to laugh, but I couldn't suppress it, I was thinking how patronising I had been. This bloke wasn't going to grovel and scrape for a living, or anything like it. He was attending Damascus University, one of the finest in the Middle East. Suddenly he didn't look like much like the victim of injustice I had painted him in my imagination. I apologised for my rudeness and as he daubed the liquid polish on, explained that getting a job in aviation in England was, comparatively-speaking, so simple that I had found it amusing that anyone should have to go to the lengths he described just to get a job at the airport.

He was plainly overawed by this. He began buffing up a mirror shine on my battered shoes (that would last, miraculously, for weeks), keeping his head down, presumably so I wouldn't see the expression of incredulity on his face. It took some time to convince him that I wasn't joking. Finally, he put his brushes down and staring absently at my scruffy trousers said thoughtfully, 'Perhaps I will come to Britain one day.'

My room looked out onto the street directly above the main entrance and I went to sleep to the steady hum of passing traffic and the march of its lights across the ceiling. But sometime in the early hours I was awoken by angry voices down in the street, and got up to investigate. Below, an unpleasant little scene was being enacted. The players, two taxi drivers, stood by their vehicles, which faced each other with locked bumpers. Clearly, some contest of right of way had taken place, resulting in a minor collision right outside the hotel. Even at this late hour there was traffic building up behind them as the two men faced off.

It was then that the bellhop made his appearance. Moving fast and with astonishing agility, he emerged from the hotel, leaping down the steps to take position between the two men. I could not understand a word they said, but the proceedings were clear enough. Whatever the problem was, Bellhop was not going to tolerate its intrusion on his turf: the combatants should take it elsewhere. The drivers interpreted this as a direct challenge and began to close threateningly on him. Something that may have been a blade appeared in the hand of one of them. This was a tactical error on his part. In an instant, the crutch became a lethally accurate weapon, wielded by a one-legged man with perfect balance and considerable aggression. The first victim took two heavy blows about the head and shoulders and immediately backed off. Bellhop now swung to face the one with the knife. The crutch's parabola fell just short of its target this time, but its threat was enough, the fight was over: Knifeman's puny blade clearly no match for the force ranged against it, he too fled. With Bellhop shouting angrily after them, the drivers retreated to their respective vehicles, sprinkling the night with a few face-saving shouts of defiance before, with an expensive rending of no-claims bonuses, they tore apart their vehicles' unwonted embrace and reversed away. The drama over, I returned to bed, assured that whatever career Bellhop turned his attention to, just like the shoeshine's, it would almost certainly work out just fine for him.

We were back at the airport by mid-morning. Jock and Dave, had returned as instructed around dawn and were able to report that *TC* was gloriously serviceable, at last. However, they were unnaturally anxious to leave and even seemed a little furtive—that is, a bit more furtive than engineers usually seem. There was business to attend to with Sayid before we could go, and that too was conducted in a decidedly secretive manner, before we were hurried out to the aircraft.

Brett climbed out of the right-hand seat to shake the kinks out of his spine and to make tea, and with a nod of consent from Billy, invited me to take his place for a while. I had been sat behind him idly watching the little green phosphorescent bug on the radio altimeter, set into the radio rack behind the engineer's panel, playing keepie-uppie with the Alps, and slowly nodding off. But for the next half hour I sat alert at the controls of my favourite aeroplane, albeit with my hands in my lap, the altimeter steady at 26,000 feet, the ASI standing arthritically at rather less than *TC*'s advertised cruising speed of 300 knots (she was after all getting old), heading 315° magnetic, watching the grandeur of the mountains slide by through a ragged blanket of cumulus. Billy sat relaxed but vigilant, scanning the instruments, monitoring *TC's* good behaviour. There was time to talk now, so I asked Jock, sitting at the engineer's panel, what had been going on so secretively in Damascus.

'Well, he fixed it for us, didn't he, Sayid,' said Jock.

'Oh, so he found a spare motor?'

'No, he didn't. Not exactly.'

'He didn't?'

'Nope.' 'What did he do?'

'He took us round to the Syrian Arab Airline's hangar at dawn and we nicked one from one of their DC6s.'

I twisted round in the seat. 'Eh? But isn't that…?'

'No. Well yes, strictly speaking. But no, it was in for a C-check (heavy maintenance). The aircraft was in bits. Sayid'll replace the motor way before the check's finished.'

'But…'

'Everybody's happy, *TC's* serviceable, we get to go home. Job's done.'

I went back to marvelling at the snowy beauty of the mountains rolling by under *TC's* nose. It was indeed possible to get anything done out there in the East. It was just a question of agreeing terms.

Per Schiphol Ad Lyneham

In a less-than charitable moment, I wondered if the designers of passenger terminal seating actually set out to make them exquisitely uncomfortable to discourage over-long occupancy. If so, they had succeeded in the present case in spades, which, judging by the discomfort I was experiencing, was what had been stored under the cushions of the one I was lying on.

We were roughing away what turned out to be forty hours in the terminal at Schiphol Airport, Amsterdam, beguiling the time with coffee, fags and uneasy catnaps, whilst we awaited the return of the DC7. We were trying to cram 220 fear-stricken calves onto two flights that should have been three. I was supposed to travel with the aircraft, but the first flight had departed without me: there was simply no room for me. "We" in this case, for no reason that I could make out, was me and Jack Bradbury. Why the Operations Manager should want to concern himself personally with the loading of a livestock flight, even going so far as to share with me the purgatory of this endless waiting, when a whole fleet awaited his dispositions back at Racebridge, was quite inexplicable.

Actually, there was one explanation; it sprang disconcertingly to mind as I lay on the bum-numbing buttoned vinyl surface of the bench, trying to keep the weight off my left femoral artery: it was another of those commercially important charters (weren't they all?) and Bradders probably wanted to ensure I didn't make a pig's ear of it. Nice. Inspiring. It was also probable that following the Isfahan saga, he didn't trust *TC* out of his sight.

We had come from the warmth of the hotel in the chill of early evening to load the first flight. Bradbury was worried. Owing to delays in the arrival of the calves and difficulties loading them, *TC* was running hours behind schedule— and there was another important charter awaiting it. So, he'd decided we should forego the hotel and doss down at the airport, so as to be on hand the moment *TC* returned for the second flight.

As if the boss's apoplectic presence was not discouragement enough, I was not in any case relishing the prospect of the task in hand, for at least two further reasons. The first was that the cargo comprised five-week-old calves, all destined for Milan and doomed to the veal trade; their only crime, that they were male and therefore of no use to the dairy industry into which they had had the misfortune to be born. The second was that, as usual, I was by no means certain of my calculations, in this case that two hundred calves could be comfortably accommodated on the aircraft. A concern much exacerbated by Commercial's insistence that—whether I liked it or not (and I didn't), there would be 220 animals to ship on two flights, for no-more legitimate a reason than that was the contract they'd agreed with the bread-head charterers, before they'd consulted me.

The day had fiasco written all over it, and once again my signature would be on it.

By the time the trucks rolled alongside *TC's* forward freight door, Bradbury had concluded whatever business he had with the bloke in the sheepskin coat, the Tyrolean hat and the air of unassailable authority, who'd arrived with the second load of calves, and had then caught the first Heathrow-bound flight out, leaving me to oversee the actual work. Dirty work, as it turned out.

Just as I had feared, there were far too many of the sad, desperate little creatures. Separating calves this young from their mothers, distresses both and the calves sought comfort wherever they could get it. As they tumbled on board, handled non-too gently by one of the loading gang, they would suck desperately at my fingers or lick at the sleeves and the front of my uniform jacket, anything to assuage either their hunger or more likely their anxiety. The cabin quickly filled up, but they kept on coming. It was clear that since the whole of the cabin floor would be occupied by them, for the purposes of my calculations, it would be a simple matter to work out the aircraft's trim by distributing their weight (on paper that is), evenly down the aircraft.

At ninety-five, the cabin was already over full. It didn't stop the loaders, they just kept going, heaving animals in on top of those already loaded and leaving them to find their own piece of floor to stand on—if they could. It was ugly and it was cruel, but the loading gang had their instructions and I had no power to stop them. It was a simple function of the contract, commercial necessity trumping animal welfare: there was no question of leaving any behind. But they were handled roughly, without pity, and that was inexcusable. It was all inexcusable and we were all guilty of a failing of basic humanity. I dreaded the prospect of the journey down to Milan, but at least there'd be somebody aboard to keep an eye on the calves, even though there would be precious little I could do for them.

Previously, I had only flown with cargo when my presence was deemed necessary. But I had begun to routinely accompanying flights since the computer affair of just a few weeks earlier. I had received a load enquiry for a shipment of IBM computer equipment to Moscow. The load was pretty straightforward— half filling the aircraft, the machines comprised wardrobe-sized tape drives with punch-card data entry terminals. (At that early stage of computing, all those bits working together had sufficient computing power to calculate Pi to ten decimal places nearly as quickly as a secondary school maths teacher in his or her tea-break). Packed in crates or transit cradles and the payload negligible, it was simply a matter of securing them properly to ensure the tender little darlings didn't get hurt *en rout*e. Naturally, I went to see Bradbury to voice my concern about this and to request that I travel to ensure safe delivery. How he instinctively guessed that I didn't really give a sod about the computers and was just angling for a jolly to Moscow, I don't know, but he did and told me to bugger off. So, one enjoyed a certain quiet *schadenfreude* on learning that one of the tape drives had arrived broken. Under the circumstances I thought it best not to meet Bradbury's eye directly for a day or two.

But the faint hope of offering any succour to the calves was extinguished when we discovered that the cabin was by now so packed that it was impossible to enter it, let alone make my way to the seat at the rear of the cabin. The skipper, Graham Coot, stood beside me on the tarmac watching the burly loader hurling animals into the aircraft, and said simply, 'This is wrong.'

He was the mildest and kindest of men and I liked him a lot, so coming from him it meant a great deal more to me than any of Bradbury's vitriolic tirades. There was nothing in Coot's tone to suggest it, but nevertheless the tacit accusation was there—this was my fault. I couldn't really disagree; I should have stuck to my guns and limited the load to 85 animals per trip.

As a last resort, a scissors truck was backed up to the aftermost window on the *TC's* starboard side—an emergency exit which was removable—and I tried to climb in. It was no use, there was simply nowhere to put my feet that wasn't already occupied by an animal. I had to abandon the attempt: the flight would depart without me.

The crew entered via their own access directly into the flight deck. Only after the routine of pre-flight checks had been completed and taxi clearance requested were the freight doors closed on the radiating heat of the close-packed calves. Later, as I stood at a window in the terminal watching *TC* climb out into a winter sky, I decided that this had been a cruel business I wanted no further part of, and promised myself I would not be involved in any future livestock flights conducted in this manner.

I had no idea quite how soon I would be required to redeem the pledge. But to reinforce my resolution (though it needed none), the crew reported that on arrival in Milan they found that more than a dozen calves had died during the flight.

I caught the BEA schedule Trident service to Heathrow, followed by an abysmally slow bus I could have overtaken on a pogo stick, back to Racebridge. It was mid-afternoon when I walked back into the Ramp, knackered, filthy and fed up, to report my return, with the plan of immediately knocking off for the day. But, as I soon discovered, other plans had been laid.

I was called straight into Bradbury's office, where he sat at his desk looking miraculously clean, fresh and rested. Bradbury's idea of preliminary niceties, at least when addressing me, was not to sack me.

'Ah, there you are. Right, I want you to ge…*What the hell happened to you?*'

I didn't need to follow the line of his gaze to the front of my jacket, to the chrome of dried-on calf-lick; to my trousers, bagged at the knee and speckled with unspeakable substances.

'And what is that smell?'

'It's sh…'

'I know what it is. You're a mess, you can't represent the bloody company looking like that.'

I didn't *want* to represent the bloody company. What I wanted to represent was a bloke going home for a bath and some scran and to sleep the sleep of the dead for about twelve hours. That was what I wanted, but the prospect of realising it had suddenly become remote.

Bradbury was turning that familiar sclerotic scarlet with hints of heliotrope that indicated the onset of disapprobation, of which I had no wish to be the recipient. So, I sealed my lips on all the things on which I wanted to vent my frustration, deciding that discretion was the better part of unemployment, and pasted on what I hoped was an attentive expression, but in my present state, probably just made me look a bit gormless.

'Right, we need to get you sorted out.' '*Do we? I could sort myself out if you'd just send me home.*' 'There's another job for you. Gloria! The DC7's heading directly to Lyneham from Milan. New crew's positioning by road. 0700hrs departure tomorrow for Changi, general cargo as usual…Ah there you are.'

Gloria, Bradbury's secretary—tall, blond, capable, looking great as usual, in a floral-print dress today—had popped her head round the door, wrinkling her nose at the agricultural smell beginning to pervade the office.

Bradbury aimed his Parker at me: 'Give him a chitty for uniform stores. Jacket and trousers.'

'Righto.' A glance at me (tolerance with a suggestion of light disgust?) and she was gone, quickly closing the door behind her. Thanks, Glaus, for the sympathy.

This was an unfortunate development. The sort of development that, some hours later, saw me on the road to Wiltshire in the gathering dusk, in the abominable car.

RAF Lyneham, a sprawling concrete wart on the otherwise-pleasant face of Wiltshire. Within its perimeter fence, squat, strikingly-ugly buildings lined a confusing network of roads and aprons. To the right of the control tower, a row of huge black hangars marched away in diminishing linear perspective. Behind the tower, beyond a cluster of sheds and stores, stood the single-storey Route Hotel with its long corridors branching away from the central nucleus of the reception area. All the buildings were overheated and everywhere the air was thick with the smell of hot paint with which the radiators were coated. At that time, Lyneham was the main transport hub for service personnel and home to the RAF's fleet of Bristol Britannia aircraft, as well as visiting civilian aircraft such as ours.

As I swung in through the gates, what is known in Yorkshire as a "lazy wind" (it blows through you instead of round you) was scouring the apron. Legging it briskly into the comforting fug of the office beside the terminal building, I presented myself to the cargo duty officer, who in turn presented me with an arm-breaking wedge of airwaybills and manifests for the flight.

Outside on the floodlit tarmac *TC* awaited, a ground power unit roaring away beside it. She would have to wait her turn for the loading gang, busy on an adjacent beaten-up-looking DC6, belonging to a dodgy Midlands outfit we often competed with for work. Meantime, all I could do was get *TC* ready to receive her cargo and be patient. Buttoning up my overcoat I trudged out to the aircraft in a biting wind that presaged snow. On board, for a change, I remembered to unplug the cabin lighting connectors beside the freight doors so as not to tear them apart and black out the cabin as the doors were raised, inserted the tailpost, then scurried back to the terminal to drink industrial-strength coffee to ward off the backlog of sleep that was becoming ever more pressing—and, for the second time that day, to languish on haemorrhoid-inducing departure terminal seating. As a special concession to my third virtually-continuous day of duty, Bradbury had sprung for company expenses and a room had been booked for me at the Old Bell Hotel, ten miles away in Malmesbury. The flight crew where already ensconced there and, once the aircraft was loaded, I would be able to join them until departure time the following morning.

As I was to discover, there would be just one snag with this plan.

I got the loading gang at about 2200 and took station on board with a clipboard ready to tally the distribution of the cargo as it came on. The inflexible rule at Lyneham was that the loadmaster had to be present throughout loading. If he got off the aeroplane, work was supposed to stop until he returned. Well, I was, miserably, freezingly, there. But it was slow progress. It was taking the gang ages to load the trucks in the cargo shed, there didn't seem to be enough men for the job and, to cap it all, shortly after loading began, they all knocked off for a meal break.

I was left alone on the aircraft, shivering, cursing the good fortune of the crew, who even now might be toasting their feet before a log fire at the Bell. Flinging down my clipboard, I returned to the terminal to resume my seat and warm myself up with a drink. How long I dozed I can't be certain, but I was roused to consciousness by the sensation of hot Bovril soaking into the crotch of my new uniform trousers. Stifling my screams, a glance out of the window told me that the loaders were back aboard, no doubt waiting for me to join them, the operation suspended until I arrived. With the icy wind mercilessly exploring the wet patch on my trousers, I hurried back aboard.

Two surprises awaited me, the first pleasant, the second decidedly not. The first was that the gang had broken their own golden rule and, without me, forged ahead with the loading, making considerable progress. It looked as though over half of the cargo was already on board. This was good news, though it meant that I would have to scramble about in the cargo to tally where the weight had been distributed. It was hardly the first time this had happened and the loading gang stood back patiently whilst I went to work. All went well until a shadowy object buried deep among boxes and crates caught my attention. Shifting a few items and using a torch taken from the flight deck rack, I went in for a closer look.

My puzzlement turned first to suspicion, then skipped everything else between and went straight to horror.

You name almost anything and we were authorised to ship it: tunic buttons, boots, toilet rolls, typewriters, stationary, stores, bedding, aircraft spares, paint, manuals, candles (I hadn't actually seen any on the manifest, but we would have carried them), tyres—for aircraft or car—chairs, tables, condoms, carboys (with non-corrosive contents), spare-anythings; an elephant's foot umbrella stand if the Air Ministry so desired. But what we were decidedly not authorised to carry was what glinted dully back at me in the light of the torch: a ten-foot-long cylinder, painted white with a chequerboard-pattern black band, stencilled serial numbers down the side and a set of fins at one end: a missile. Clearly *sans* warhead, since the other end terminated in a blank plate. But it was still, unquestionably, a missile.

How it had ever been assigned to our flight, nobody seemed to know. But what our diplomatic clearances for the countries we would overfly between here and Singapore expressly forbade, (not to mention our insurance), was the carriage of weapons or ammunition of any description. There was no question, it would have to come off, even though to do so would require the removal of tons of freight already loaded to get at it.

The loaders looked at me and I looked at the loaders. We were in an invidious position here, viz a viz the apportion of blame. They should have known better than to load the thing in the first place. On the other hand, if I had been there instead of in the terminal anointing my groin with meat extract, I could have prevented it. There again, they were guilty of breaking their own rule by recommencing loading without me. It was a tricky one, but nobody wanted it escalated to higher formal proceedings, so we all just quietly hated each other and got on with shifting the thing, before anybody else with rank and a predilection for officiousness got involved.

0200 and the unloading and reloading finally completed, I made my way to the car beneath a cold glitter of stars, just beginning to diffuse into a scattered cloud blanket moving in from the east. It was bitterly cold; just as well, it would help to keep me awake as I turned out of the base and floored it for, Malmesbury, the sewing machine engine pushing my egregious little car up to a dizzying 50MPH.

Abbey Row, Malmesbury, deserted and peaceful at that hour. To my right the darkened mass of the abbey where Æthelstan, considered by some historians to have been the first true king of England, has slept for more than a thousand years. Also, where from the tower up there in the darkness, an ill-judged early venture into aviation was attempted back in the 11th-century, when the monk Elmer of Malmesbury stuck on a pair of wings and leaped from it. He is reputed to have flown 200 yards before gravity reasserted itself and he piled in, breaking both legs, correctly blaming his lack of a tail for the untidy end to his experiment.

And beside the Abbey, the Old Bell Hotel, also largely dark but for a single light burning in the lobby. Encumbered with my overnight bag and an armful of documents, I tried the door: locked. I knocked. No response. Rang the bell: nothing. Put down my stuff and knocked again. Hammered on the frame with my fists. Still nothing. The lobby yawned warmly at me, only the light behind the reception desk betraying any sign of occupation. I had been assured there would be a night porter to let me in, but a further desperate ten minute's exercise transferring my knuckle DNA to the door frame proved I'd been assured wrongly. In frustration, I grabbed the wrought iron handles and rattled the doors against the bolts, gave them a couple of kicks for good measure. I even whistled piercingly through the letterbox. All of which the lobby loftily ignored. Finally, beaten, I grabbed my stuff and trudged exhaustedly back to the car, to head back to Lyneham.

I don't know what made me open my eyes, but it was fortunate that I did. A double fingerpost road sign, atop an earth bank marking a fork in the road, was hurtling towards me. I hit the brakes and hauled right on the steering. The nearside wheels hit the bank, the car pitched over 45° to the right and came to a sudden halt an inch or two short of the post, my head hitting the side window hard enough to encourage full wakefulness. I staggered out of the car, momentarily disorientated. The wind was icy but it helped. I looked at the signpost. The places it indicated in either direction meant nothing to me: I was lost.

I reversed off the bank and spent a few minutes removing vegetation from behind the bumper and the wheel-arches. Then, winding all the windows down to promote wakefulness, I set out, grimly determined to find Lyneham—though preferably not if it killed me. After an age I found it, turned into the carpark, and that was all I remembered until the pain woke me up. I had slipped sideways until my head rested on my overnight bag on the passenger seat, my legs almost at right angles to my body and with the gear leaver jammed hard into the side of my knee. It was the pain of this that had woken me, but worse was to come when I got out of the car and tried to stand up: both my legs from the waist down had gone to sleep. But when I hobbled about like an unconvincing am-dram Long John Silver and the blood began to return, the pins and needles it produced were excruciating.

That was it, I'd had it. The ignition was still on and the windows were open. I fixed them, grabbed my bag and the documents and limped off to throw myself on the mercy of the duty officer. He took one look at me and wrote out a chit, hardly listening to the babbled account of my petty misadventures. The chit got me a room in the Route Hotel, normally reserved solely for transiting personnel. Like all military establishments, it was clinically clean and tidy. Anonymous, brightly-lit corridors with highly polished floors and mathematically-placed doors, identical but for their numbers, stretched away in diminishing perspectives. I might have been just as lost as I had been at the crossroads, but for the little map the desk clerk had given me. The room was small, clean, with a bed and a cabinet beside it. It may also have had a gorilla and a mariachi band for all I knew. I couldn't care less; I hit the sack so fast that I almost made it to the horizontal before all the sleep I was owed finally cashed the cheque.

Rattatatat ta ta ta, rattatatat ta ta ta! I remember thinking as I emerged groggily from deep sleep that, whoever was knocking on my door, was unconsciously doing it in 9/8 time: Joe Morello on *Blue Rondo à la Turk.* Had it been he in person, I should have made it to the door with greater alacrity. As it was, it took a supreme effort to drag my sorry, unwilling blanket-wrapped carcass there to face the impatient countenance of Todd, the first officer. As he quickly made clear, the problem was that nobody knew where the hell I was. And as I had all the ship's documents with me, the flight was going nowhere until I was found. Clearly, the note of my whereabouts I'd handed to the clerk on the desk last night had gone astray and it had taken some time to locate me.

Out on the ramp, under a lowering sky sulphurous with latent snow, *TC's* crew were getting on with the pre-flight: I was not so late after all. I took the documents on board, got the loadsheet signed, bade them *bon voyage* and returned to the terminal to await departure. Only when *TC* was airborne could I at last knock off and go home. As the first flakes of snow began to fall, the doors were closed, the steps pulled clear and the ground engineer, standing a few paces in front of the aircraft's nose so as to be visible to the flight crew, began exchanging obscure hand signals with them as they set about starting engines. One by one starters whined, props turned—slowly at first until the cylinders fired—then, coughing blue smoke from the exhaust stubs, blurring to silver disks. With all four engines running, the ground power unit was disconnected and hauled clear behind its tractor. Chocks were pulled from the wheels and the engineer stood aside, waiting to exchange the final clear-to-taxi signals with the pilots.

He waited some more. The engines ran on. The snowfall thickened. Still no signal from the flight deck. I held my breath: another problem? A minute or two more, then my spirits sank as the engineering steps where wheeled back on and the ground engineer sprinted aboard. Several more trying minutes passed until, the problem, whatever it was, was resolved, the engineer reappeared, steps where pulled and *TC* rolled.

She had hardly dissolved into the blanket of nimbostratus covering the airfield, before I was driving out of the gate. The Abomination however did not appear to share my eagerness for home. Less than five miles down the road a small explosion, accompanied by a starburst of sparks, burst from beneath the dashboard. The wipers, the heater and the indicators stopped working, and the engine faltered. Thereafter, the best speed I could coax out of it was 25MPH, and I completed almost all of my journey at that speed, with the window down to prevent the windscreen from steaming up and to enable me to reach around to clear a hole in the accumulating snow, so I could see where I was going. Then, just a couple of miles short of my destination, the fault miraculously disappeared. At which point, I can only think that the pin had been withdrawn from my wax effigy.

It was dark by the time I reached Racebridge, and actually colder inside the car than it was out. Shivering despite my heavy greatcoat, I decided to get a hot drink and thaw out before going home. Having scrounged a cup of tea from Loaders, I walked into the Ramp office to established myself on the nearest radiator. I was just beginning to feel worthwhile again, when I spotted Fenner.

Unfortunately, he'd spotted me first and in three of his ridiculous slow-motion leaps he was across my bows, moustache all a-twitch.

'What's all this about a missile on *Tango Charlie?*' 'There's a hell of a flap on.'

The price of a cup of tea and a warm posterior, had suddenly become prohibitively expensive.

Heat

In Ops the atmosphere is unbearable. I walk through the door and the heat, which has been building steadily as I ascended the stairs, hits with tropical ferocity. It's mid-August. All the fans have been liberated from Nav by 0900 and all the windows are open—with no apparent effect. An hour ago, just for the hell of it, I got Jeep to obtain an actual for Bahrain—it's two degrees cooler than the office apparently—until I discover he's got me Bournemouth.

Okay, it's hot. But I see that Sally Trainor is making things hotter.

Bustling about the calm seated bulk of Captain Bill Healey (it's a bit like surfboarding round Gibraltar), with the wedge of met and NOTAMS I've just brought from AIS, I pretend not to notice what's going on so that I can surreptitiously enjoy the spectacle of Jeep losing the battle with his libido. Sally has come up from the crew room on some post-flight business and, finding herself at leisure whilst Jeep speaks on the telephone, has decided to indulge one of her little weaknesses, that of tormenting hormonally over-active young men. So, kicking off her shoes, she has draped herself across the desk in front of him and swung her legs up so that she is now reclining comfortably on one elbow whilst directing a desk fan at her face. Her eyes are closed, her cheeks flushed, her hair blowing as she bathes in the cooling breeze. Occasionally she pulls at the collar of her blouse to allow the air to circulate to other overheated places— places that Jeep will be dreaming about for most of the rest of the day. I can't be quite certain at this distance, maybe it's just the fans, but I am almost sure—yes, she's making a quiet, contented little noise low down in her throat: she's purring. A tail and some ears and she'd pass for one of her own anthropomorphic cats, the ones she is so besotted with.

While all this is going on, naturally she affects to have no idea that Jeep even exists on the same planet—which is probably the planet Pussycat in her case. Jeep looks as if he has been hit by the Ops copy of the MEL (a big, heavy manual), which in another ten seconds will be exactly right, if he doesn't get it together down in his Fruit of The Looms and pay attention to this Saturday morning, which is trying to come apart on us, again. I should have Sledge with me today—my own private albatross—but he is at Bisley watching people blow things to fragments with heavy-calibre semi-automatic weapons. I am afraid that Sally's charms would be entirely lost on Sledge—he'd probably tell her to gerroff his desk and to stop crumpling the July issue of Guns & Ammo. Sad, very sad. The one advantage of Jeep, apart from his being such good fun, is that it is possible to disguise one's borderline incompetence behind his inability to do anything that doesn't involve either batteries or his scrotum—or both.

Phoenix—it's a gross misnomer when it spends so much time *in* the ashes—is down as usual. I have never really got on with technology: I had one of those infallibly-simple Zippo lighter once—it is flint, it's wick, it's petrol: what could go wrong? It didn't work for me.

Dick Pullman, the chief pilot is in his office with Keith Tollworth our training captain and judging by his bilious expression, is not to be trifled with. They make a dangerous and unpredictable pairing—and must be watched closer than a bar girl checking her pay slip. And for goodness' sake, Captain Les Morris is doing the Banjul, which means he'll want three different routes and he'll be working out a drift down from bloody Southend. Yes, of course there is no point, but that's the point for him, time-consuming and ultimately fruitless exercises, the worst aspect of which is his inclination to involve us earthlings in his dark alien practices. Les's problem is that he has brain capacity to spare after he has got through allocating some of it to flying, and he just has to do something with it. Though he's pleasant enough, the man is a sick parody of normality.

More pleasingly, the unassuming little man with the slightly baffled air who has wondered in, as if by accident, is Captain Dennis Clark, reporting for his Palma—not that he shows any sign of being aware of that. Good old Dennis, he's my kind of pilot and probably not half as incompetent as he seems.

'Er, what am I doing here?' (On the other hand.)

'Apart from looking nonplussed do you mean, Dennis? How about checking in for something?'

'Yeh. Hello Les. Yeh, that's it. Las Palmas innit?'

'Palma I think Dennis: bit more to the left, not so far down, still populated by unmitigated Spanish bastards who hate us just because their summer streets flow with our English vomit and we expose our buttocks to their womenfolk.'

'Yeh that's it, I remember. Good.'

The phone rings. I make the mistake of reaching for it instead of leaving it to Jeep. But since he has now gone into geo-stationary orbit round Planet Pussycat, who is still too busy being fabulous to notice him, (Oh, do pack it in the pair of you), I pick up.

'Son son, tell me this and tell me n'more…'

(Christ.) 'Hello Tony.'

'Are you alright Mike? You sound a wee bit outta sorts there, m'boy.'

'Anthony, it's bloody sodding SaturDAY, right? DEE AAY WHYYY—day, not my time at all. I should be in my box with the soil of the homeland, sleeping the sleep of the undead at this very moment. But no, I'm here. Jed wouldn't let me swap for the nights again. Thank you, boss, up yer bum. The programme is teetering on the brink of spontaneous confusion, it's hotter than Sue Luscombe's knickers in here, but nothing like the fun, and (I lower my voice), and Les is doing the Banjul so he'll be wanting to know the square root of a gnat's gonads before we get him away. So, y'know Tony, I'm not ecstatic right now.'

'Copied. Okay I'll cut to the chase, shall I?'

It's a nice idea, but Tony and terse, or trenchant come to that, are just words that begin with T and have no other point of relevance between them. It's about flight plans, some dreary tosh about difficulties routing inbound transatlantics via EXMOR, GIBSO and SAM (navigation waypoints). I suggest routing via EMERSON LAKE and PALMER. He tells me they aren't in the data base. It's going to be a long one this if I don't shut it down.

Whilst I am doing this, my peripheral vision notes Sally's departure with a flick of her tail and a smug "gotcha" expression, and the arrival of the svelte Danny Huq, bearing a brown envelope. Jeep gets out of his chair, adjusts his privates and wanders over to see what has just spewed from the telex, ignoring the phone which has begun to ring. Out in the broiling heat of the car park a flash of pinky-yellow—part of Pringle's Blood-Stained Vomit range of cardies—announces the arrival of our Deputy Reichsführer. At the best of times, his approach is hardly an occasion for unfettered rejoicing, but right now he's about as welcome as a landmine at a clog dancing competition. At that very moment, the ramp radio crackles into life with Joe's (our man on the tarmac), unmistakably flustered tones. Even at the remove of a telephone line, Tony is able to detect that I am developing an anxiety spike; ever the sensitive soul, he wishes me luck and rings off.

My skin crawls. If I had fur, I'd look like a lavatory brush now. I feel the dark wings of the shitehawk beating the air about my head. I may be marginally incompetent, but my nose for trouble is in a class of its own. Hurriedly, I drop my sketch pad into the desk drawer and clear the screen of those eighteen flight plan re-requests since 0900, whilst Jeep hides his Hot Wheels radio-controlled truck in the waste bin, covering it with telexes. Ignoring the phone, I plump for answering the radio whilst Jeep walks to the board with a telex and starts the decline for us.

'Romeo Alpha rolling at 1145.'

No! This cannot be right. Not 1145, it cannot be 1145, it has to be 1130, on schedule. Nothing else will do. Our Commercial bloke from upstairs, "Slick" (so dubbed by Flick owing to his marked preoccupation with his appearance), stood in this very office not twenty-four hours ago, pale beneath the careful tan, Don Moss pullovering away at his elbow, explaining that the charterers of the Gerona programme had expressed deep dissatisfaction with the consistently late departures of their flights, (at least we're consistent), and there was even talk of "repositioning the product" if our performance didn't improve immediately.

'But we had an on-time slot, Joe. What the f… (Oops, radio procedure) … What happened?'

'Catering went to the wrong aircraft. Somebody passed them the wrong stand numbers.'

I look at Jeep. Jeep looks at me. I notice that he has now put up PK's ATD, in fatal red: 1145, it glares accusingly at us from the board. Moss's tread is even now audible upon the stairs. We are finished: Nemesis on final approach. Moss has maybe two hours dual VFR—probably on a tethered balloon—owns the tailwheel bearings of a bug-smasher no sane person would take higher than the grass it stands on, yet he acts like he's got aviation sown up.

'We can't be late…' I stammer weakly. Jeep looks at the telex. The outer door swings open.

'Right.' He turns abruptly, removes the offending red with a single swipe of his fist and pencils in 1130 in lovely, on-time, sap green.

'You can't...' I begin. The door swings open. He can, he has, and if it wouldn't ruin both our reputations, I'd kiss him right now.

With quite amazing *sangfroid*, Jeep winks and to avoid getting asked any awkward questions quickly answers a phone, as Don Moss enters. Taking my cue from Jeep, I fade into crewing where even Will's audible indigestion is preferable to the company of Captain Pullover. Meanwhile, Danny Huq waits patiently for attention, watching our charade with the faintest of smiles playing about his Errol Flynn moustache.

What is it with Danny Huq? I mean he's not quite for real. He never gets flustered, he's always immaculate—just look at those fingernails, he probably spends more time on his manicure than I spend in the bath—and he's always, always, always right. I make a mental note to check out his back when he leaves. I'm curious to see where the batteries go.

Don Moss stands looking at the board, sort of inviting conversation, whilst I sort of avoid it. Jeep, standing right in front of him, is able to meet his gaze and even to smile, safe in the knowledge that as long as he is talking on the phone Moss can't collar him. Jeep continues with one of those monosyllabic conversations full of words like "yeah" and "right" interspersed with a whole range of differently-inflected "mmms". Meantime, I frown over a crew list and look preoccupied. At last, Moss loses interest and goes off to do business on the golf course, or whatever else gives him pleasure when he is not persecuting Ops.

Emerging from Crewing to speak to Danny, I find out that the telephone conversation Jeep was having was with the duty controller over at Big Al was actually about the reason for the delay to *RA*. Jeep covered brilliantly, extemporising neat replies to the controller without giving anything away to Moss, who was stood right in front of him. The boy is a revelation, a positive revelation. Of course, we'll have to restore the right ATD later but, by the time the unpleasant brown substance explodes odiferously in Ops, me and the lad will be on days off and gone like a cool breeze. I really must see about getting Jeep on my shift. In any case, it's about time Sledge moved on—to Sam Ford's shift for instance. I think the clash of matter and anti-matter there would be quite entertaining to watch.

Danny Huq gives me the benefit of his perfect bridgework as I approach, pushing the bar envelope towards me across the counter. I look carefully at the details written on it and suppress the sudden feeling of exultation I get at having at last nailed Danny, who is obviously here to point out some little error or other. Only, there isn't one.

'Lemme see, old chap. Yup, 554, Gerona, today's date. One one-hundred-pound float. Looks good to me, mate.'

'Me too. I'm on the Banjul.'

Sod it. As I swap the envelopes, I thank heavens that at least the flight deck has got their correct paperwork: I know that because I saw them swapping their folders over just a moment ago. Captain Tollworth sweeps in as Danny turns to exit. (Nope, couldn't see where the batteries go.)

'Yes Keith?' I say, trying to sound positive.

'Nid Omyo Ampha etoff onime?'

Here we go. I really haven't time for his appalling diction right now. My options are clear: the first one is to bundle him into the Astra and get Jeep to run him up to GCHQ for decoding. But the second option, since his speech ended in a clear interrogative, is the simpler one; with a fifty/fifty chance of success, I go for it: 'Yes Keith.'

'Esellent.' He turns and leaves.

Yess! I punch the air like those footballers do on *Match of the Day*. Cracked it. I can't help wondering what he wanted though.

First Officer Wassname (never seen him before) walks over to hand me a slip of paper. The phone rings. In the background I notice bar girl Jill, newly-arrived from Athens, dropping an envelope of bar takings in the deposit safe, or trying to, and Len from Customer Relations arriving (not on a Saturday, perleeease!), armed with his pad and biro, which probably means that he is looking for information about a spilt cup of coffee on a flight last Christmas: there's a scalded privates claim in. I need that right now, I really do.

'Is this XK's fuel figures? Only this burn-off wouldn't get you to Clacton, let alone Banjul.'

'You put three noughts on it, don't you? Shall I do that?'

'Oh yeah, right, sorry. No that's okay.' I pick up the phone noticing that, from the southerly view of Jill—which benefits from her frequent participation in some sort of near homicidal national-level ball game—that the float safe deposit tray has jammed again and she is struggling to free it.

'Hello, Ops.' (I have absolutely refused to do that 'Hello-HCA-Operations-Duty Officer-speaking-how-may-I-help-you?' bollocks that Tony is trying to institute).

'Hello Mike.'

The unmistakable tones of Stuart Dance, my fellow duty officer. 'Always a pleasure, Stuart.'

'Oh, having a bad day, are we?'

Astute as usual. 'It's me. It's a day shift, mate.'

'Right. Have you seen my oppo today?'

Since they both managed to wangle flying sponsorship from the company, Greg and Stu are now rare sights around hanger F. 'Fraid not. I think somebody mentioned that he was flying this afternoon, so I expect he is east of here somewhere trying to identify Kent. It's only a thousand square miles so…'
'It's fifteen hundred, actually.'
'…Yes, thank you, Les… (Who the hell would know that? I was making it up. The man's not normal.) …It's only fifteen hundred square miles, so he could be some time.'
This flying training business has proved a sad revelation for Greg. The course has been no real problem for him, although the way he tells it, it comes over like the Dam Busters' raid. No, his work will be fine. It's just that Greg has been getting his early nights in and arriving half an hour early in the mornings with more pens and highlighters than is quite normal for a grown up, slogging his guts out for top marks and worrying himself sick about his results—eventually to come an acutely-galling second from top in the class. Whereas, Stu will be out most nights getting hammered and fruitlessly trying to mate with anything lawful, will turn up for business at the crack of five past nine in the mornings, occasionally with pyjama bottoms under his trousers, to jot the afternoon's complex navigation exercise on the back of an envelope with the sucked stub of an HB, and will go AWOL on some sort of bender for a full 24 hours prior to the final exam—only to pass, easily, with a virtually faultless paper. This is

particularly hard for Greg to swallow, but it's salutary lessons for him on the futility of going up against jammy natural brilliance, and the need to learn how to come second gracefully on occasion.

'Righto, if you see him tell him I'll meet him in The Bell at eight o'clock.'

'Will do Stu. Bye.' In these idle moments between one crisis and another, I am free to gulp my Red Label and to admire Jill's astonishingly taut figure. Oh God, Jeep has caught my eye and moving over to nudge me in the ribs, leans confidentially towards me.

'Are you thinking what I'm thinking, ey?'

'Possibly lad, but not in so many words. Now isn't there some appalling cock up you should be getting on with making?'

And then that moment comes, quite suddenly, when the sum of all an incompetent's fears coalesce into one great ball of crap, threatening brown oblivion. It goes like this.

'Mark to base. RA returning to stand. I think he's shut an engine down.'

Jeep over by the window: 'Moss just turned his car round. He's coming back.'

Jill moves to the doorway. I wonder fleetingly what that shade of lipstick is called: *Sudden Air Sea Rescue* perhaps? 'The bar money is stuck halfway into the float safe. Can anybody help?'

'Got the wedge wedged, ey?' I think it's the rising hysteria that makes me talk this way.

I tear off a telex and pretend to read it to give me time to think, but the floor trembles slightly and I register Bill Healey approaching. Jeep almost flings himself across the room to help Jill. Good luck to him—struggling shoulder to shoulder with the safe is about as close as he is ever going to get to her.

'Ah Mike, have you seen this NOTAM?'

'No Bill, but I've just seen this.' I hold up the telex. I can't quite believe it. Not today *please*. Bloody Banjul closed between 1700 and 1900. AARRGHHH! It's the space shuttle *Endeavour's* number one alternate as adverse weather conditions are presently forecast for the landing area. No no no. Oy, NASA, do you know you've been stitched up? I mean a shuttle costs what? A squillion vermilion bucks and you don't even get an engine? Should have bought the GLX model. *Endeavour's* got four of America's finest—plus a token Oriental—up front, and two thousand geezers back at Kennedy doing everything for them, right down to emptying the ashtrays, yet a bloody three-knot crosswind, somewhere in Panama, writes off the whole of North America. It's a paperweight that's what it is, *Endeavour*, a hundred and fifty-tonne paperweight with Marley tiles on the nose, and it's going to close Africa just when we are due to arrive.

Len Borer, wearing his Customer Relations hat, steps forward just at that moment, blissfully unaware of the tragedy unfolding before me: 'I wonder if I could have just a quick word, Mike?'

No Len, that's a big fat negatory, you bloody-well couldn't. Suddenly Dick Pullman materialises at my elbow. I flinch with the suddenness of his appearance. He is holding a red marker pen and a green one, waving them accusingly in my face. Keith Tollworth is there too, flying wingman in Dick's five o'clock. He has a copy of yesterday's log page and probably wants to know how I—we—managed to snatch defeat from the jaws of victory, again, with the Orlando going three hours late. Now Don Moss enters the office, still in his car. Jill Squeals as *Endeavou*r passes over her head to jam itself into the float safe drawer, and Bill Healey flies out of the window…

I sit up in bed, chilled and sweaty at the same time.

I'd like to think that it never got as bad as that, but I'd be lying. In the old days, I can remember it getting exponentially badder than that, on several occasions and for real. The film was one such.

Shaken

The line of trucks drawn up outside the freight shed in the gathering dusk already seemed endless, so I watched with mounting unease as yet more joined the end of the line. Had I got my sums wrong? How was all the stuff ever going to fit on the aircraft?

The business had started a couple of weeks earlier with a phone call from Ron Cudney up in Commercial. It was a noisy morning in the Ramp and I could barely make out what he was saying. But, asking the lads if they would conduct their business a little more quietly, only earned me four suggestions of what I might otherwise do if not satisfied with the present arrangement—two of them gross. Nevertheless, Cudney persevered and it became clear that he was trying to pass me the details of a projected load. There followed a scramble for paper and pencil and when he asked me if I was ready, I nodded. It's the sort of dopey thing people do when talking on the phone. But maybe he'd heard my neck creaking, because he immediately launched into the recital of a list that became evermore surreal as it progressed.

'Six brute arc lamps,' he said.

'Six what?'

'Brute arc lamps. They have them in film studios.'

'Do they? Right.'

'Next. Five thousand rounds of 9-millimetre blank ammunition.'

'What! You mean bullets and things?'

'Just blanks,' said Cudney, 'no "things".'

'Well how big are they?' I said.

'At a guess, I'd say nine millimetres.'

Oh, good one. 'I mean, how big are the boxes?'

Cudney sighed several times—the hydraulic braking system on his patience was losing pressure. 'Look, can I just give you the list first and I'll let you have all the weights and dimensions later?'

This struck me as about as pointless an exercise as it could possibly be, but I just said, 'Go on then.'

'Alright. Ten dummies.'

I said: 'Don't bother with the small stuff. Just bung them in an envelope and I'll give it to the skipper to look after.'

Cudney ground his teeth, I could hear the enamel cracking: 'Not those sort…Mannequins, dummy people.'

'Oh, like they have in shop windows?' This load was getting weirder by the minute.

'No, these are recumbent.'

'Recumbent?'

'Yes. They're lying down.'

'I know what recumbent means.'

'They are dead.'

'Existentially speaking, aren't all dummies?'

'These are meant to be dead. Shot. Fallen in battle. Killed in action. Right?'

I wrote "Ten dummies. Recumbent. Killed," wondered if Cudney might benefit from a few days' holiday, and said 'next.'

'One Bell helicopter.'

'WHAT?' I was getting repetitive.

Cudney corrected himself: 'Well it's two helicopters, actually. But the other one's an autogyro. Much smaller.'

After that, the conversation degenerated to the point where we were no longer communicating in any meaningful sense. And what with the noise from the office, Cudney just gave up and rang off, leaving me none the wiser for his call. Not many minutes later Bradbury called me into his office. Right after I'd got through flinching because Bradbury had called me into his office, I discovered that Ron Cudney had been on to him.

'Ron Cudney's been on to me,' he said. 'Get yourself over to Pinewood Studios.' (No preamble as usual. He always gave me the impression of being a man with a scorpion in his underpants.) 'They're making another James Bond film,' he told me, (Ah, so that's what Ron was on about) 'and we're in the running to ship the props and equipment to Tokyo.'

'Ooh, exciting,' I thought. *'I've never been to a film studio.'*

'It's a big job, lot of money involved. But I'm told there's a lot of stuff to go. It'll be the DC7, of course. So, get to the studios as soon as you can, have a look at the load and confirm we can get it all on. Commercial need the go-ahead so they can accept the contract before some other bugger grabs it.' And he went on to mention some of the others buggers who'd sacrifice a goat and burn a church for a job like this.

'Ooh, still excited.'

'So, don't cock it up. It's important; I'm relying on you.' *'Er, not quite so excited now.'*

'It will all be down to you: just make sure it goes without a hitch.'

'Ok, not overly excited anymore.' A moment ago, it sounded like fun. Now, suddenly, I was holding a grenade with the pin out and nowhere to throw it.

By early afternoon that day, I was driving the Abomination through Buckinghamshire when to my astonishment, through a curtain of trees to my right, I spotted what looked like…but no, surely not. But yes, it was: a snow-capped mountain peak. Now, my geography had never been what you would call rock solid, but if memory served there were no mountains anywhere in the Home Counties. Only later was I to discover that what I was gawping open-mouthed at, while trying not to run off the road, was a representation of the top 120 feet of the Japanese volcano Shinmoedake, built to scale, for what would be the fifth James Bond film, *You Only Live Twice.*

Gaining entry to the studio was nothing like the security obstacle course it is today. Simply dropping the name of Harry Brown, the man I had come to meet, at the famous mock-Tudor gatehouse, got me directed into a labyrinth of buildings and soundstages where, eventually, I found my man in a small cluttered first-floor office. As I soon discovered, Harry Brown was the studio's go-to man for anything that needed—well, going to. This was only too apparent from the constant stream of visitors and the persistent jangling of the telephones on his and his secretary Jill's desks.

Harry was something of a legend in the business, a big, affable ball of energy, indefatigable at seventy-five, known and respected by actors, directors, crew, secretaries and tea ladies alike. If somebody needed a hundred French tunic buttons from the Napoleonic period, or a return flight to Sidney, or a taxi to Windsor, Harry was your man.

Despite the many interruptions, we soon got down to the tedious business of deciding how the packing of the cargo should be done. I was concerned that when it arrived at the aircraft, every item would be clearly marked with its weight in kilos. To this day The UK clings to the last remnants of the avoirdupois system, but back then the use of the metric system was rare indeed—except in aviation, where it was employed extensively. Without clear weight markings, I explained, it would not be possible for me to work out the loading and the trim of the aircraft. Mr Green told me that though some of the packing had already been completed, he would see to it that the weights were re-marked the way I had requested. However, the majority of the cargo was still scattered across several sites around the studio, he said, and was yet to be packed. This offered me a brilliant opportunity to dress a skive up as an essential part of my work, and to suggest a visit to these sites to assess the cargo. Harry cheerfully agreed, and set off at a cracking pace on a guided tour of the studio.

In a dusty storage room, we came across the remnants of the set for the Elizabeth Taylor/Richard Burton epic *Cleopatra*. Harry told me that originally it was to have been shot wholly at the studios, but bad weather had dogged the production, eventually forcing a shift to sunnier climes. I mentioned that I had seen the gilded royal barge constructed for the film moored in Naples harbour. He told me that owing to the prohibitive cost of transporting it back to the UK, it had been left there to rot. Parsimony and profligacy seemed to hold equal sway in the movie business.

Passing the open door of a small sound stage (movie-people's talk for a studio), we spotted a group of female dancers inside dressed in toreador pants and multi-coloured t-shirts, rehearsing a routine. I came out slower than I went in, and backwards, until a little further on we found ourselves on the outskirts of picturesque Spanish village plaza, complete with adobe-covered houses and a central fountain. The feeble English sunshine was being supplemented to Mediterranean standard by a phalanx of arc lamps, behind which various crew hovered, as Cliff Richard and The Shadows repeatedly circled the fountain on bicycles. This was *Finders Keepers*, a dollop of teen froth which wouldn't trouble the Oscars much—nor cinemas for very long, if memory serves.

In one of the many gloomy corridors a tall elegant figure in a lightweight blue suit greeted my guide with cordial familiarity: Roger Moore, a couple of films away from getting his own licence to kill, still going about his Saintly TV duties. In another long corridor hung with framed posters from a host of classic movies, glass cases containing beautifully-detailed models of cars and ships used in some of the productions, lined the walls. In one stood an immaculate foot-long replica of a Rolls Royce, its front bumper realistically mangled. Clearly the budget had not stretched to damaging an actual 1930 Phantom II Sedanca de

Ville. So, with CGI and other advanced trickery still some decades away, an anonymous craftsman had lovingly recreated the car in miniature—then bent it. In the Special Effects department where Harry led me next—it looked like a carpenter's shop—here the geniuses who ran the place could sink the Titanic, or blow up a castle, or simply make someone disappear in a puff of smoke, with a few multi-coloured stars thrown in, if the lily needed so gilding. In one corner stood a 500cc motorbike equipped with rocket tubes that I was assured worked perfectly—and without scorching the rider's legs. While along one wall three aqua-sleds were parked, equipped with compressed-air spearguns that had been used by the baddies in *Thunderball*. Harry said that somebody had actually been shot with one of the harpoons (accidentally of course, there is a limit to realism), but he thought the man had survived. These were the people who had installed twin machine guns and a working ejector seat in an Aston Martin and built a full-scale rocket that would actually take off, for the current production.

Stepping quietly into another working sound stage, we came across an elegant, minstrel-galleried French drawing room of the Revolutionary period. This was a set for *Carry On Don't Lose Your Head*. As I watched, up on the gallery, a stunt man was going through the routine of grabbing a chandelier and swinging across the room on it, to disappear through an opposite window. Except that best-laid plans aft gang agley, and at each attempt the stunt man missed his target by a couple of feet, instead hitting the adjacent wall with a resounding thud. After each collision, he would hang stunned in his safety harness for a few seconds, before insisting—against the advice of his mates, no doubt eager to take the job from him—on having another bash—literally. He was replaced a couple of times with a sandbag to try to establish an accurate parabola through the window. It made no difference, he was still regularly hitting the wall when we turned away, unable to watch any longer.

As we headed for the door, my attention was caught by a little scene being enacted in the shadows behind the set. Here, seated around a makeshift table, engaged in a cut-throat game of poker, was seated the cream of British lavatory humour: Sid James, Peter Butterworth, Kenneth Williams and Charles Hawtrey—from the look of their respective piles of cash—all being taken to the cleaners by Joan Simms.

But time was pressing for Harry and, after giving me some directions to orientate me so that I could find my way back to his office, he left me to wander more or less at will. No doubt he had better things to do.

114

A brief, decidedly bizarre stop in the canteen to munch on a sandwich among doomed aristos and swarthy blokes in grey combats, and I was on my way again. After a bit of a search, I followed the flow of major activity to find one of the Bond sets. Here, a scene in the office of Tiger Tanaka, head of the Japanese secret service, was being shot. In it, Connery enters the rooftop office and Tanaka (played by Tetsurŏ Tanba), invites him to sit in front of the desk. Tanaka then presses a button and the desk swings round to face Bond. This was achieved, I noticed, by putting the desk and chair on a low platform fitted with what looked like domestic castors and having a couple of prop blokes lie on their bellies just out of shot, to swing the contraption round by hand. Glamour in the movies, I was discovering, was barely screen deep. Two monitors on Tanaka's desk displayed an X-ray of Bond's thorax and I could see that he was not in the best of health—there appeared to be a Walther PPK in his left lung.

I watched fascinated as the actors struggled to deliver a just a few words each without something ruining the take: an anonymous twit at the other end of the studio hammering a bit of wood, the desk swing being performed too quickly, too slowly or too jerkily; or one of the actors fluffing a line. The takes were endless. By the time I left to head back to Mr Green's office, I was pretty solid on both actors' lines.

It was clear that the cargo was not anywhere near ready for inspection. Pity: I would have to return. That was what I told Bradbury, and though it aggravated his scorpion, he had little choice but to acquiesce and a few days later I was back at the studio.

This time I was taken straight to a shed to view the cargo. Everything had been crated, each one stencilled with its contents and weight. There was a lot of it, and right in front of the stack stood 'Little Nellie', the autogyro that would be flown by its inventor, Ken Wallace, for the aerial battle scenes with the SPECTRE helicopters. I had done my sums, played around with bits of graph paper to represent the cargo on a diagram of TC's cabin, spoken to our vastly-experienced loaders—and would have left a toad at the crossroads at midnight if I'd thought it would help, until my uncertainties crept away into a dark cerebral recess to whisper amongst themselves. It just had to be ok. Nevertheless, it still looked like a whole mountain of stuff. That distant, persistent *ting-a-linging* I could hear wasn't just my tinnitus.

Before I left, Harry's secretary Jill took me briefly to the volcano set to be shown inside. As I negotiated a crowd moving mostly in the opposite direction in a dark walkway leading to the set, I bumped into a big solid figure in combat gear. We mumbled our apologies; it was only when I heard the clipped lisping Scots accent that I recognised it was Connery.

The set was astonishing; the volcano I had assumed was just an empty shell, was Bond's arch-enemy Blofeld's base, complete with rockets, control room, helicopter landing pad and a working monorail that ran around the inner circumference of the crater's base. The million-dollar set featured lots of Bond-movie signature stainless steel, nestling amid rough-hewn rock. A massive sliding door 70 feet in diameter, disguised on its upper surface as a lake, plugged the crater high above our heads. I stayed long enough to watch the door slide open and for Bond, leading a team of Tanaka's ninjas, dressed in the grey combats I had seen in the canteen, rappel from it onto the helipad to launch their attack on the base. There was lots of smoke and bangs and flashes and people saying 'Arrrgh' and falling over. Then it was time to get back to the real world.

Later, I learned how nearly the whole production, might never have been realised. A team, including Lewis Gilbert the director and Ken Adams the Oscar-winning designer of the set, had been in Tokyo scouting locations. Booked to return home on BOAC flight 911, they missed it, having been unexpectedly invited to watch a ninja demonstration. The Boeing 707 left without them. Shortly after take-off it encountered clear air turbulence, broke up and crashed near Mount Fuji, with the loss of everyone on board.

Now, as I eyed the line of anonymous trucks drawn up beside the freight shed, it was time to stop worrying about my judgement—it was too late for that by at least a decade—and to get on with the job. *TC* stood ready on the ramp, her fore and aft freight doors raised, and the nightshift loading gang already fretting by the cargo shed door, itching to get stuck in. I'd been in my "office" (the little partitioned rat-hole off the Ramp Office) most of the day, had knocked off briefly in the afternoon and was back for what would be a marathon session straight through to the schedule take off at 0500 the next morning. I thought that this would be one long shift. I was right—it was pretty much the only thing I got right all night.

Still uncertain about the load, I decided on the cautious approach (hardly my customary *laissez-faire* MO), and much to the annoyance of the loaders asked them to weight some of the cargo. Walking down the line of trucks, I picked one at random and had a few boxes removed to the freight shed scales. This proved reassuring; the weights neatly stencilled on the side of the boxes, in kilos as requested, proved to be exact. By now, the loaders looked ready to run me down with the truck if I didn't get out of the way and let them get on. I had no choice, reluctantly I gave the go ahead to begin loading and let slip the dogs.

As the night wore on, chaos was born, grew to maturity and was crowned king before dawn. First it was HM Customs, interesting itself minutely in proceedings, demanding to look at everything. Then Harry Brown, who had arrived with Ron Cudney from Commercial, began to prioritise what must be carried in the event that anything had to be left behind. But he was constantly changing his mind, and Cudney just hovered in my background to ensure that nothing upset his customer. Up to my eyes in it by 0300, I asked the night duty officer for some help with paperwork, and got a blunt refusal. He thought my job a pretty cushy number compared to the slog of shifts and probably relished the thought of me going down in flames.

The race was on: Me v The Loaders, and the devil take the hindermost. As the cargo was brought on board, I was supposed to tally its weight and mark its position in the cabin. Painted white lines on the aircraft's floor delineated sections or 'bays', each one of which had a maximum weight and, depending on its position along the fulcrum of the cabin, a greater or lesser effect on the aircraft's centre of gravity. Now, whereas the loaders main aim was to get all the stuff on as quickly as possible, so that they could thin out back to the crew room to drink tea, play cards, scratch their privates, belch, fart and get their heads down, my overriding concerns were to ensure I got all the weights and knew which bay every item was being placed in. I also had to make sure that the floor loading and maximum bay weights were not exceeded. And while that was going on, I was constantly running estimates of the trim on a graph to make sure it fell within the aircraft's safe envelope. Moving cargo after it had been stowed because of load or trim problems was anathema to loaders, and I had no intention of anathing them.

First on was *Nellie*, the autogyro. With her main rotor blades folded back like the ears of a vexed cat, it was placed right at the front of the cabin, where it was lashed to the floor and boxes of all shapes and sizes packed carefully around it until it was snugly cocooned. After that, a veritable torrent of cargo began to flood in through the rear cargo door.

Six loaders plus a forklift and driver, versus me. I was losing track already. I stopped them occasionally to scramble in among the boxes searching for

117

missing weights, while they shot "sod-me-what's-he-up-to-now?" glances at each other. On one such occasion I stumbled across a body in the gloom. It gave me quite a turn until I realised it was a dummy. The loaders probably thought we made a pair.

We must have been three quarters through the loading. It was the early hours, spirits were low, it was as cold as a penguin's bum and it was still dark. By now, I was struggling with umpteen lists, pens and trial loadsheets and trying not to drop anything, when a tread heavy enough to make TC tremble heralded the arrival on board of Greg Thorner, our chief engineer. Big Greg's appearance was not always entirely welcome, not just because he had the sense of humour of a mortician with haemorrhoids, but because his arrival often presaged bad tidings. This was one of those occasions.

'How's it going, Mike?' He didn't wait for an answer, he just let me have it: 'We're going to put a spare engine on board.'

He might just as well have said: 'We're going to bomb Basingstoke.' It would have made as much sense to me. A spare engine? There wasn't enough spare payload to carry me—I wasn't going—let alone an engine. Besides, considering he was the engineer in charge of *TC's* serviceability, shouldn't he have had a bit more faith in the quality of his own work? A spare chuffing engine? Hadn't *TC* got enough already? There were quite a few out there on the wings last time I counted.

I didn't actually say any of that, naturally. I was young, I was junior in experience and seniority to just about everybody, and anyway he was a big bloke with a monobrow and prehensile arms. So, I settled for asking weakly what such an item might weigh.

'The engine and its stand together,1500 kilos. It's on its way over.'

'Not on its own accord, I hope.' I may have been a bit hysterical. I think he thought I meant it. I had to try to tell him that the thing was simply impossible. 'I…umm…I don't see how we can get it on. We don't have the payload for a start. And anyway, look, the aircraft's nigh on loaded. Unless we unload it all again, it'll have to go right on the back by the rear door: 1500 kilos right aft is going to be a bugger to trim…'

Greg shut me down mid-whine: 'Sorry (he bloody-well wasn't), not my problem. It has to go. Offload some cargo if you have to. Do whatever you have to, but the engine goes. Ok.'

The "OK" was rhetorical. He was gone, leaving me working my mouth like a landed pike, aghast at the prospect of either trying to work out a way of carrying the engine, or explaining to Jack Bradbury and Commercial—maybe even the MD Himself—why I had left either the engine or some of the near-sacred payload behind. It was a choice between being boiled in oil or burnt at the stake. I settled for an appeal to the Court of Procrastination and decided to try to get the engine on *and* all the cargo. There didn't appear to be any other way to save my miserable skin.

I suspended the loading while we awaited delivery of the engine, so that it could be loaded as far forward as possible. This would mean that it could be placed just forward of the rear freight door without removing any of the cargo (the anathema thing). Not ideal, but a lot better than putting it on last, right down aft by the toilets, where its impact on the trim would be so much greater. The engine came. We saw. Were appalled. Put it on. TC reverse genuflected in response and the tail post inched closer to the ground, after which loading continued.

But we got the job done and as the footlights came up on a chilly but clear morning sky, I trudged back to the office to complete the load and trimsheet. It would soon be showtime, only I felt a bit under-rehearsed for this one.

Many discarded loadsheets later, I had it done. Morning was already well under way and TC's crew were checking in. I had struggled to make the figures add up and TC was a bit tail heavy, but by the time John Shepherd, who had been on the Iran trip and was the skipper today, came to inspect the loadsheet, all was ready. He wasn't ecstatic about having to reduce his fuel load to accommodate the extra weight, nor was he applauding the tail-heavy centre of gravity, but since it was within the aircraft's limitations, he checked through the figures and signed—right next to my signature.

0700. A low sun was unrolling long carpets of shadow across the tarmac as *TC* lurched heavily away towards the runway, to a ragged derisive cheer from the night shift: the flight was hours late. As usual I had stayed for the take-off; my task would not be complete until the aircraft was on its way. The day shift was arriving now, preparing for a busy schedule. I kept out of their way, drinking tea and trying to stay awake as I watched *TC's* laboured progress down to the far end of the runway. She would be taking off towards us, on runway 09.

In the Ramp Office, in our idle moments, we would gauge an aircraft's take-off performance from runway 09 by its relative height above a railway bridge, after it had lifted off from the eastern end of the runway. We would first watch the aircraft's take-off run until it disappeared behind the end of the south passenger pier, by which time it would be airborne. We would then cross to the other side of the office, to the rear windows, to estimate its height relative to the railway bridge (though some distance beyond it) and thus rate its climb performance.

TC sat for some time, distantly, at the far end of the runway, the ever-thorough John Shepherd no doubt ensuring that the pre-flight checks were carried out punctiliously. But at last, a halo of blue smoke rising behind her showed that take-off power had been applied against the brakes. After a few moments, during which TC sat waggling her tail like a cat about to pounce, the brakes were released and she began to roll. It would be a long roll, I expected that; she was at maximum take-off weight and would take time to achieve flying speed.

But she rolled. And rolled. And rolled some more. I noticed that some of the shift had now stopped what they were doing and were also watching. *TC* continued the run, but did not from this angle—nearly nose on—seem to be gaining much speed. She came on, engines flat out, streaming the blue smoke that had earned her the nickname *Torrey Canyon* (a tanker which sank off Cornwall in 1967, causing a massive oil spill). I began to squirm and I forgot to breathe for a while, until my autonomic system insisted upon it. I watched in horror as she passed out of sight behind the tip of the south pier, her nose wheel still firmly planted on the runway.

The room fell silent. Somebody swore under his breath—it may have been me. In a body we turned, moving quickly to the rear window. My mouth was ash-dry. Where was she? Jesus, what had I done? And then the old girl was there, airborne. But there was precious little to celebrate: relative to the bridge she was visible through the arch—she was *below* it. We had never seen that before and maybe it had never happened before. It was happening now. In any case, *TC* was clearly in poor shape. Her climb angle was virtually zero as she struggled to maintain flying speed, let alone climb. The lads around me broke into exclamations of astonishment and relief, with the occasional sharp sideways glance in my direction. There may also have been one or two thinly-disguised accusatory remarks. My name was on the loadsheet: this one was down to me, that was the thinking. I was too stunned to do anything but stand there, staring dumbly after the retreating aircraft. It took some time, but I watched until it became no more than a speck and finally dissolved into the morning haze. Blue oil smoke hung on the still air over the runway for some time, until the vortices of a jet taking off finally whipped it away.

I stayed in the Ramp, with my fingers crossed and my teeth gritted. Exactly what I was waiting for, I preferred not to think too much about. Whatever it was didn't happen: there were no sudden phone calls or urgent radio messages, nothing, just the bustling routine of a normal day.

I slunk quietly away, hoping that nobody—especially the crew—had noticed just how badly *TC* was flying this morning. Think drowning man, using an anvil for buoyancy.

"You nearly killed us," was John Shepherd's trenchant opening line to me, over a crackly telephone line from Istanbul. To be fair, I couldn't claim all the credit, I'd had a lot of help. But clearly, as lead would-be assassin, contrite silence was what was required now.

I had gone home, slept fitfully and slunk back to the Ramp that afternoon, trying to maintain as low a profile as possible. For the next hour, nothing happened and I was just beginning to come to the incredulous conclusion that I had managed to blag this one, when Jack Bradbury appeared at my door, beckoning me to follow with a crooked finger. Entering his office, I noticed that the handset of his telephone was lying on the blotter. Bradbury pointed to it: "John Shepherd, for you."

There followed an excruciating couple of minutes during which the ever-phlegmatic Shepherd recounted the crew's adventure that morning, in remarkably restrained tones. That *TC* had so nearly not made it into the air was only too obvious. In fact, she had not come unstuck from the runway until she'd reached the piano keys marking its end. She'd gone off on full emergency power, Arthur the flight engineer's hands clamped over the throttles to keep them all the way forward against the stops. He was still in that position ten miles out, and *TC* was still on emergency power as she crossed the Channel coast. All aircraft can take off at heavier weight than they can land (the difference being the fuel consumed during the flight) and since it was obvious that *TC's* load had somehow exceeded her maximum permitted take-off weight, there was no question of turning back. The flight would have to continue to its tech stop, Istanbul, to burn off sufficient fuel to make it light enough to land.

John didn't need to tell me that if they had lost an engine at any time during the take off and climb out it would have been all over. He told me anyway. By the time they reached Istanbul, *TC* was flying ok, but there was no question of her going any further loaded as she was. The spare engine would have to come off. Not only that, but the cargo would have to removed and re-weighed before continuing. If I thought that was bad—and I did—John made it more so by finishing his diatribe with a very simple, direct question to which, as yet, I had no answer: 'What went wrong?'

We finished our conversation with John interspersing my many stammered apologies with mildly-worded requests that I investigate. Promising to do so, I rang off and waited for Bradbury to fire me. At the very least, I expected him to shoot me with the humane killer. He refrained from either. To give him credit, he only repeated Shepherd's demand for answers, telling me to get on with it. Then, just as I was leaving, added a little more woe to proceedings which were already woeful enough.

'We're sending a Bristol 170 down to Istanbul to bring back the engine.'

I nodded and left before he told me that also all the firstborn of my tribe would be slaughtered. Could it get any worse? I had assumed that *TC* would swing by Istanbul to collect the dumped engine on the way back from Tokyo. However, for reasons never explained to me, other councils had prevailed and she was to be re-routed on her return journey, missing Istanbul, necessitating the long and costly flight of a 170 to Istanbul to retrieve it. The case for my prosecution was building nicely. The Bristol 170 was a dreadful bit of antiquated kit which—with a top speed of just under 230 mph—could only be considered a success as an ugly exercise in how to approach a standstill in the sky. It looked like a builder's skip with wings and boasted the performance of a rheumatic vicar climbing a hill on a rusty bicycle with a flat tyre. Nevertheless, with its large nose doors, it was useful for carrying cars and horses—and, for that matter, orphaned aircraft engines marooned in the Levant.

The answer to whatever had gone wrong clearly lay back at the studio and I headed back to Pinewood. The investigation didn't take long. What I discovered was, that when I had walked down the line of trucks outside the freight shed and chosen one of them at random, I could not have picked a more unsuitable candidate for checking the accuracy of the weight markings on its contents. The truck contained only Panavision camera equipment, the boxes marked with the maker's weights and accurate to the ounce. The rest of the cargo however, didn't add up to the manifested weight. It appeared that whoever had been given the job of converting pounds to kilos had very little idea how to do it and had guessed it. It had not been an educated guess. Some case markings were shown in pounds, when the figure actually represented kilos—more than twice the weight. There were so many discrepancies between the cargo manifest and what was loaded on the aircraft, that it was unlikely we would ever know just how overloaded *TC* had been, but it must have been in the tons, possibly two or even three.

Bradbury accepted the explanation, but, though he didn't actually say so, clearly thought my part in the debacle had been far from glorious. John Shepherd graciously accepted my explanation. But I was much chastened by the incident. I also had to take some sledging from the lads in the Ramp and the story, somewhat dramatised, even found its way into an episode of a TV drama series about a dodgy airline. As it turned out, to add salt to the wound, *TC* acquitted herself admirably throughout the trip. The spare engine was never needed and all the trouble its shipment had contributed to might have been avoided if there had been just a little more faith in the old girl.

Christmas

In Ops, once again Christmas is approaching, close enough to smell its flaming brandy sauce and rampant commercialism.

It is night time and I am alone in the office. Strictly speaking I am not alone, according to the roster Sam Ford is my number two. But though he has a radio with him, he is not here in person. His person is somewhere nearby, at a party, trying to make it with a stewardess he's had a crush on for a while. Though his interest in her is potentially mutual, he will be getting hammered with such a grim intensity of purpose that the target of his affections will simply give up the fight. She's not likely to be into troilism—her, Sam and his demon. A psychoanalyst would have a field day with the lad. But wherever he is and whatever state he is in, if I needed him, he'd get here, and still be able to function sufficiently to be of practical use. I really have no idea how he does that.

I won't need him. The movement board shows two flights tomorrow, not early, and there is just a bit of paperwork, while I indulge in what I like to think of as "self-pity light." In this case, it is an affectation which may be innocently enjoyed, because the fact is I hate parties: the darkened rooms, the blaring conversation-obliterating music, the paper cups of flat beer, the predatory atmosphere, the desecration with hurried fornication of hosts' bedrooms that had been innocently set aside for coats; worst of all the feeling that your disengagement is noticed, that you have to keep making up purposeful moves (like striding out to the kitchen for more of the flat beer you don't want), so as not to appear to be the party's Johnny-no-mates. I am not interesting at parties, and I'm not interested in them. So, by way of compensation, there is the righteous melancholy of being left out to be enjoyed; the outsider bravely holding the fort, taking one for the team. It's a harmless indulgence.

Christmas is pretty much the same around most airline offices. Some companies push the boat out with the decorations. In Ops we don't. We exhume a couple of ragged streamers from the bottom of a filing cabinet and decorate the walls with all the cards we get from companies who don't give a cloud of reindeer breath for Yuletide, but just want to remind us, albeit obliquely, of their outstanding invoices. A balding six-inch Christmas tree also appears to adorn the top of the AFTN telex machine, where, while printing is in progress, it sheds needly dandruff it can ill afford to lose. Then, sometime on Christmas Eve, the National Air Traffic Control Service launches Santa One, their annual stab at Yuletide frivolity. Thereafter and until Christmas morning, ATC position reports will pop up in between the real traffic as Santa and the reindeer speed around the world at incredible speed, delivering illusions to the pure of heart.

The lead up to the festivities has been, as it always is, frenetic. So many people, quite unaccountably, seem to need to be somewhere else at Christmas. It's all very tiring to watch, more so be involved in. But finally, a day or so before Yule Zero, it's all over, the strain drains away, the airport is suddenly deserted, skeleton staff rattle around doing their skinny thing—which isn't much—and everybody awaits (with baited enthusiasm in my case), the commencement of festivities. The only present I really want for Christmas is New Year's Day, but apparently you have to wait until all the other ballyhoo is out of the way first. An instance in which the concept of deferred gratification is rather less than rewarding.

On this evening, just up the road at the slab of strenuously-mocked Tudor that is the Regis Hotel, the works' thrash will by now have negotiated the celeriac soup, (terrine alternative for the rebels), landed the inevitable turkey and be considering either the immolated Christmas pudding or the default trifle, whose identical recipe, without its festive paper coaster, is also available throughout the rest of the year. The cheese will be served straight from the fridge and the coffee from an urn of instant secreted out the back. (I've done gigs there and never want to see another guinea fowl again, ever. So, I know whereof I speak.)

These enjoyably-misanthropic musings are rudely interrupted by the telex machine clattering into importunate life. It's the machine that reports things that you may need to know, (not the AFTN machine next to it, the one adorned with the Christmas tree, the one that waffles on endlessly with position reports and ATC flight plans and may be ignored most of the time.) So, I must get up and have a shufti, just in case it's anything I need to deal with.

It is something I need to deal with. I toy momentarily with the idea of pretending I haven't seen it, because it promises pain-in-the-assery conflicting with the more restful plans I have for the evening. The signal comes from Aviolé, the grungy Spanish outfit we've occasionally used in the past, strictly in extremis, for sub-charters when things have gone terribly wrong for us. And they do have to have gone *terribly* wrong before we resort to the vaqueros of Aviolé. For the company is a blot on the face of Aviation, their rattling Boeing an afront to the environment and everything about their operation redolent of *laissez faire* incompetence. That they have an Air Operator's Certificate at all is a miracle. The signal informs me that their aircraft is crook in Madrid and sub-charter availability is requested to move their stranded passengers to Frankfurt.

Now, recently, we have received *ex cathedra* instructions from Upstairs (couched in unnecessarily pettish terms, I thought), to actively pursue opportunities such as this. Profits, we are told, have been disappointing of late and our lords and masters at Golding have begun rumbling at our backs like a pack of attack dogs on unreliable leashes. So, despite the fact that I am more or less certain that we can't assist Scary Air S.A., I must at least look into the possibility. After which I can log it, in suitably flowery terms to indicate the thoroughness of my investigations, then forget it, put the kettle on, revert to my original plan.

This intrusion on the quiet night I had planned has almost made me yearn for the data entry drudgery that has become a feature of our nightshifts since the recent introduction of a rudimentary computer system for Crewing. The monitor is the size of a small family car, boasting a screen the size of a wing mirror, upon which jerky little green florescent figures march endlessly until, after the couple of hours it has taken the processor to meander through its calculations, they are burnt semi-permanently onto one's retina. So cumbersome is the programme, that every single member of crew must have a manual entry made against his/her name, every night, whether they have worked or not. It takes about an hour longer than it used to take to do it with pencil and paper. It will not be long before Crew Scheduling upstairs tires of discovering most mornings that the night D/O has been too busy—or at least claimed to be so—about his own duties to spare the time to do their filing for them, and an outside contractor is engaged to take over the task. Though it offers brain-addling tedium, at least when compared with the sub-charter, it has at least the advantage of predictability.

Reluctantly, I call the Big Bro engineering supervisor. He has the gall to tell me that *Golf Delta* is not only serviceable but cleaned, cabin dressed and, on completion of a routine inspection, will be ready to roll shortly. This blow is compounded by a glance at the movement board, which informs me that the programme does not require *GD* until tomorrow afternoon. I retreat into Crewing's cubicle to look for an alibi in the roster, only to receive a further setback: the requisite flightdeck crew—captain, first officer and flight engineer are available, on standby and with their customary insufferable professionalism, may be relied upon to answer the phone, forensically sober and alert if needed. But there is hope yet, for although many cabin staff approach their duties with the same professionalism as their counterparts north of the flightdeck door, there are undeniably some among them more interested in their nails, their hair, who is single and/or available amongst the flight crew and which room the night-stop party is to be held in. And the girls are no better. I need eight cabin staff. I have four on standby, at least one of whom falls into the unreliable category. Many are on leave, we also have two Christmas trips out, one in the New World, the other in Africa. So, even with our quiet Racebridge programme, we are short of cabin crew. It looks like the reprieve I have been waiting for.

Then the phone rings and *plus ça change*. It's the outside line. I pick up. It's Jed, with preternatural bad timing, calling from the Regis. I can hear the DJ in the background against a soundtrack of unbridled revelry.

'How's it going, dog-breath?'

This is horrendous (not the epithet, that's just standard for Jed, the unrepentant vulgarian), no, it's his ringing up just at this moment, with that question. On three hundred and sixty other nights in any year, there wouldn't be a rabbit's chance in a foxhole of him doing that. Now, tonight, just at the psychological moment, he's on my six, presenting me with the insurmountable problem of hiding the sub-charter from him.

I do what I can, but I don't have much to work with. I daren't not mention the big Spanish elephant tramping around the office, but at least I can try to hide it in the jungle.

'It's quiet, nothing worth the mention. Just a sub-charter request from Aviolé, a Madrid Frankfurt. We don't have enough cabin staff. Oh, and I think the HF set is on the blink, coz I can't...'

An amateurish effort: Jed is not to be distracted by that. 'What's wrong with it?'

'Well, it sounds a bit crackly when...'

'Not the HF, dickhead. Aviolé's Boeing?'

'I don't know. As our Irish cousins would say, "They have it broke." What am I, an engineer?'

'You're not even a bloody ops D/O most of the time. How many cabin-staff have you got? Do we have an aircraft? Catering?'

It goes on like this and reluctantly, I have to admit that yes, we do have an aircraft, and probably catering, though I haven't enquired about it yet; and yes, we do have flight crew, but we only have four cabin staff on stand-by, and one of them is well, a delightful person, but flakier than the paint job on Aviolé's Boeing, so I'll be amazed if she answers the phone.

'Right, hang on, do nowt for the minute, you're good at that, toad. I'll call you back.'

There is barely time to call him a fornicating Mancunian toe-rag, before the phone goes dead. As I delete the telex I have been preparing, offering Aviolé a polite "sod off" in the form of my best wishes whilst regretting that we have no availability, I wonder what has got into the normally indolent Jed to make him want to indulge in these commercial heroics. What does he know that we don't? There is just long enough for me to become mildly paranoid about this, before he is back on the line, accompanied in the background—though not that far in the background—by Hendrix, sawing through *All Along the Watchtower*.

'Right listen up. I've had a whip-round for volunteers amongst the cabin staff and I've got six.'

'But Jed, they'll be legless, by now, surely?'

'Nope, all sober and all on days off. Haven't touched a drop and they're ready to knock off here and go home. What ETD you working on?'

I'm too shocked to learn there are so many sober cabin staff at the party, (who the hell is running it, the Sally Army?), to have an immediate answer...to anything.

Hendrix Launches into his solo, it's cracking – and from the way things are shaping up, so is mine.

Since the volunteers are all off the roster effectively, crew rest is not a consideration; their duty will begin when they report for the flight. So, only the standby crew's duty is dictated by their roster. They begin at 0400.

'Say 0600 STD?'

'Sounds about right. Even you should be able to get the flight plans right by then. You'll have to get on to Commercial, get them to sort out a contract with

Aviolé. Who's on call? It's Slick isn't it? And you'd better get onto caterers right away…'

Hendrix steps on the wah-wah and the Strat weeps. I know just how it feels.

'Jed, if you'll forgive me interrupting your diarrhoea – sorry, diatribe – why don't you come over and bring your crayons, so you can draw me diagrams too?'

He tells me that sarcasm, in terms of wit, is lower than a snake's belly in a wagon rut, and I point out that so poverty-stricken is his imagination, that he has managed to combine two tedious clichés in a single short sentence. He tells me that if he had anything to do with it there would be no short sentence for me, which is a better effort. Then he spoils it all by reverting to type, telling me to fuck off and putting the phone down before I can respond.

Hendrix is finished, but it looks like I'm just starting.

An hour later the sub-charter has become a certainty. Slick has talked contractual mumbo jumbo with Aviolé. (I have a mental picture of him sat on his bed in his silk jammies, talking to Madrid on the phone whilst the ice in his bedtime Old Speyburn melts beneath the bedside lamp.) We are taking all six of the volunteer cabin staff from the works' do, (there have been more since then, which is nice, but their sobriety could not be credibly established.) The aircraft is ready and my flight plans are nearly right. Catering was no problem. Similarly, handling will be no problem, since we require little. Being empty outbound, we won't even need a stand. *GD* will depart from the North Park, to where she's has been banished while idle, and will only require a start-up crew and somebody to wave the tear-stained valedictory hanky when she rolls.

0515. The fag end of the shift when sprits are at their lowest ebb, but there is work yet to be done. The crew is in, one or two cabin staff looking suspiciously bleary for 'stone-cold sober.' But if they are not, it's goodnight Vienna for their career, should they be discovered. The pilots are working on the paperwork laid out on the crew room desk. The crew bus is throbbing away outside the front entrance, ready to take them to the aircraft. It's basically a morning like a hundred other such mornings: routine, quiet, unhurried.

Only, no. The Lord of Misrule is about to make his seasonal entrance, and if he appeared, in this instance, in the guise of the Engineering Supervisor, I should not be surprised.

'Morning. Engineering Supervisor here. There's a problem.'

See? I'm not surprised. He tells me that the routine inspection they were carrying out on *GD* has revealed a crack in something called the number one engine thrust bolt mounting. I say oh dear, so you'll have to get another one then. No, they bleedin' won't, says he. What they'll have to do is drop the engine to inspect the whole of the pylon front spar mounting. He then goes on (and I do mean goes on), to enlarge on the likelihood of also having to have a look at the angle strakes, the pylon spar web and, while they're about it, the rear monoball mounting. But since he lost me back at "There's a problem" and I wouldn't know a monoball mounting if it were plonked on my desk with a sign reading *monoball mounting* on it, I see no point in further discussion. Cutting to the chase, I demand to know when we can have the aircraft, having momentarily forgotten one of the unspoken golden rules of aviation—not to dis Engineering, since they have the means to destroy us. And it is possible that my tone may have irritated the supervisor for he tells me that he can't say when the aircraft will be available, because he is grounding it pending an ultrasound inspection. And what is more, if the mount or any of its component parts is found to be wanting, then tough titty, because they don't have one to replace it, in which case I can stick my aeroplane up my bottom because it is Christmas and he has a list of jobs as long as his technical explanations—and every bit as boring—to do before *GD* gets a sniff at a fix.

I tell him this is unacceptable and he professes heartbreak at the news.

Henceforth, the downward trajectory of our fortunes is as inevitable as the bed chart of a nonagenarian with double pneumonia and a blocked oxygen line.

The crew are all here, their enthusiasm for the project dribbling away with their duty time. The cabins staff's dreams of supplementing their Yuletide budget with a few quid in flying pay evaporating like the morning mist now visible outside the window. We have no aircraft and we're not going to get one. An hour ago, cringing with embarrassment, I telephoned my beleaguered counterpart in Aviolé Ops with the ill tidings. He received them with frigid Castilian dignity and punctilious politeness, before abruptly ringing off to resume the search for a solution to the now rancid delay I had dumped back in his lap.

But with just fifteen minutes to go before the shift ends a kind of symmetry, which in any other circumstances would be pleasing—not this one—is achieved when the telex erupts with a message from Aviolé. Unexpectedly, their crap-heap Boeing has become serviceable and will operate its own Frankfurt/Madrid flight—after which, *it will be available for sub-charter should we require it.*

Double portion of chagrin with a side order of humble pie. Aviation is a bitch, and then you fly.

British Standard Sheep

As previously averred, the trouble with making promises, such as the one I'd made myself at Schiphol over the calf flight, is that one day you may be obliged to honour them.

The showdown came in the form the oleaginous Simon Glover, calling from Commercial. To say that he was my least favourite person in a department I wasn't that keen on anyway, understates my antipathy by a fairish margin. The only thing more important to Glover than his inexorable—execrable—rise to power, was his determination never to allow any of the shite he distributed to splash back onto himself. And at this, he was most adept.

But his delivery of poisoned chalices was second to none, and never bore even a trace of his fingerprints. The serpent voice with its reassuring tones, the friendly helpful manner; the soothing delivery, so convincing to the unwary that the disquiet they felt was perfectly understandable, but that everything would work out just fine. The snake oil was of the highest quality. But, after Schiphol, which he had authored, I was onto him: behind the cloak of the smooth spiel, lay cold venality and ruthless ambition, between who's pincers I had no inclination to be caught.

This time he was trying to sell me the idea of shipping 120 sheep on the Dc7, to Nice. It took me ten minutes to pick the essential details of the load out of the verbal gruel he was serving it up in, before I told him I would investigate and call him back. Putting the phone down, I went in search of Max Cannon's gruff wisdom.

'Oh Christ, it's Wonderboy. What is it this time?'

Max, it seemed, was in a good mood this morning. I told him about the sheep.

'A hundred and twenty on *TC?* You reckon? What breed are they? Southdowns? They're short-wools, they are. And full grown? They'll be big buggers, then.' A pause for thought. 'It's the wool, see, very thick. Roll your sleeve up and poke about in there and you'll be up to your elbow before you touch mutton. Mm, wouldn't like to say. I reckon a hundred and twenty's pushin' it, meself. Tell you what, there's a field full of 'em—I'm sure they're Southdowns—other side of the railway line. Why don't you nip over and have a butchers? Ha! butchers, geddit?'

A rutted track ran down beside a pub and a couple of cottages and the Abomination trundled down it shedding sump bolts and other bits it considered superfluous, until a five-barred gate did the job its name suggests. It led to a large field full of big sheep mowing wet grass for elevenses. To get some idea of the mass of the load, I tried counting them, unaccountably losing track at around thirty. So I gave up, and mentally photographing the scene, returned to the office.

I was going to have to work it out a bit more scientifically, on paper. My maths wasn't much above barely adequate, but in any case, assessing a load of live animals by volume and square feet seemed inappropriate. So, I had to come up with a more practical, simpler method of working it out. The result was, I like to think, a minor triumph of logic: the British Standard Sheep. I decided that it would be thirty inches wide and five and a half feet long. I then spent the rest of the morning fitting rectangular graph-paper sheep in blocks of five, onto a scale diagram of TC's cabin floor.

I felt pretty stupid. Very much more so when Mr W happened by, pausing to inspect my paper flock.

'What are you doing?' He had a way of getting straight to the point like that.

I explained that I was attempting to load sheep onto the DC7, and that there were 120 of them, including the two he was standing on.

Carefully peeling the strays off his shoe and putting them back on the desk, he said, 'They're square.'

I said it would be more accurate to describe them as rectangular, going on to explain that they were my British Standard Sheep, and that one had to use a little imagination.

Watkins looked at me for a moment. Then studied my "sheep" through half-closed eyes, turning his head this way and that. Then, without a word he made off towards his office. At the door he paused and looked back.

'Take some leave before you go bloody daft.' And when I told him I hadn't any leave owing, he nodded: 'You'll will go bloody daft, then.'

Thus encouraged, I soldiered on. It was a tricky load to work out, partly because nobody seemed to know exactly how big the animals would be or how they would be penned. So, with unpleasant memories of the debacle of Schiphol still fresh, I laboured long at my desk, shuffling my stupid little bits of paper, fitting them repeatedly into *TC's* 80' x 9' cabin, (it would be rather less by the time the necessary penning was installed.) Glover called twice; the first time to chivvy me up for an answer; the second, dropping the mask of amenability, to offer what amounted to blatant harassment. And by 1300hrs he was incandescent. But I would not be rushed, determined as I was to take as long as I needed to get this one wrong.

Eventually the dog-eared bits of paper and repeated infantile jottings began to work out to a consistent figure. I went over my calculations again and again, acutely aware that the sheep, with their heavy fleeces, would require sufficient spacing to prevent them overheating. Having obtained from my deliberations the same result repeatedly, yet still unsure, I took my figures once more to Cannon. They got his blessing and I returned, much encouraged, to the rat-hole to call Glover. I was fairly confident of my figure now, but just as confident that Glover wasn't going to like it.

I was right. I am sure he gave a short scream, though it could have been somebody goosing a secretary (a routine occupational hazard at that time) in the background. 'Ninety?' he gasped. 'That's pathetic! That can't be right. There must be another way.'

There was: we could shoot them all and stack them five high down the cabin. Job done. I didn't say that. I just stuck to my guns, suggesting that a DC3 could be used to carry the remainder. He wasn't listening, persisting with the unworkable idea of getting all 120 on *TC*. I stuck to my guns. Impasse. He rang off.

I got the uneasy feeling that I had won the battle, but was about to lose the war.

Half an hour later the artillery opened up, blasting me into astonishingly small fragments. It was our beloved director, Giles Woodman, in person, he of the strange sideways-windswept hair, the unhealthy pallor, the supercilious expression. Glover had been busy, ruining the knees of his trousers.

You didn't have a telephone conversation with Woodman, you just waited for the transmission to end, so you could slam the phone down and scream into your desk drawer.

The transmission went thus: 'These sheep depart at 1100 on Monday morning. They are all to go, understand? This is an important charter (really, another one?) Make sure everything runs smoothly.'

That was it. No discussion of my estimate, nor was my opinion sought: neither mattered. I was simply expected to get it done. What was clear to me was that on Monday morning a colossal clanger was going to be dropped from a lofty place, and I had no wish to be beneath it when it landed. There really was only one honourable thing to do in the circumstances. But since I had no idea what that was, I took the day off instead, feigning sickness.

Though the airport was a considerable distance away, throughout that Monday I could hear the deep and mournful tolling of a great bell. It came clearly to me over the intervening miles and spoke of an absolute gothic balls-up.

Tuesday dawned bitterly cold and I took my time walking from the carpark to the Ramp office, so as to give the icy wind time to bleach the colour from my cheeks. Feigning sickness can be an excellent way of avoiding unpleasant consequences; after all, nobody wants to beat up on a dying man. But there are some basic rules. For instance, if you are complaining of a sprained left ankle, limping with the right is inadvisable. If it's tonsillitis, smoking is out, naturally. Stomach trouble? Don't bolt your lunch even if your famished; you can get through three courses if you take long enough over it, while telling everybody it's revolting but that you haven't eaten for three days. And do make sure that your chosen ailment suits the purpose to which it is to be put. I learned this lesson early at school when a classmate, wanting to avoid swimming, told the sports master that because of a skin condition he wasn't allowed in the water. It earned him a gruelling cross-country run. Hardly the desired result.

As I sauntered towards the office, I began manufacturing the symptoms of the bilious attack I was going tell everyone I had suffered. Pausing outside the door to button my coat to the neck, I entered, pale-faced and dry-lipped (I hadn't licked them for half an hour), my shoulders hunched, a pained expression pasted on, and a slight shiver to indicate a temperature. A theatrical masterpiece.

Nobody noticed.

What I quickly noticed to my horror, looking out of the window, was that the livestock trucks were still here. Then—looking beyond them with the chill I had been affecting becoming a reality—that *TC* was also still here. I was dumbstruck: this wasn't just a cock-up; it was a bleating disaster.

Little attention may have been paid to my theatricals, but plenty was paid to me the moment I entered the Ramp.

Fenner, fluttering in from Flightwatch: 'What happened to you yesterday? Hell to pay here. Sheep all over the place. I suggest you get your finger out and shift them.'

And worse still Bradbury, striding through from his office: 'You, get your arse out there. I want those bloody sheep out of here by noon.' Adding ominously, 'Then come and see me.'

Woodman, on the blower from London. 'This flight has been delayed twenty-four hours because of you.' (*'Er, just a minute'*). 'It's cost us a fortune. Get it moving. Top priority. Expedite!' End of transmission.

So, I really didn't need Cannon, blundering in from Loaders, all flatulence, indiscretion and bluff banter. 'Ah, there you are,' he chuckled (after all, none of it was down to him). 'What a carve up yesterday. I got a hundred of the buggers on and they were coming out through the flightdeck door. 'Uge they are, 'uge. C'mon, let's get weavin', son.'

And as I was leaving, Watkins with his eternal smile. 'Cocked it all up, have you? Yes.'

Then, as we passed each other in the doorway, Penny Butler (looking pert and pretty this morning—the only thing that did), gave me a sympathetic smile, but offered little comfort. 'You're in trouble, I'm afraid.' I agreed that that was a fair assessment, but doubted that she was half as afraid as I was.

It was an awful day. Whatever we did, we could get no more than a hundred animals on board. I suggested what I had suggested when the load was given to me, using a DC3 to ship the twenty or thirty animals that couldn't be got on *TC*, but Woodman vetoed that idea on grounds of expense. Cannon came up with the idea of laying planks on top of the penning to form another deck. But we quickly discovered that there just wasn't enough headroom, and in any case how would we get the sheep up there? Now Woodman made his contribution to the day by sub-chartering one of Big Bro's Britannia aircraft (which I suppose was still cheaper than using our DC7 and a DC3). But, a curious choice since the Brit's cabin was only three feet longer than *TC's*. But with the double-decking and the Brit's bigger payload it looked like we had a solution. That was until some dozy clot from Big Bro's Traffic department came out to tell us (when the loading was two-thirds complete, if you please), that the Brit would fly much prettier if they put a ton of ballast on to trim it. That left us in the same position as we had been with our DC7. We were back to square one.

136

Then Woodman solved the problem for us with a cracking idea, which was both elegant and simple. We should, he told us, load ninety of the sheep on *TC,* and the remainder on one of our DC3s. It was a great solution. I just couldn't help wondering where I'd heard something like it before.

I learned all this the next day, in Bradbury's office, just before he sacked me. It had to be done of course—a sacrifice to the Gods of Commerce to shift blame and explain the balls up. It wasn't a really serious sacking, not one that would prevent Spanavia from employing me again, at least twice, in different capacities. But for now, I was *persona non grata.* So, with only the quiet satisfaction of knowing that I had, albeit dishonourable, honoured my Schiphol promise, I handed in my ID and the unused humane killer and stepped out to an uncertain future.

Expensive

In Ops it is the weekend. Which means that when the metaphorical crapola explodes all over the day, the people most eminently suited to clearing it up are either busy mowing the lawn, or indulging in displacement activity to avoid mowing the lawn—or, euphemistically or otherwise, mowing somebody else's lawn. And one or two others are in such deep doo-doo of their own, that they probably wish they were here. But they're not, none of them are, which leaves me to deal with it.

It's the oldest and most venerable member of the fleet, *X-Ray Mike,* on the ground in Orlando and doomed to stay there until further notice with a damaged leading-edge slat—twenty-foot or so of metal which, when extended, produces extra lift during take-off and landing. Though there are quite a few of these handy gizmos arrayed along each wing, they do all need to be working in unison or the aeroplane develops an unpleasant tendency to roll over and play dead. So, no slat means no flying, which translates into 300-odd frustrated holidaymakers milling about Orlando airport, getting crosser and sweatier by the minute—and more pressure on Ops than on Santa with a broken sled and a dead reindeer. And I'm going to need some Santarish magic if I'm ever to find a spare this side of the Season of Joy.

Today my assistant is Flick, Felicity. She and her pal Angie came to visit Ops on work experience when they were but pubescent sixth formers. So impressed was everybody (possibly at how cheaply they could be got to work for us), that the following year they were recruited to join us permanently, as ops assistants. But any idea that they were dewy-eyed little innocents was extinguished faster than a porch light in an air raid: they were bright, cynical, sharp-tongued and shockingly world-weary for their years. And working in Ops wasn't doing much to restore their lost innocence—which I suspect had been irretrievably waylaid long before they came anywhere near Hanger F.

Flick is on the phone. She likes a party does Flick. Boy, does she like a party. But so much fun does she have at these parties that it seems some unspecified assistance is required to see her through. From the snatch of conversation, I overhear *en passant* (I am heading for the radio), this appears to be what is being negotiated. Whatever it is she is scoring, it's not a cricket match. But, when her deal is done, I'm sure she'll be joining me in the crapola to lend a hand with the shovelling.

I am trying to contact *XM's* crew on the ground in Orlando via HF radio, so we really don't need distractions such as that represented by the approach of Captain Martin Cable, in mufti. Since he appears nowhere on our crew list today, and since he also has "previous" as it were, he is clearly up to something— possibly involving mowing somebody else's lawn—and seeking our cooperation in it, "complicity" being too ugly a word.

Broadly speaking, what happens in Ops may be relied upon to stay in Ops. It's not that we are immoral, rather that we are tactically amoral: after all it is not our business to make judgements on the behaviour of our workmates (not least, lest we too are so judged), only to ensure the smooth running of the operation. Disgruntled pilots do not facilitate smooth running. They must be gruntled at all times, so that when our operational hard rock meets an equally unyielding place—as it surely will sometime—they will be there for us, to cushion the impact; extending a discretional duty hour or whatever else we need them to do beyond the call of duty, in order to avoid the apocalypse. It is our place neither to encourage nor decry their actions, only to do what they occasionally ask of us. Discretion then, is our watchword—with maybe just a seasoning pinch of the Nuremburg Defence. Notwithstanding, I have no inclination just now to become entangled in one of Martin's webs, and I flee into the little cubicle that is Crewing. At least, I would have if Ella the duty clerk hadn't chosen just this moment to exit. Ricocheting lightly off the ample sufficiency of her bosom, I am returned swiftly to Ops—as Martin enters, making fatal eye contact. Careless of me.

'Could I have a word?'

Well sod me, of course you can, Martin, coz yes, what we really, *really* need now is a peccadillo to go with our AOG. His request boils down to telling anybody—specifically anybody who is married to him—who calls, that he's going to Alicante tonight. Now, we do have an Alicante tonight, only Martin's not on it. But we are not going to offer that information, are we? No, we're simply going to say what he asked us to say: that he's going to Alicante—and whether he actually is or not is none of our business. For all we know he *is* going, with his bucket and his spade and his trousers rolled to the knee. You see how it works? Yes, it is as disingenuous as an estate agent's property description, but we can claim that we have not lied, since we are only passing on the message. Shabby? Possibly, but it gets the job done and nobody has to die.

So, ok, got it Martin. Yet he is still here, haunting the office; Banquo's ghost. One wonders if there isn't somebody…sorry, some*thing*…he should be doing. But I think I know what's detaining him. Though we have been required to provide diplomatic services for him on previous occasions, it seems that he is concerned that his message has not yet been conveyed to the rest of the shift— at least not in a sufficiently obvious manner to reassure him. Which means that I must now do this again, with the crayons, floridly enough to convince him that we all have the brief. I walk back to Flick. She cups a hand over the phone and attends. I lean close to her ear and whisper, pointing histrionically in Martin's direction. She nods. I enter Crewing to repeat the performance with Ella. Then I head back towards the HF, winking conspiratorially at Martin as I go. He repeats my signal and, apparently satisfied, the ghost vacates the battlements.

I try again on the HF and this time, combining the wonder that is shortwave skip propagation with the Faustian pact I have made with Satan for my soul, I am able to talk to *XM*'s crew over four thousand miles distant, on the ground in Orlando. Guy Vaillancourt is the skipper; tanned, handsome, gravelly-voiced, efficient and authoritative, looking to me for solutions; me, the Ops duty grunt, pale, ordinary, marginal ability and no solution yet. It is an uncomfortable position to be in with Guy whose testosterone is oceanic. So, I resort to what I am good at, the dispensation of unguents sufficient to calm the savage breast, in the hope that it will buy me time enough to figure out either a fix or, failing that, an escape. I tell him that even as we speak a team is all over the problem. He won't have bought a crock like that, but he confines himself to encouraging haste, before handing me over to fat Barry the flight engineer for some tedious technical thick-ear about part numbers.

It's going to take some doing, finding this spare. It's an obscure bit of aeroplane, it's Sunday, America is a big place and I'm going to be doing my search by telex and phone, with the added bonus of a four to seven-hour time difference, depending on which side of the continent the spare—if I ever find one—is located. And then, suddenly, the situation takes a turn for the better when

Sam walks into Ops. I don't ask why he's here when he's not rostered to be (he's always up to something), but accept his offer to muck in with the AOG.

Sam Ford was my "assistant" (he's somebody else's now), but I use the term loosely, for Sam, despite his youth, is no more my assistant than I am Bilbo Baggins's chiropodist. His problem is that, when it is unoccupied, his unconscionably clever, restless brain is predisposed to morbid introspection. Thus, he is a study in perpetual motion; constantly fiddling with flight plans, tinkering with the computer, checking NOTAMs and met forecasts, anything to mask the siren call of his demons. He survives on weapons-grade black coffee, a near-suicidal Marlboro habit and a predilection for the miserabilist Mancunian rain music of The Smiths. In his rare quiet moments, he pens poetry, which is not without literary merit but tends to feature his less than ecstatic view of existence. He's the only man in the outfit you might stumble across reading Camus, or opining on the poetic legacy of the Hughes/Plath relationship. So, the idea that he is in any way subordinate to me, other than in the titular sense, is fanciful. But, since we are not in competition in any way, we co-exist very amicably, he pretending to be my assistant, me pretending I know what I'm doing—neither of us convinced by the other's charade. He's only waiting for one of the DOs to die or go mad before he gets his own shift. I wish him luck—with the proviso that it's not I who ends up supplying the vacancy.

So, simply by his presence today my difficulties are halved. Whatever I farm out to him I can forget about, in the knowledge that it'll be done. He's already working at the computer as I begin my own hunt for a spare in the midst of a sudden flurry of minor embuggerances: somewhere beneath us Big Al starts an engine run in the hangar; Flick, on a tea run, slops some of it over my paperwork, and Captain Martin bloody Banquo Cable trundles back onto our battlements, looking a bit furtive. I can guess what it is, he's allowed too much time for us to grasp his explanation of the Alicante thing (what does he think I am, a blundering amateur? And how did he spot it, anyway?) So now he has time to kill. I bend to my task—we all do—to forestall any inclination he might have to start making idle conversation. Earlier, I caught him reading the terms and conditions on the back of his library card. Now he picks up one of the clipboards from the hooks on the wall behind the desk and starts reading. Yes, he's actually reading a NOTAM; really, you have to be suicidally bored to do that when you're not even flying. If Banquo was even half as annoying as Cable is right now, I can quite sympathise with Cawdor having him knocked off. If Martin dares to start a conversation about the emergency engineering work temporarily shortening 08 at Charles de Gaulle, I will have to knife him to the ground with the office scissors.

Half an hour later we have, rather miraculously, found a flap (in a warehouse in Los Angeles), Martin is cleaning his nails with the pointy bit of a staple remover, and we have another visitor, if he ever makes it through the door.

First Officer Colin Murray, diffident, polite, a bit anxious, is a welcome visitor, at least more so than Banquo over there. For a start, he has a bona fide reason for being here today. However, it is by no means clear that he is in a fit state to fulfil any function, if you don't count falling down. He appears to be attempting a very poor impression of Richard the Third as he enters—or tries to enter—Ops. Activity stops for a moment as we turn to watch the strangely stooped figure, twisted to one side, as it struggles to manage the door and its flight bag and to walk at the same time. It makes it as far as the crew room table in slightly less than an age, dumps its bag on it, then hovers over a chair, clearly unable to lower itself into it without assistance. I get there first.

We learn that it's his back, his L4 and L5 in open revolt against their intervertebral disk. How he did it is unclear, but since Collin's not the sort to scale the north face of the Eiger on his day off and would probably prefer a buttered scone and a cup of Lapsang Souchong, it's unlikely that it was anything recklessly heroic. The problem now is that it is a big, BIG day for Collin, for today he is to be transformed, metaphorically speaking, from the ugly caterpillar that is First Officer Murray, into the beautiful butterfly of Captain Murray. That is, he will if he can pass the command check he is due to take this afternoon. It requires him to complete a return flight to Palma, in command, his every action performed beneath the gimlet eye of Keith Tollworth our training captain. It will not be an easy day for a fully-fit and alert man. So how it's going to pan out for a bloke with a spine like a lighthouse staircase, who can't even sit down (or it transpires, stand up), without assistance, is at best a moot point. However, there is steel behind that mild facade, as I am about to discover.

'Christ Collin, you can't do this. Knock it on the head, I'll call a standby.'

'No no, I'll be fine, thanks.'

'But you can't even sit down.'

'Yes, I can. It's *sitting* down that's the problem. I'll be fine.'

'But...'

But there is no more time for buts, for there are other pressing matters to attend to, not the least of them the AOG spare. In any case, Captain Tollworth has arrived in Ops, looking formidably purposeful. As I return to my desk, I note surreptitiously that he gives Collin about 20 seconds to explain his Quasimodo-like posture, to establish whether he wishes to proceed with the check and—having received the intelligence that his examinee is imbecilically determined to do so—gets right down to business. Good luck, Col, you are going to need it.

Shimmying past Banquo to get to my desk, I must now figure out how to get the spare from Los Angeles to Orlando. Sam, hanging on the phone, tells me he already has the answer. I just hate it: "It's a *what?*" I ask, failing to keep the note of incredulity out of my voice.

He cups a hand over the phone and repeats: "A 727. It's sitting on the ramp at LA, ready to go in an hour."

'But we're shipping a bloody twig, what do we want with a 727?'

'The alternative is a Piper Arrow at Van Nuys and we'd be strapping the slat on the roof. What does an Arrow cruise at, a hundred-odd miles an hour? Be in Orlando by Tuesday. There's nothing else. What do you want me tell them?' He waves the phone.

'Ask them how much?'

Sam speaks into the phone, listens for the answer, jots something down, covers the phone again. 'Forty thousand dollars.'

'Forty thou…? I don't want to buy the bloody thing! I just want to borrow it.' This is a nightmare, mainly because it involves a decision which, ultimately, will have my name on it. 'Tell 'em we'll call back. I'll have to talk to the Pullover first.'

This is the problem: we have what to all intents and purposes is a 20-foot metal plank, to be shipped two and a half thousand miles. But all we have to transport it in, is either a huge 180-seat Boeing 727 airliner, in whose hold we could easily lose the spare and be challenged to find it again without a torch; or the alternative is a little Piper Arrow bug-smasher, parked at Van Nuys, twenty miles away from the spare. Only it's not really an alternative because the spare won't fit in it, and even if it did, a burger van with a flat tyre, driven by a tree sloth, could drive from LA to Orlando in half the time the Piper would take to fly there. And that would be before factoring in the refuelling stop it would require en route. In other words, it's the 727. So now I must speak to Don Moss—not my absolute favourite pastime—since he is the finance director and will have to authorise payment of the opportunistic fee being demanded by the 727's owners.

Before that, I ask Sam to get *XM* back on company frequency PDQ, before they wander out of the flight deck. Since they can do nothing until they get the spare, they'll be in search of something more engaging than their broken aeroplane and endless cups of cat-piss galley tea.

Meanwhile, Martin has finished cleaning his nails, reading the notice board—from the operating instructions for the photocopier to the antimalarial Maloprim reminders—polished his shoes with the flight watch board duster, made a cup of tea with the last of our milk and, at last, sodded off. Following him out are Keith, and Greg the flight engineer on the Palma, making for the crew transport downstairs. Collin is dawdling over his paperwork and we know why. I nip over to him as soon as the others are out of the door and take both his hands in mine. With his knees firmly locked in the straight position, I heave and he rises out of the chair with a suppressed yelp of pain. This is lunacy. He plonks his hat on his head, not quite straight, I hand him his bag and he walks, like a condemned man to the scaffold, very circumspectly to the door. We wish him good luck, although I am privately convinced that if he even makes it down the stairs, it will probably be headfirst. En route he passes—albeit imperceptibly slowly—In-flight Director Polly Trainor and Flight Attendant Hanna, members of his Palma cabin crew. They follow his agonised progress open-mouthed and silent, Hanna's hand poised mid-air to collect the bar float Flick is trying to give her. As he exits Flick, ever helpful, supplies the answers to their unasked questions.

'It's his back. Knackered, innit. If you ask me, he's not fit to drive a hard bargain, never mind a bleedin' plane. How's your first aid? You'll probably have to carry him off…'

Leaving Flick in charge of crew morale, I head for the HF from which is blossoming Fat Barry's unmistakably bucolic tones. I am at pains to establish beyond doubt that the part we have located is the correct one. We recite the serial numbers back to each other a couple of times.

'Yes, that's the one,' agrees Fat Barry.

'You're certain. Sure, Positive?'

He sounds a bit irritated, possibly offended by the tautology of my insistence: 'Yes, that's it. Definitely.'

'And you won't need anything else?'

'Yeah, a bottle of Craigellachie and a box of fucking coronas.'

Oh, joy unbounded, Fat Barry is pleased to joke. As punishment, I extract another couple of minutes' worth of reassurance from him that the part we have is indeed what is required, and all that is required. Then, promising him an ETA in Orlando as soon as we have one, I sign off and ring The Pullover at home. I expect a blizzard of searching questions, followed by a flat refusal and instructions to sub-charter our flight, leaving *XM* on the ground in Orlando until a part can be shipped out from the UK. Something like that. But no, to my horror he gives me the go ahead. Now, either I'm paranoid or I'm right in suspecting that he's been waiting to get me for years. I'm too paranoid to know which for certain, but if it is the latter and anything goes wrong, this could be his chance. Reluctantly, I give Sam the nod, he picks up the phone and we start the process of uniting the flap with the expensive 727 and shipping it eastward to Florida.

It is eight hours now since we found our spare and progress has been made. Sam, his work here done, has gone home to prepare for a party, which means that yet again he will ensconce himself in a corner, get rapidly hammered, make a mild pass at somebody and top off the festivities with a faceplant in the venue's flowerbed, until the chill of morning dew rouses him. Flick has turned her attention to the flight watch board, to the ugly red chinagraph scrawl of the acronym "AOG" against *XM*'s flight, and it has become a happy little Humpty Dumpty figure with spidery arms and legs. *XM* is still an AOG, but with the recent intelligence that the required part has arrived in Orlando, there is every hope that the aircraft will be serviceable soon and Humpty can be erased from the board. Sitting uncomfortably at the crew room desk, doing a bit of paperwork, is Captain—*Captain*—Collin Murray. He made it. God knows how, but he made it. His promotion will make a pleasant addition to the skippers' roster; mild, quiet and polite, he is unlikely to be giving Ops a hard time about anything, unlike some we could mention.

Which is not to say that Ops—more specifically Greg—wouldn't be responsible for giving him at least one hard time, albeit unintentionally, in the very near future.

Invited to take a flight deck ride on one of Collin's flights, Greg took his place on the jump seat directly behind the skipper. This seat is designed to swivel to the right through ninety degrees from its normal fore and aft position, for ease of access. Crucially, it also features a locking mechanism to prevent accidental un-commanded swivelling in flight. But, in the bustle of pre-take-off procedures, Greg overlooked this, possibly dreaming distractedly of the day when he himself would sit in the captain's seat, wearing a uniform not unlike that of a U-boat commander, suavely handing out his orders, whilst surreptitiously checking his reflection in the side window. (All of which, in the fullness of time, would come to pass.) But, for the present, he had to settle for the role of lowly spectator. With the aircraft lined up on the runway and cleared by the tower to go, Murray called for take-off power. The first officer advanced the throttles and the big jet trembled against her brakes as the needles of the N1 gauges began their climb. A moment more, the brakes were released and the aircraft lurched forward. The sudden momentum this produced elicited an instant response from Greg's unlocked seat and it rotated smartly 90° to the right, away from its fore and aft position. To save himself, Greg grabbed wildly at the nearest static object, the back of Murray's seat—and missed. Instead, his hand closed around the wire of the skipper's headset and his continued momentum caused it to whip round so that one earpiece now covered Collin's eyes and the other, the suspiciously-thin vegetation on his crown.

With the aircraft gathering speed and now blinded by his headset, Murray's yell of surprise froze Greg's blood. Aghast at what he had done, he could think of no other strategy than to reach over the back of Murray's seat, take an earpiece in each hand and twizzle them back to their correct position over Murray's ears.

Thereafter, the take-off run continued as normal, with Greg slumped down in his seat, cringing with embarrassment. But truly it may be claimed, that he is the jammiest of us all, for even as he awaited the castigation that must surely follow, to his astonishment he found Murray effusive in his thanks *for saving the day*. How Murray came to this conclusion rather than the very obvious one that it could only have been Greg who was responsible for losing the day in the first place, was a mystery and remained so. All that mattered to the bemused Greg was that, miraculously, in an instant he had been transformed form flightdeck pathogen to Employee of the Month.

Like I say, Greg and the smell of roses are inseparable.

It has been a long shift (at 12 hours all our shifts are long, it's just that some can seem interminable, especially when there's an AOG in them) and as the evening draws in, I begin to cast the occasional glance down to the parking bays beneath our windows, where shortly I expect to see Irish arriving to relieve me of the watch until 0700 tomorrow.

146

Dermot "Irish" Reid is not the slightest bit detectably Irish, it's just another instance of my inveterate inclination to allot nicknames—in this case rather obviously prompted by his name. He is quietly-spoken, friendly and easy to get along with. In his spare time, he flies executive jets for rich people who can afford such baubles. He seems to slide imperturbably through his shifts; whether this is attributable to the luck of the Irish—except that, as I say, he's not particularly Irish—or any great skill, it is impossible to tell. But somehow, things seem to work out about right for him—as evidenced by his handling of another tricky AOG, earlier this year.

The aircraft was en route from Tenerife to Manchester when it developed a technical fault, requiring a diversion to base. As the repair was going to take some time, it was decided that the increasingly-frustrated and angry passengers, marooned in the transit lounge, should be put on a replacement aircraft. Effectively, this meant sub-chartering the flight to another company. But it didn't take long to discover that there were no such aircraft available, anywhere. This was after all the height of the summer season, when every company was working flat out on the holiday trade, storing up fat for the lean winter months when the fleets of charter companies could sit expensively on the ground for lack of work. Now Irish was faced with an apparently insoluble dilemma: there were no aircraft to sub-charter, yet if he held 350 passengers in the transit lounge while our aircraft underwent the lengthy fix it required, there was every possibility of a riot; a rampage, broken crockery, flying furniture. A solution had to be found, and quickly.

What Irish came up with was simple, unorthodox and a bit bonkers. First, he made some phone calls to establish his plan's viability. Then, just as I had done today, he called Moss at home for authorisation, who was incredulous: 'Say that again.'

'I want to charter a train, from here to Manchester. I've found one. It's available. They can have it here in a couple of hours.'

I don't know if any of the rest of us would have come up with that solution. It was daft, but since all other avenues had been explored without success, even the Pullover had to admit that letting a train take the strain solved an otherwise intractable problem. So, the go ahead was given, the charter was arranged, and an hour and a half later the bemused passengers trooped aboard a diesel to rattle away to Manchester. The day had been saved.

As if summoned by my recollection, Irish's car swings into the car park. At that very moment two telephones begin to ring, just as Angie, Irish's assistant tonight, enters Ops. There is a slight pitch difference between to two telephone bells, which, to my ear, produces an unsettling, somehow premonitory dissonance. Flick reaches for one, Angie fields the other.

I'm scribbling a note for the shift handover to Irish as Angie says: 'Hello Mrs Cable.' My blood turns to ice. Angie has not yet been briefed on the Martin/Alicante business and might be about to…

'No, I don't see him on the roster tonight…'

…put her foot in it. I grab for the phone, registering as I do so, that Flick's call is from across the water. 'Hello Orlando,' she says, chirpily. I worry about that, but I don't have time to worry enough about it because I'm worrying too much about Martin Banquo Bloody Cable, his peccadillo and his puzzled and doubtless suspicious (he's got previous, remember), missus—and the protracted and messy divorce that could result from this massive failure of Ops's diplomatic protocols. Nemesis on short finals. I take the phone, frantically cobbling together a plausible explanation…

'Mrs Cable, Mike the duty officer. No, you're quite right, Martin's *is* on the Alicante. Yes. Angie's just come on shift: not quite up to speed yet.' (Old fashioned look from Angie, who's not only up to speed, but not overly chuffed at being scapegoated to save Cable's arse.) A bit of serendipity comes to my aid now—it's nice to have a bit of good luck: 'We've got two Alicantes tonight' (we do, see?), 'Martin's on the second one.'

Satisfied, Mrs Cable's wronged-wife radar stops pinging. She gives me a message to jot down, some quotidian fluff about getting the BMW serviced, and rings off. I reach for the other phone Flick is holding out to me. That bit of good luck? It's about to run out. Already. I raise an eyebrow. Flick says: 'Engineers, Orlando.' Behind me I hear the door opening: Irish is in Ops. I take the call.

'Where's the fitting kit?' He's got quite a thick Floridian accent, but I get the thrust of it first time. He explains anyway: 'We got the slat, but we need the fitting kit that goes with it. We don't have it.'

Well of course you bleedin' don't. Despite getting Fat Barry to repeat himself more time than Jed's digestion to ensure they'd have everything they needed to fix the aeroplane, actually, it turns out they don't. Nice one. Irish saunters in raising a hand in greeting, which I return, absently noticing the clock on the wall behind him. No fitting kit means we blew a whole sack-full of cash for what our

American cousins would variously describe as bupkis, Jack, diddly. I've hired a huge aeroplane that could easily have accommodated the entire Manchester United football team, reserves, coaching staff, groundsman, boot boy (if they still have such a thing) and the board of directors to carry just a piddling aluminium plank two and a half thousand miles, seemingly for nothing.

There is only one thing for it. It is now 1903 and officially I am off shift. I turn to Irish: 'Must dash. It's all as per the board. Oh…' I hold out the phone… 'And there's a call for you.'

Rocket Man

Being only lightly sacked from Spanavia and certain to be taken back when my scapegoatery had been served, was like sliding down a snake in a snakes and ladders game; it was just a question of waiting for the roll of the dice to get me to a ladder and the climb back—if not to fame and fortune—at least to a comfy office chair and somewhere to park my tea. Meantime, my penance awaited me in the shape of Monk Aviation's draughty hanger, out on the southern extremity of the airfield, far from the glamour of the terminal and the bustle of the ramp.

Monk operated domestic and European routes with De Haviland Doves, one DH Heron and a couple of the ubiquitous DC3s. It also offered excruciatingly tedious employment for the recently dishonoured, such as myself, who ought to think themselves lucky to have got any kind of airport work at all. This was reflected in the pay and conditions: both unspeakable. I didn't think myself lucky. I was wretched: a wretched bloke given a wretched job. But if I was hoping to pay my rent and get remission for good conduct, then I should have to stitch my lip and get on with it.

"It" was a position described as "aircraft cleaner." Only, it didn't involve cleaning aircraft in the way I was familiar with, represented by sweaty people in tabards bustling through recently-vacated cabins picking up trash, while trying not to gag on the lavvies and the sick bags. No, this cleaning entailed removing paint—every last vestige of it—from the exterior surfaces of aircraft which were undergoing heavy maintenance. For this, we were equipped with a set of overalls, a Civil Aviation Authority-approved scraper (a five-inch strip of metal hardly sharper than your elbow) and a tin containing a substance manufactured by sadists, with which to afflict Humanity and infringe its human rights. Masquerading as a proprietary-brand paint stripper, if it came into contact with exposed flesh, it could strip skin quicker than a tank-full of piranhas ending a hunger strike, and it produce extremely painful burns if not washed off very quickly. Not surprisingly, eyes were especially vulnerable. So much so, that an eye shower—a strange device that looked like a set of binoculars for a giraffe—was installed in the hangar.

By far the worst part of Monk's meagre induction process was the issue of an atrocity I had not encountered since my first job on leaving school—a clock card; a fearsome object whose time stamps turned accusingly red seconds after our 0800-start time, costing the miscreant 15 minutes' pay. Thus, recidivists could expect considerable accrued deduction by the end of the week, as well as unwelcome attention from Jock the hangar foreman. Repeat offenders would be invited to explain their dilatoriness to Personnel.

As if the foregoing were not enough, the work itself produced in me terminal ennui. A Dakota's construction includes, amongst other things, a googolplex of rivets. Our job was to apply the stripper, then scrape every last vestige of old paint from every rivet. Laying on my stomach on a wing for hours on end, chiselling away at fragments of paint, not only put me at serious risk of falling asleep and executing a faceplant in the paint stripper, but of going totally postal with boredom.

If work at Monk could be represented by the metaphor of a uniformly-grey sky, at least my time there was briefly illuminated, Asimov-like, by two suns. The first by my workmate and friend Tony Novak, ginger-haired with deep-set blue eyes and a ready smile, like me he was also passing through on the way to better things (indeed it would have been challenging to pass through to anything worse—maybe a waterboarding or tickets to a bagpipe concert.)

One winter morning, Tony was tasked with cleaning the number two engine electrical bay of a Douglas DC4. This was accessed via a small hatch on the underside of the nacelle. Beneath this, on the floor beside the ladder, a large tray had been placed to intercept oil drips from the engine. Having first checked with the engineers that power to the aircraft had been cut, he placed a pair of stepladders beneath the engine and, armed with a brush and a can of cleaning fluid, ascended, edging the upper part of his body into the cramped bay. He had not long been engaged in brushing the cleaning fluid onto the bay walls, when tea break was announced. With an anticipatory welling of gastric juices, he climbed down, set his brush and tin aside and departed for the canteen.

On his return, collecting the brush and tin, he wormed his way back up into the bay. However, Tony was now labouring under two misapprehensions, which were to have a spectacular effect on the events of the next few minutes. The first revelation, as he squeezed back into the bay, was that in his absence some nameless cretin had restored the power supply, without clearing it with anybody, and the bay was now a buzzing nest of electrical serpents. Horrified, he immediately began to retreat down the ladder, holding the brush above his head as he exited through the cramped hatch. That was when a big blue spark arced across from a bus bar to the metal jacket of the brush. Second revelation: the cleaning fluid he was using was flammable. It ignited. In the circumstances, Tony thought it best to let go. This was understandable but unfortunate, as the blazing brush fell into the can and instantly a roaring ball of fire engulfed the bay. Things were not going well for him, yet fate had not quite finished with him. For in his haste to descend the ladder, he knocked the tin over and it fell past him into the drip tray below, which contained a further devil's brew of fuel and oil. As a great conflagration blossomed beneath the wing of the DC4, Tony fled, his right sleeve ablaze from cuff to elbow.

Engineers gravitated at speed from all corners of the hangar towards the blaze, armed with hastily-acquired CO_2 extinguishers and fire blankets. Whilst Tony's arm was put out with the blankets, the extinguisher-wielders quickly doused the fire. Tony survived unhurt apart from a temporary reduction in eyebrow density; the DC4 likewise unharmed, emerging from its adventure smoked like a breakfast kipper, but otherwise undamaged.

In the circumstances, it was bad luck that the fire had not spread out of control, as shortly afterwards we were obliged to return to our insufferable work. I suppose the fact that Tony had not been barbecued was sort of a compensation.

The second highlight of this dreary period, was Chris' rocket.

Chris—slight, twitchy, ingenious—had, like Tony and I, been driven by necessity to spend a few purgatorial months at Monk, before escaping to something worthier. But restless soul that he was, he needed constant mental stimulation or he was inclined to find something, anything, to engage his unused capacity—with not-always constructive results. In Monk, he could hardly have chosen a less suitable venue for his restless curiosity.

His solution to the vacancy in his working day was to build a rocket. If the logic of the decision escaped me, it probably escaped him also. But he needed something more to do than scrape paint and, as he also liked pyrotechnics, building a rocket was the obvious answer. So why not? was his unassailable rationale. He was just as likely to have chosen self-drive flying lessons, and as there were more than enough aircraft available to facilitate that desire, by comparison the rocket seemed like a good idea. Thus, over the next couple of weeks, he gathered the materials he would need from around the hangar, mostly from the waste bins. The solid fuel, who's exact chemical make-up was never revealed to me, he developed at home in his dad's garage. The projectile itself consisted of an e eighteen-inch-long aluminium tube, one end of which he blocked with plastic filler, fashioned with great care into a perfect nose cone. Three small fins were attached at the other end for longitudinal stability and construction was complete. It only remained to load the fuel, which he spent considerable time on, tamping it down so that it was packed hard into the whole length of the tube. With a fuse added—a piece of string impregnated with a dilute mixture of the fuel, "*Monk 1*" was ready for launch. All that remained was the choice of launch site and a take-off slot.

Appointed observer, I joined Chris one lunchtime well down the side of the hangar, out of eyeshot of the foreman's office. The rocket looked a bit like an anti-aircraft shell which, on reflection and given the location, it might well have turned out to be. But such thoughts did not come to cloud our anticipatory joy. Chris had placed the rocket in a narrow container, half buried in the ground to prevent it falling over during launch. Conditions were perfect; a calm, dry day with good visibility. All was set. A quick look round to ensure we were not overlooked and Chris lit the touch paper, before retiring in the best traditions of Bonfire Night.

There was the briefest of pauses while *Monk 1* smouldered, considering its ignition. Then, with a protracted *Fffwhoosh!* and at quite incredible speed, it streaked skyward atop a perfectly-vertical column of white smoke that hung motionless in the still air as the rocket infringed the Racebridge air traffic control zone, en route for God-knew where.

We stood together, momentarily awed to silence by the force of its departure. If we were expecting to see it again, we were to be disappointed. It never returned. Given the sheer dynamism of its launch, it was hardly surprising. I imagined it achieving escape velocity and, who knows, maybe it's still out there, ploughing its lonely course across the vastness of space, en route for Proxima Centauri with its message of work for idle hands.

One frosty morning, not long after, we were gathered for the ritual of tea break in the shack attached to the side of the hangar that served as our rest room. Opposite us, visible through the big window, was the huge grassy bank that served as a blast shield for engine runs. Parked tail-first against this and facing

153

us stood three DC3s. Having been late in by a couple of nanoseconds and discovering that all the seating had been bagged, I collected my tea, unwrapped my cheese roll and leant against the table. This gave me an uninterrupted view of the parked aircraft.

As I sipped my tea, I wondered out loud who was positioning *Tango Echo,* since all the engineers were here in the shack.

'Me,' said the man next to me engrossed in the sports page of his newspaper. Without looking up he said, 'And yes, I know it's tea-break, but thanks for reminding me.'

Sarcasm. Nice.

I looked again. Yes, *TE,* the one at stage right of the line, was quite definitely moving. Not only moving, but gradually picking up speed, heading directly for us. Then I noticed something else, several somethings else: DC3s are towed tail first, but there was no tractor attached to this one and, as the engines weren't running either, it followed that it must be moving under its own momentum on the slight incline. Nor was there anybody in the cockpit. (Towed aircraft always have somebody in the cockpit to apply the brakes.)

I lost it a bit at this point, because instead of issuing a clear, articulate warning, I began shouting incoherently, spraying masticated breadcrumbs, waving my arms, jolting elbows and spilling tea, succeeding only in annoying people for vital seconds. It was not quite the response I had intended. But suddenly, the room cottoned on and there followed a charge for the door. I'm not proud to say I lead it as I was the nearest, but with no intention whatsoever of heroically arresting *TE's* advance. I just wanted to render vacant possession before she reduced the shed to matchwood. Others, more courageous and quicker-witted, overtook me, running to meet the aircraft. With reckless disregard for his own safety, my sarcastic interlocuter, crossed in front of the oncoming runaway, sidestepped the blades of the port propeller, dropped into a low crouch as the wing swept over him, then launched himself in through the open rear door. A nutter, obviously. Others clapped onto the horizontal bits of the tailplane, planted their feet and began slithering. Two or three grabbed at the undercarriage, hopping and chasseing to avoid the big wheels; a couple clung to the door frame. One moron even made a wild grab at a static discharge brush on the trailing edge of the starboard wing. It's an itty-bitty piece of wire and the DC3 weighs seven and a half tons in its underpants: the brush came away in his hand. He stood stupidly looking at it until the horizontal stabiliser reminded him of its approach by smacking him in the back of the knees and bowling him over. A more scientifically-minded soul flung a chock under the port mainwheel. It was a nice try, but *TE* ran it down with hardly a pause and the chock tripped up one of the struggling anchor men at the tail.

Just when an unholy marriage between aircraft and tea-shed seemed inevitable, Sarcastic reached the cockpit and stamped on the brakes. *TE* stopped dead, her tailwheel lifting momentarily from the ground. Everybody else kept going, sprawling over elevators, barking shins on undercarriage struts, falling and rolling in cursing heaps. It was invective that mutated rapidly into whistles of relief, for *TE*'s nose had stopped just shy of six feet from the shed. Luckily, nobody was hurt and Sarcastic, the man who had saved the day, but who's negligence had caused the debacle, was soundly rollocked. Not only had he left the brakes off, but incredibly he hadn't troubled to chock the wheels either.

Incidents of this kind, though uncommon, were not unheard of and could produce quite spectacular results. Such as the one I witnessed on another occasion when two engineers were towing a Boeing 707 in the rain. As they approached its allotted stand, the tug driver applied the brakes. The ramp was slippery, the tug's wheels locked and, impelled by the sixty-ton bulk of the 707, it began to slide. The engineer riding in the cockpit of the 707 applied the brakes, but nothing happened, which was when he noticed that the brake pressure gauge stood at zero. The Boeing was fitted with an emergency system, but unfortunately the engineer was not familiar with the aircraft and didn't know how to operate it. The result was not only embarrassing for the 707's owners, but costly too. It ran past its allotted bay and on to the next which, as luck would have it, was occupied by a BAC 1-11. As I watched in horrified fascination from my passing van, the Boeing mounted its smaller neighbour, riding up on its starboard wing. Engine pods crumpled, the wing buckled, the 1-11 tipped under the weight of the 707's amorous onslaught and its undercarriage partly collapsed.

Not long after the DC3 incident, Big Brother also sacrificed one of its precious Vickers VC10s on the altar of negligence. Fortunately, the aircraft was in a hangar which was completely deserted at the time, or there might have been loss of life. The aircraft had been placed on jacks preparatory to an undercarriage retraction test and an extra supporting jack had been placed under the soaring tail with its four heavy engine pods. As work was also in progress on the engines, the tail had been cocooned in scaffolding to provide catwalks for the maintenance staff.

Crucially, the locking ring on the tail jack had not been tightened and, in the middle of the night, when the shift was away on other duties about the airport and the hangar was quiet, the jack lost hydraulic pressure and failed. Slowly, the nose of the aircraft began to rotate roofwards and with a terrible protracted buckling crash, audible all over the airport, the VC10's big flying tail descended through the scaffolding to plant its engines on the hangar floor.

For some time following the accident, the line's normally polished image was somewhat tarnished. Their shame they hid behind double-locked hangar doors, guarded by granite-faced security men. Rumours regarding the cost of the damage varied between the unconscionable and the frankly fanciful. But whatever the final bill came to, it could not have been less than eyewatering.

To us outsiders who thought Big Bro haughty and puffed up with its own importance, it came as a revelation to discover it also had a heart. For the line treated the miscreant with great benevolence. We had expected that, at the very least, the man responsible for the blunder would dangle from the hangar flagpole for his error. But no such thing. He was probably smacked on the back of the hand and had his Swarfega confiscated—he was certainly demoted—but he was not sacked. The less charitable suggested he was paying back the £1million-plus repair costs through deductions from his pay.

At about this time a telegram arrived, instantly dissipating the ennui that had dumped its bags in my hall and was threatening to move in permanently. I had barely registered the fact that it was the time of the Hadj, when Muslims all over the world make the once-in-a-lifetime pilgrimage to Mecca. In one month, the last of the Islamic year, two to three million of the faithful make the journey, airlines playing a major, highly-profitable role in the undertaking. The telegram came from one of the companies which only recently had not required my services. In terse phrases, it reversed its decision, offered Faustian wages for a month's work and informed me that a ticket for the schedule service to Rabat awaited my collection from the Royal Air Maroc desk at Heathrow. Elated, I hurried to my would-be employer's offices, where I discovered that nobody knew first thing about my recruitment. A further 24 hours spent pestering them for information yielded no results, until finally I had to admit defeat and in a stew of frustration, trudged back to the hangar.

A few weeks later I ran into Mike Ashington, who had himself taken leave from Spanavia to work on the Hadj in Rabat. He confirmed that they had been desperately short of staff, that the station manager had personally authorised my recruitment, and all I had needed to do was pick up the ticket and fly down. I think "oh bother" was the term with which I greeted this revelation.

Mentally fossilising at Monk, but still not quite rehabilitated into polite aviation society, the cargo duty officer vacancy at Loadstar I'd seen advertised in the local paper offered—if not quite full rehabilitation—at least a return to looking wistfully in at its lighted window, hoping someone would spot me and let me in out of the cold. Anyway, I sped along to the interview, said things that presumably they wanted to hear, and got the job.

Lodestar operated half a dozen Canadair CL44s, essentially Britannia aircraft converted for freight work. The CL44's main feature was its swing tail, which opened to ninety degrees from the fuselage so that large cargoes could be slid straight in, thus avoiding the difficulty of manoeuvring loads through a side freight door. We shipped supplies to Nigeria during the Biafran war, Formula One cars to the Brazilian Grand Prix, fine champion bloodstock, sheep, pigs, even some weapons.

But what I recall most, was our determined effort to kill the people of Sudan—though to be fair we were really only a party to killing them, rather than the perpetrators. We facilitated this by shipping a constant stream of fags—twenty-five tons at a time—to Khartoum. They may have been lethally-addictive harbingers of sickness and death, but looking on the bright side they were a doddle to load. Packed as they were in nice square carboard boxes, it was just a matter of stacking them neatly down the aircraft and erecting a few crash nets between them to prevent the whole load joining the pilots on the flight deck in the event of unexpectedly-fierce braking forces or, on the other hand, knocking the tail off the aeroplane if excessive momentum was applied in the opposite direction. In either of these circumstances, cigarettes would certainly have been injurious to health.

Whatever else I did at Loadstar, I have no recollection of, other than the leaving of it. On my way home one evening, I had run into a smiling Mr W and jokingly asked him if he had any vacancies back at Spanavia for an ex-aircraft cleaner and tobacco baron, with delusions of grandeur. He told me to "Bung in an application," observed that I still looked a "scruffy bugger" and went on his way chuckling, leaving me to stare after him in astonished silence. Clearly, a sacking from Spanavia's Operations department didn't cut much with Mr W's Traffic department and to prove it, two weeks later, I attended an interview with him. The venue a little grander than his old place down on the ramp; we now sat in an office high up in the terminal building with a panoramic view of the airfield where, down on the taxiways, double-glazed into silence, aircraft crawled spider-like about their business. The atmosphere of the interview was much the same as it had been on that first day when he'd given me my start in aviation. Only this time, he didn't mention the job once, until right at the end, when he asked when I could start. And that was it, banishment served, I was back to my original job, a lowly traffic officer once more, out on the ramp, dispatching flights: manky working conditions, long hours, hard graft, so-so wages and occasional anarchy: a glorious prospect.

While I had been away, the Ramp and Operations offices had been shifted from the relatively cosy apex where the central and southern piers met, to the bleak out-flung arm of the north finger. Quite what advantages this new accommodation had to offer over the old place was not immediately apparent, but given the company's renowned parsimony, it was probable that they were cheaper—much cheaper, given the austerity of the place.

With a little wangling on my part, I was assigned to my old shift, under the ever-benign rule of Tim Frazier. Here I met for the first time the husband-and-wife team of Glyn and Jill Williams. Glyn, the shift supervisor and second in command, had transferred from our outstation in Wales; Jill, originally from our Liverpool office at Speke (now John Lennon Airport), was the movement controller. Glyn sported a full beard and a thatch of untameable-wiry hair, his dark eyes exuding a Rasputin-like intensity that strengthened the illusion that Owain Glyndwr was come amongst us to avenge Wales. At first glance, he seemed bigger and more ferocious than he actually was; but on closer inspection, it quickly became apparent that he was of decidedly slight stature and wasn't a bit ferocious except, as I was to discover, intellectually. He never wore his hat because it looked ridiculous perched on top of that mass of hair. He slouched around with his jacket unbuttoned and his tie—quite invisible anyway behind the beard—always loosened. Intelligent and clever, he was full of nervous energy, slept less than six hours a night, ate a spartan vegetarian diet and pursued a somewhat austere lifestyle with few creature indulgencies. He was idealistic, principled, and probably would nowadays be described as a bit bi-polar. He had little time for bureaucracy and none for religion. Believing himself fortunate to have been born in circumstances that meant he would never go hungry, and that he would be healthy and literate, he was acutely aware that for many that modest aspiration was denied. He felt it his duty therefor to help them, especially the young. It soon became clear, almost from our first meeting, that though he enjoyed aviation and would always be interested in it, it was simply a stepping-stone to something more fulfilling. (And so it proved. Eventually he went on to train for and work in social services, dealing with young offenders.) Yet, he was not the least bit dour, quite the opposite. Despite his occasional bouts of depression, he was great company, with a fine sense of humour based on a heightened sense of the ridiculous. He was also a kind and an utterly-reliable friend. Jill was also smart, practical and, like Glyn, widely knowledgeable about the business. This unrivalled experience came from their work at outstations, where the same person might undertake everything from checking in passengers, to marshalling aircraft, or searching for lost luggage. There seemed to be nothing that they didn't know something about, and with me and Tony Novak (the accidental DC3 arsonist from Monk), ramp dispatching, and a couple of others on loadsheets, we had a happy team. Okay, we also had Babington, amiable but thick-headed and quite hopeless. His mental arithmetic was beyond abysmal and Glynn was often to be seen fretting silently at Babington's shoulder, while the latter, with tongue-jutting concentration, scratched away at a scarred loadsheet.

Tramps

Another Christmas day in the Ramp, a place that was never pretty, so scruffy that you wiped your feet when you went out. But today, in the absence of cleaners, it was a shocking mess, failing to achieve even its customary seedy standard. The room uncharacteristically quiet now since the night shift's departure amid shouted exchanges of seasonal greetings with the oncoming day shift. The teleprinters silent, their last messages—mostly pictures of Santa Clause and reindeer formed by the intricate arrangement of hundreds of Xs—still hanging from the carriages. The Ground Movement Control ticker tape machine, normally in constant snickering action with flight arrivals, having wished all stations a "Very Merry Christmas", officiously prefixing its message with an 0326Z timestamp, thereafter had fallen silent. That was over three hours ago and since then, nothing. The waste bins were stuffed with crushed cans, the source of the sour smell of stale beer which hung on the air; forms and manuals cluttered the desks, and the floor was a scruffy mosaic of flattened cigarette butts and discarded paperwork. Behind the entrance door, adding to the unlovely appearance of the place, were the special dust collectors; two electric motors, bolted to the floor, powerful, expensive and quite useless. A few years previously, the company had decided to install a compressed air message delivery system between Check-In and the Ramp office, down which to send passenger manifests and the like. It took weeks to install and months to get it working properly—which was when HM Customs pounced on it, having suddenly realised that the canisters, whizzing through the pipes at thirty miles an hour, constituted an excellent means of transporting contraband landside to airside, and vice versa, completely bypassing all their controls in the process.

Out on the otherwise-deserted ramp, a single BAC 1-11 sat silently on stand, nose in, staring blankly at its reflection in the pier windows.

Lounging sleepily in the movement control office were Pete Wallace and Pat Cole. The shift had been split into two duties to allow everybody to spend at least

160

part of Christmas Day at home, and they had drawn the early turn. Wallace tall, amiable, with a deep educated voice; Cole ex-RAF, tubby, with big sideburns and a bluff manner. At their elbows stood paper cups each with an inch or two of scotch remaining. Early, even for such serious drinkers, but after all it was Christmas.

They were both sinking gradually into REM sleep when the ticker tape rattled suddenly into life. They both stared at it blankly. If this was another frivolous message from GMC, then they should know better: they had sent their greetings, it didn't require further embellishment. Grudgingly, Cole hoisted himself out of the chair to read the tape.

'What? They've given us a DC6, finals for the North Park.'

Wallace sat up, 'Whose?'

'Don't know. I'll call them.' He reached for the direct line to GMC but it rang before he could lift the receiver. He listened, grunting occasionally, jotted a note and put the phone down. Reading from his note he said, 'Griffon Flugt DC6 B, fag freighter en route for Khartoum. Diverting with an engine snag. Great.'

This was the one day of the year when only fools and adventurers would think of flying. It was not immediately clear to which category the DC6's crew belonged. Their aircraft, a battered, ill-used and poorly maintained cargo hack would surely only be flown by fools. Whereas her three crew, two Icelandic pilots and a British flight engineer, seemed not the least foolish, exuding rather something of the aura of amiable buccaneers. They certainly looked the part: the cigar-smoking skipper was grey-haired, fortyish, moustachioed beneath a startlingly red nose, and rather stocky. His first officer, mid-twenties, handsome, blond, slim, quieter than the other two. The flight engineer, chewing unceasingly on the stem of an unlit pipe, was short, tubby and clean-shaven; somewhat American-looking with his close-cropped hair. For uniform, they wore twill trousers, windcheaters or leather flying jackets over open-neck shirts, and each carried a battered flight bag that looked to have fared no better than their aircraft.

As ministry-appointed handlers obliged to supply ground support to any *ad hoc* movements into Racebridge, it fell to Spanavia to meet the DC6 when it limped into its allotted space on the North Park, with an oil pressure drop on her number two engine. En route for the Middle East with a cargo of cigarettes, her weary crew expressed the hope that they would get the rest of the day off—a hope they hoped in vain. A phone call to their boss earned them a blunt refusal and instructions to get on with it. It seemed that the Sudan's craving for tobacco was not to be denied at any time, let alone by a Christian holiday.

In the circumstances, the crew were philosophical about their fate, accepting it with stoical shrugs and rueful smiles. They were a pleasant trio and while Cole and Wallace tried to find some engineers to show interest in their delinquent engine, they came into the Ramp office to drink coffee and to shoot the breeze. Basically, they said, the aircraft was the airborne equivalent of a tramp steamer, looking for work wherever it could be found. Flying from one charter to another, wherever they were needed, they might not see home for many days at a time.

Asking where they had been recently garnered exchanged looks between them of disgust at the recollection of a shipment of sheep meat to West Africa. In an aircraft whose ability to maintain level flight was at best questionable, refrigeration was never going to be an option. The cargo, being already "well hung" when loaded in France, by the time it reached the heat of Dakar, stank. So much so, that the authorities there immediately vetoed its unloading and even had the aircraft, complete with cargo and crew, towed well clear and downwind of the terminal building. There it sat under a baking sun, the crew gasping for breath as the cargo continued to decompose, until the authorities finally took pity on them and allowed them to disembark. The cargo however was taken out, dumped and burnt, and for a few hours downwind Dakar reeked like a giant kebab shop. The aircraft was then unceremoniously and with scant regard for safety, hosed out with disinfectant and the crew themselves subjected to the humiliation of fumigation, before they were allowed to leave. It was only after take-off that the final horror of the trip was visited upon them. As the aircraft settled into the cruise from the climb, a tidal wave of cleaning fluid emerged from hiding to flood onto the flightdeck, eventually to drain away to God-knew where amongst electrical circuitry, control cables and other sensitive bits beneath the aircraft's floor, never to be seen again.

In the Ramp, there was some admiration for the crew's—especially the skipper's—determination to see the job through. Many another pilot would have walked away by now to safer flying in more salubrious conditions. Not these three. As the skipper said: as long as the old bus would fly, he'd stay with her. A remark that was to prove prophetic.

Despite our best efforts, no engineering support could be found to fix the engine. So, it was topped up with oil, the crew bade us farewell and by 1330 they were airborne. Within half an hour they were back, predictably with the same snag. It was then decided that, even given their relaxed approach to crew duty hour limitations, they would have to night stop, in the hope that the engine would be rectified the next day, when there would be more staff on duty. Meanwhile, hotel accommodation was arranged and off they went to their rest. The next day they got the fix the engine needed and made ready to depart. Before they left, they brought in cigars, a case of beers and even some scotch for the staff in the Ramp. They had been an easy-going, undemanding crew despite their predicament, and generous to a fault. We wished them well, raised a seasonal glass to them and bade them goodbye.

Three months later, on the 6th of May 1974, whilst on approach to Nurnberg, the aircraft struck trees four kilometres from the airport and crashed inverted, killing all on board. A possible cause of the loss was given as airframe icing. But a further contributing factor was certainly the captain's blood alcohol level, which was five times above the permitted limit—the significance of his red nose becoming suddenly apparent. At least he got his stated wish, to stay with his aircraft. Sadly, as it turned out, he stayed a little too long.

Treachery

In Ops we are to deal with outrage, treachery and a technical unfortunateness, not necessarily in that order. There are to be other ingredients in our day, but of lesser moment. Sledge is my wingman and, puffing about out there on the ramp, is the bunteresque Marco, our permanently-perspiring, semi-hysterical passenger rep, whose task it is to monitor how Big Bro handles our passengers—or fails to, as the case maybe. And as I am presently to discover, the latter maybe how the case may be.

Thus far, it has not been a bad day at all. Not a single member of cabin staff has reported sick for duty, (a notorious minority cannot be relied upon to fulfil all of their rostered duties; whereas, generally, pilots tend not to report sick until their eyes roll up in their heads and they have no detectable pulse); the weather is benignity itself, everywhere; there are no problems up at check-in, even the baggage belts, who's design pairs the sturdiness of a ping pong ball with the dependability of a train service timetable, are working properly, sending bags off to destinations not necessarily shared by their owners. And so on. So, we are in good shape. There is tea at my elbow, sunshine outside, Sledge filing things that don't really need filing, which prevents him doing anything more destructive and explains why I have him filing things that don't need filing. There is even likely to be an on-time ATC slot for the Tenerife, and all the pilots' paperwork, including their flight plans, each waypoint nicely underlined just the way the big jessies like them, are laid out with the other flight documents on the crew room table next door. With four of my twelve hours done on the last of my hated day shifts and not a cloud in my sky, the bird of paradise is sitting on my shoulder.

Sadly, I'm about discover that my bird recognition is no better than my aircraft recognition.

The phone rings on the big centre console (the one that Tony has had built to his own blueprint, apparently in feet when he had intended inches. It is the only reasonable explanation, and has resulted in a monstrosity that looks like the bridge of the starship *Enterprise,* dwarfing all who sit at it.) Sledge picks up. It's not good. I haven't the faintest idea what 'it' is yet, but judging by his bitten-in-the-groin-by-a-pitbull expression, I am about to discover that the bird of paradise is in fact my old pal the shitehawk.

Sledge goes into an *en garde* with the phone and says, 'Engineers.'

My hand, outstretched to receive, shrinks involuntarily from the handset. Engineering? Nooo. I'd sooner take a call from the anybody, even those ambulance chasers who keep calling me about the accident I didn't have in Stirchley (wherever that is) last October, but not Engineering. It's never good when engineers call, because they never call with anything good to say. There'd be no point. Ergo, it's not going to be good news now. That's not pessimism, that's being realistic.

There is no pleasure in discovering that I am right.

I take the phone. The niceties don't take long—there aren't any. Jed (now Ops manager since Bernie's ticker finally called time and he departed for what in aviation is sometimes referred to euphemistically as *Angel Fleet*), who has been talking on the phone in his office, slams it down, shouts 'Fire in the hole!' and farts loudly—we can hear it through the closed door—then wisely decides to vacate his office, carefully closing the door behind him in a prescient contribution to the yet-to-be declared war on global warming. Relieved of the burden he was carrying, he ought to look happier. He doesn't. He waits patiently by my desk while Engineering, without so much as a *gardez l'eau!* empties its own load all over my day.

'*X-Ray Mike,*' says a Glaswegian voice with, do I detect, a note of supressed triumph?

'Yes, I believe that's one of ours, mate,' I observe facetiously.

'Well it's nae yours noo. It's ours. Number one engine change.'

There's more to the conversation, a lot more. But since it is studded with my unseemly Anglo-Saxon profanities and his unintelligible Gaelic asperity, it is best not recorded here. Precis must suffice. It boils down to this, that somewhere in the offending engine there is a reservoir of oil. In the base of this reservoir is a plug. It is magnetic so that any metallic particles shed from the engine are attracted to it and can be spotted when the plug is removed for examination. In this case, the plug from our number one engine has emerged with enough metal swarf on it to make a decent-sized pan-scourer. The bottom line is that, without question, an engine change is required.

There is a question, actually: do we even have a spare engine? And come to think of it, there's another: how long is it going to take to change it if we do?

Sauchiehall Street, on the smug end of the phone, reassures me that we do have an engine, but spoils it all by going on to say that they don't have anything else yet—like tooling, hangar space, the time or indeed the people to perform an engine change and he will let me know when they do—possibly before Hell freezes over, possibly not.

I believe there is something else they don't have—the slightest inclination to haul our chestnuts out of the fire. I don't say that of course or they'd knock off for a week on the pretext of finding the right spanner. I give the phone its cradle, not gently, and look up at Jed: 'Problem,' I say unnecessarily since he has copied the exchange.

'Yeah, well you've got another one,' he says.

'No, see, I already have a problem, so I don't need another one. He should have said he has a problem whatever it is, and incidentally I don't want to know what it is—then we'd have one each? He doesn't say that.'

I suddenly remember there is other stuff I'm supposed to be doing. 'Sledge, delay signal for the Tenerife.'

He turns to his keyboard. 'When?'

Askance. 'Now, of course.'

He rolls his eyes. 'No, how long do you want to estimate the delay to be?'

'Oh.' I'm losing focus here. 'Indefinite for now.' Back to Jed: 'What?'

Even as I'm asking this, the shitehawk shakes its feathers and does its thing. Suddenly I realise that the Tenerife crew are all about to check in for duty. It's far too late to stop them, they won't have an aircraft to fly and they will have gone out of duty hours long before they do. So, we've lost them, all thirteen of them. I'm still realising this (I can be quite a slow realiser in a tight situation), as Will, the duty crewing wonk, emerges from his cubbyhole to the right of my desk, having overheard my half of the conversation with Engineering.

Jed says, 'My office. Get this sorted first.' He says it like I'm sorting my sock drawer, not a bloody disaster. But he's gone before I can think of a suitably snarky riposte. What he wants me for I have no idea, but it's an extra niggle to add to the portfolio of anxieties I'm mustering.

Through the partition window I can see the Tenerife flightdeck crew filtering into the crew room, which means all the cabin crew will already be downstairs in their crew room. I wave an arm, starting at Sledge and ending at the new arrivals. With a bit of additional eyebrow semaphoring, Sledge gets it and walks out to give the flightdeck the good news. Will comes to join me, a frown of concentration on his dark gypsy features. He is one of the lads, a recently-retired steward with a reputation for being at the epicentre of good times down route. He knows the system and how to squeeze the pips out of the crew duty regulations. We're going to need that.

I open my mouth to speak. The phone in front of Sledge over there on the bridge of the *USS Enterprise* rings. My phone rings. Captain Dirk Lawrence, late of Cape Town, but decades here in the UK, ambles into Ops, In-Flight Manager Hanna Giles, the senior stewardess on his Tenerife, freshly arrived from downstairs bringing up the rear. Jed emerges from his office, cup in hand, heading for the tea-making facility in the stationary room.

'Got it sorted yet?'

He doesn't stop for an answer, the question being entirely rhetorical since I have hardly had time to finish silently screaming yet, let alone begin dealing with the problem. He knows that, he's just winding me up. He likes doing that. I resist the overwhelming temptation to hit him with a shovel. That would be quite out of the question—there are no shovels in Ops.

Sledge answers his phone, it's Flight Enquiries. I answer mine and get the check-in supervisor over at Big Brother. Captain Dirk Lawrence stops in front of the desk, smiles affably, and composes himself to wait until I am free to speak or to leap to my death from the window—whichever decision I arrive at in the next two minutes. Dirk is always composed, always pleasant, one of our cooler skippers and a good one to have on a bad day.

Hanna steps out from behind Dirk, into the light. She is at least 5'10", but Dirk is easily a head taller. She too is composed, patiently waiting until I am free to talk. Elegant, refined, polite and cool, her loudest declaration is reserved for the declamatory shade of the lipstick she favours. Hanna is the last person you'd imagine would be involved in a torrid affair with a married manager. So, you'd be wrong, because she is. It's been going on for some time now, but so loyal are her friends that nobody has breathed a word about it to anybody. Not that they needed to; like any other "secret" affair in a close-knit company like ours, everybody right down to the lady with the dayglow trainers and the smoker's cough who comes in to clean the offices, knows about it.

Sledge smothers his phone to tell me Flight Enquiries are concerned that our Tenerife has been flagged as indefinitely delayed on the flight information boards in the terminal, and they are beginning to field questions from our passengers. They want to know what to tell them.

Asking the check-in supervisor to hang on a moment, I cup my phone. 'Well how about telling them it's in-sodding-definitely delayed, just like it says on the board? And we'll let *them* know when *we* know.'

Sledge nods and starts passing on the message, only more diplomatically. Back to the check-in supervisor. She asks more or less the same questions and gets more or less the same answer, with a promise that I will keep her updated on progress—a promise I may keep.

I put the phone down and Dirk and Hanna step forward. Dirk opens his mouth to speak, but I say 'Christ, the catering!' Dirk steps back, Hanna performing a chassé to avoid him. I grab the phone again and call flight kitchens. I need to get the catering off *X-Ray Mike* before it's dragged off to the hangars, where it will either rot in the carts or be plundered by feral engineers. That done, I turn to Dirk. Just then Jed raps his knuckles on his office window to attract my attention. I look at the patient, tolerant expressions on Dirk and Hanna's faces, then at Jed scratching his arse in his office, and prioritise.

'We're goonered for now, Dirk. Engine change. Good news is it's number one.' (The number one engine is one of the two wing engines and it's a much simpler job to change than the number two engine, which is built into the tail and is a time-consuming sod of a task to complete.) 'I don't know what we're going to do with you yet.'

Dirk nods and retreats to the crew room, Hanna, with a resigned smile, tells me she'll let her crew downstairs know, and they are both gone. Bless 'em; no stupid questions, no time wasted—I'm too busy wasting time myself while I figure out what to do, without anybody else wasting it for me. Like Jed for instance, who's making come-hither signs through the glass. He'll just have to wait.

Will comes to join me and we stare at the board together. All we have up there is the Tenerife departure at 1230 and a Malaga at 1400.

'Swap 'em?' he says.

'The crews?'

He ignores that. 'Oh, the aircraft, right. We can hold the Malaga crew at home for how long before their duty hours start?'

Will folds his arms. 'Four hours.'

'Ok, so we switch the Tenerife to *Golf Delta* which is on stand and more or less ready to go, and delay the Malaga crew at home for as long as we can, or until *X-Ray Mike* becomes serviceable. And if it doesn't become serviceable before the crew run out of hours…'

'…It won't matter, because we'll have gone home by then.' Will's grasp of the essentials is really quite edifying.

'Okay, let's do it.'

It's all fairly routine operations work, but the AOG and our chronic shortage of crew makes the outcome highly uncertain. There now follows an organisational scramble to make the new plan work. The first priority is to hold the Malaga crew at home to prevent them coming on duty until *X-Ray Mike* shows signs of being serviceable and we can call them in. This is not as straightforward as it might seem. A scheduled duty such as theirs does not require them to be contactable—unlike a standby—as long as they report for their flight at the proper time. Thus, they might be occupied in any number of activities, from the mundane to the biblical, rendering them incommunicado. Some of them may already be on their way. So, it going to be a gamble how many of them Will can reach to stop them reporting for duty. With the decision made, he ducks quickly back into his crewing cubbyhole to hit the phone.

I get Sledge to stop whatever it is he's not doing properly and call Big Bro to inform them of our aircraft change. I call Engineering—teeth clenched, bum puckered with anxiety—to inform them of our decision, hoping against hope that they won't veto the change with any technical abstrusities. But Sauchiehall Street appears to be on-side for this one, at least for now, so we're done. I bang the phone down and pick up for the flight kitchens to get the catering switched over. The flying time to Tenerife is an hour thirty-five longer than it is to Malaga, so they have different refreshments. I don't know why either.

While I'm doing that, Dirk appears before me. With the phone still to my ear I aim my biro at the board. 'Aircraft change. Yours is now *Golf Delta*, Stand 39. Depart ASAP. New flight plans to come.' Dirk nods, performs a *volt face* and exits to inform his two flight deck colleagues.

Even with this revision, the Tenerife crew are tight on hours. According to the crew duty regulations, in the present circumstances, their maximum allowable duty time from report to going home is twelve and a quarter hours. The flight time to Tenerife and back is nine hours, with at least a further hour's turnaround on the ground in Tenerife. But since the crew are already here and pre-flight has eaten further into the allowance, they really need to get away within the hour. As a last resort there is also the last-chance-saloon of a Commander's Discretion Report, which basically requires the captain of a crew that has overrun its flight time limitations to write a grovelling letter to the Civil Aviation Authority to justify what happened. So, it can be achieved, it's just that it would be infinitely better if the rest of the day's problems would just Fox-trot Oscar and leave us alone to get it done.

But no, Ops doesn't work like that. Whatever the day deals out, you suck it up and sort it out, or you get out of the chair and let somebody who knows what he/she is doing, do it for you. As I can't do that, I'm sucking.

It takes over an hour to get the crew out to *Golf Delta,* during which new flight plans are produced (an easy job for once, since they are identical to the original plans, the only change being the aircraft); to change all the documentation, to get the aircraft fuelled and the cabin dressed to receive passengers, to obtain an ATC slot and a whole grocery list of other details, before it finally taxies out, as reported over the radio by a near-incandescent Marco.

Meanwhile, there has been silence from Engineering. The problem of the next flight has been festering away in the back of my mind like that tub of cream cheese I forgot was in the back of the fridge. While we have been sorting out the Tenerife, my Nietzschean nihilism has sprinted ahead to convince me that the Malaga engine change will, ultimately, go to hell on a handcart and we shall be powerless to resolve the situation. Engine changes such as ours might be performed swiftly—if you believe in the Tooth Fairy, Father Christmas and you're the chairman of the Esperanto Society. In real life, the job commonly takes twelve hours, or a lot longer in some cases. But it won't matter which applies, because our crew will have gone out of hours long before that and we won't have another crew available before tomorrow at the earliest. That being the case, we shall have the welfare of 347 irate, hungry, tired, murderous passengers to arrange. Two options are available to us, neither very attractive, both expensive, messy and injurious to our reputation. The first is to HOTAC the passengers (aviation-speak for finding them hotel accommodation). At this time of year, locating enough hotel rooms anywhere near the airport will be like trying to find serving staff in B&Q on a Saturday afternoon. The second option—which would certainly be our *second* option—would be to sub-charter the flight to the dodgy Spanish charter outfit we've used, *in extremis,* in the past, whose sole advantage is that they're likely to be the only company with an aircraft to spare—their prehistoric 707. With its threadbare carpets, leaky toilets and uncomfortable seats to distract passengers from pondering too much on the old bus's mechanical shortcomings, it's a good job they won't get to see the flight deck whose appearance, even to the layman, is unlikely to encourage confidence. In short, it is an aircraft to inspire awe—as in awful. In any case, it will take an age to get here from its base in the Land of the Conquistadors, and it is just as likely to arrive with a level of unserviceability to match our own aircraft's, the difference being that in their case, it won't necessarily stop them from flying it. One tries not to shudder visibly when occupying the duty officer's chair, it betrays weakness.

I sidle into Will's crewing bunker to discover what success or otherwise he's had in delaying the Malaga crew. He swivels around to me in his chair, adopting a reassuringly relaxed pose and doing the xylophone thing on his teeth with a pen.

'Yes, we're good. I got all of them, bar three cabin. I left messages for them. We might get two of them, probably not Sharon Barclay, she'll be off having her shellacs redone or a colonic irrigation, or whatever. But it doesn't matter if we don't stop them, I've got enough stand-bys to call out to cover them and we're legal to go one down anyway.'

I nod and back out. Sledge is taking another call from Check-in, fending off an increasingly-frustrated demand for information about the Malaga that he doesn't have. I pat him reassuringly on the shoulder as I pass by, heading for Jed's office to find out what he's been itching to talk to me about for the past hour. I've a feeling that it won't be anything pleasant. (It's not paranoia if they really are after you, is it?)

'How's it going?'

'That's a friendly start. So, it's worse than I thought.'

'Glad you asked. It's a bag of shite, as if you didn't know. Engineers don't answer the phone—I'm calling the wheelhouse of the *Marie Celeste*—so I've no idea if they even got the bonnet up on *X-Ray Mike* yet. We've got till 1800 then the Malaga crew are on duty, whether the aircraft's serviceable or not, and they'll be out of hours to do the flight by 2200-ish. Are we going to get an engine change done by 2200? I don't think so. Will we find HOTAC? I don't know. Can we sub-charter…?

'…You don't know that either. I get it. Shut up, you're getting boring. I'll check with upstairs for authority to sub-charter. But don't do it till your certain we're out of time.'

That's an afront. 'And shall I get some more eggs so you can carry on teaching me to how to suck 'em?'

'You don't need eggs, toadface, you already suck…'

Further schoolyard badinage is interrupted by Sledge, leaning in at the door. 'Er, punters getting really restless. Check-in is requesting LRVs?'

Light Refreshment Vouchers will buy each passenger a cellophane-wrapped doughy wedge purporting to be a sandwich, and a hot drink—neither hot nor very drinkable—from the cafeteria in the terminal.

I look at Jed: 'Three quid? It'll keep them quiet for a while.'

He nods agreement, I say 'Three quid' to Sledge who goes off to carry the good news to the check-in supervisor, and we've just spent over a grand to buy ourselves a short reprieve from the rebellion that is brewing in the terminal.

So, back to business: 'Yes Jed?'

'I've had a complaint.'

'Have you? Try a course of penicillin, that should clear it up. And stay out of Soho after dark.'

'Hysterical. Choose your next witticism carefully, it may be your last. (He's quoting Goldfinger: not a good sign.) I've had another complaint about you from a captain.'

'What do you mean *another?*'

'What do you mean another?' Jed has an annoying habit of doing that, repeating your words back at you, only in a whining nasal voice you hadn't used. He does this when he wants to grate on your nerves. He's grating now like he's making a cheese omelette.

'I get more complaints about you than anybody else.'

I choose to ignore that calumny. 'Who's complained?'

'Dickie Bird.'

Dickie, apart from being a matchless example of nominative determinism, is also a prime tosser. I say, 'But he's a tosser.'

'I know he's a tosser, but he's complained so I've got to look into it. Where were you on the eighteenth?'

Blank. I have no idea. I say: 'Buggered if I know. I haven't a clue.'

'That's what Bird said too. He's buggered if he knew where you were when he was trying for over an hour to contact Ops on the outside line…' Jed consults his notepad… 'between 0100 and 0210.'

'Well, I…I was prob…I…' OK I'm floundering here, I haven't a strong grasp of where I was the day before yesterday, let alone way back in the mists of a couple of weeks ago. Who needs that kind of stuff?

'Yes well, while you were busy with: "Well, I prob…er er" (Doing the mimicking thing again), he was trying to go sick for his 0700 Faro so you'd have plenty of time to call out a standby. In the end, lucky for you, Fizz was passing through on her way home from a party and she took the call.'

This is making less sense to me than IKEA flatpack assembly instructions. How come I don't know anything about this? I say: 'I don't know anything about this. So, who called out the standby to replace Dicky?'

Jed looks at me askance. He does a good askance. 'What? *You* must have, you pillock. It departed on time. I think we can assume it didn't go without a skipper.'

'I don't remember doing that. Maybe Crewing called somebody out…'

'Don't think so—there was no crewing officer on.' And then, in a suddenly dangerously decisive tone: 'Right, this is what's going to happen. You've obviously done too many nights, you're turning into a chuffin' owl, and not a very wise one.'

'But…' I begin.

'No buts' he finishes. 'You can't remember an entire shift. You can't even tell me where you were, or why the office was un-manned for over an hour. You need to be kept an eye on you do, so I'm pulling you off shift for a while. You can do nine to five.'

I am aghast. Not only will I have to be in here during office hours, subject to the random importunities of the petty martinets whose empires grind their grist during the day, but everybody will know my shame.

'I…' More inchoate protest is cut off by Jed who's into his stride now.

'Tony will take your shift pattern until further notice, effective from the end of your shift today. You can take two rest days then start back on office duty. And I will be looking further into what happened on the eighteenth. Whatever you were up to, it better have been kosher, that's all I can say.'

'Jed, honestly I…'

'Out fool. Get that delay sorted before you go home.'

I walk out like a zombie. Stunned. Banjaxed. As if the day wasn't bad enough already, suddenly my reputation (I suppose I have one, though whether it is one I want to keep, I'm not sure) is imperilled *and* I'm going to be on permanent days. I'm not that keen on daylight.

Further morbid introspection is mercifully interrupted by the phone on my desk. I pick up and the following conversation takes place.

I say: 'HKA Ops.'

'Is that HKA?'

'What? No, it's Mothercare. Plank.' 'Yes, this the HKA duty officer.'

'Can you tell me when your Malaga flight will be departing?'

'This doesn't sound right.' 'Excuse me, who is this?'

'I'm a passenger on it'

What? 'Then you've come through to the wrong number, sir. You need Flight Enquiries. I'll give you the number…'

'No, I don't want Flight Enquiries, I want *you* to tell me when your flight will be departing.'

'That's what Flight Enquiries is for, to supply you with that information.'

'Only, they don't know. That's why I'm calling you.'

'OK, well the way it works is, when we know we tell Flight Enquiries and then they tell you.'

'They're bloody useless, they can't tell us anything. That's why I'm calling you.'

Thickhead. 'Yes, the reason they can't tell you anything yet, is because we don't know yet. That's why we have an indefinite delay on the flight at the moment.'

'Well how much longer is it going to be?'

It's bloody indefinite, you prawn. That's the main thing about something that's indefinite—it's sort of, well, indefinite. 'That's the indefinite part, sir.'

'That's not good enough. We've got families here with young children. Everybody's tired…'

'Excuse me. May I just stop you there a moment? You see, you've come through to Operations where we are trying to resolve the problem…'

'You're not making a good job of it, are you?'

'Well, at least part of the reason for that is that I'm wasting resolving time talking to you. Which is why we have Flight Enquiries and why you should be speaking to them.'

'This is unacceptable. Can I have your name?'

You mean 'may?' Semantics I know; I suppose I'm getting cross. 'Yes. If you would just like to give me yours?'

There is a moment's hesitation before he says: 'Walk…Si…Simon Walker.'

A bloke who stumbles over his own name? Right. As luck would have it, laying in front of me is a copy of the Malaga passenger manifest, shed by Marco when last he passed through.

'Please hold on a moment, sir.'

I scan the manifest. Twice.

'Would you confirm your name again for me, sir?'

'Simon Walker. Come on what's your name? I'm going to make a complaint about this. We'll be seeking compensation.'

'Have you checked in yet?'

'Yes of course, hours ago.'

Gotcha! As they are won't to say at the lower end of Grub Street. 'I see. Only, your name doesn't appear on the passenger manifest.'

'They must have missed it off.'

'Excuse me, are you actually one of our passengers?'

'Yes. Well…Yes.'

'You're not, are you?'

'Yes, I am.'

I don't have time for this. 'Forgive me, you're *not*, are you?'

'Actually, it's my brother-in-law and family. I'm calling on their behalf. They have been stuck here in the concourse for hours. Now, you have a legal duty to…'

Oh good, all I need now is a smart-arse. 'Excuse me, Mr Walker, excuse me, if I may. The thing is, as I have said, we pay Flight Enquiries up there to deal with, well, flight enquiries, so that we down here can get on with our own job.

Only, you are preventing me from doing that. So, you're delaying not only your brother-in-law and his family, but everybody else on the flight. And, as you are not even one of our customers, I'm going right away now.'

'Hold on. We need to know when we are going to get away…'

'The next thing you here will be the dialling tone. Goodbye Mr Walker.'

There is more from Mr Walker, but I have no idea what because, as promised, he's telling it to the dialling tone. The phone rings again. It's him. I put down. We perform the ritual twice more in rapid succession, until he realises that this is a contest he cannot win, and quits. Having got the line back I grab the phone, punching in for Big Bro Check-In. Peeved would describe my attitude, only nowhere near adequately. This is little short of treachery.

While I wait for a reply: 'Sledge? Try Engineers again, will you?'

Check-In answers. I ask for the supervisor. She answers brusquely. I go into a rant about their unprofessional behaviour, demanding to know the name of the person who passed our Ops number to a passenger. She doesn't actually say so, but her tone sound like '*Stuff you, if I knew who it was, I wouldn't tell you. Your passengers are driving us nuts up here.*' I tell her that that's what we pay them for, that we will be making an official complaint and that we want the name of the…all that etc. I know my impotent rage is wasted on her, so I finish weakly demanding that she instructs her shift not to repeat the offense, warning that if it is repeated, she will be in the frame for it. Clearly, she is terrified by the prospect, in much the same way that Russia would be terrified if Barnsley declared war on it.

I hate everybody and everything right now. But specifically included in my silent misanthropic hit-list are Jed, passengers, aeroplanes—especially aeroplanes—day shifts, work in general, today in particular—and did I mention Jed?

Sledge tells me: 'Engineering still doesn't answer.'

Perfect. When things are this bad there is really only one recourse: the eternal solace of tea. (Thank God it's not booze; my liver would be in a pickle jar at Barts by now.) I head for the kettle. Halfway there, I am struck by a sudden thought. I return to my jacket which is draped over the back of my chair, and pull out my diary. Why I hadn't thought of it before, I have no idea. I fan through the pages, locate the date I want and stare at the scribbled note. Recollection floods back.

Moments later I am striding into Jed's office, holding my Letts before me like Moses bearing The Tablets: 'Jed, I wasn't on.'

'What are you mithering about now, I'm busy?'

'What? You're busy, reading *Asian Babes?* I wasn't on shift on the eighteenth.'

'What are you talking about, buffoon? I've got the roster here.'

'Yes, but your copy probably hasn't been amended since knitted tank tops were cool. I had a gig on the eighteenth. (He knows about the band). I took a leave day. Tony did my shift.'

We look at each other blankly. This does not compute. The idea of Tony being in anyway delinquent is preposterous. A man so diligent that he takes a radio with him to the lavatory—to "fire the morning canon" as he so delicately puts it—is not going to abandon his post for over an hour. There is something wrong here. We are unable to question Tony as he is on leave, so further investigation will have to wait.

'Anyway, it wasn't me. So, I'm in the clear? I can have me shifts back?'

'No, you bloody-well can't. I'll investigate further. You can stay on days, you sloppy sod.'

'What? That's not…'

'Out cretin!'

I halt at the doorway. 'Barbarian!'

He doesn't look up from his reading: 'Yes, but I might gentle my condition. Whereas you will always be a useless git. Now get that fucking AOG sorted.'

Dumfounded to discover that the arch philistine is able to paraphrase the Bard, I am unable to think of a suitable rejoinder and trudge disconsolately back to my desk.

It's 1800 when Sledge wiggles the handset of his phone at me: 'Engineers.'

This will be to tell me they've got the stepladders up and have gone off to find some fitters who give a tinker's cuss about fixing our aeroplane. I know it's going to be tomorrow, before they say it. (I was told once that I should be the president of the Society of Pessimists, my adviser clearly not realising that I would think there'd be no point.) I don't want this day any more, really. The other lads, the sharp ones, would relish it: Greg would have three different scenarios worked out, very likely in different coloured inks; Stuart would amble nonchalantly through it all and somehow it would work out alright, like always;

177

and Sam, fuelled by Orc-strength black coffee, would get it done with his usual clinical thoroughness, leavened with a dash of grim intensity.

I take the phone.

'Hi, it's Engineering,' says Sauchiehall, unnecessarily.

'Always a pleasure,' I say. He ignores that; either he doesn't have time for insincerity or his radar isn't working.

'It's done,' he says.

What is? Your lunch? My career? 'Done?' I repeat stupidly.

'Aye, your engine, it's in. We've to dae a run yet—mebbe half an hour—then we'll put it on 36 for yea.'

This is quite extraordinary; they've done an engine change in—a glance at the clock—six-and-a-half hours. If that's not actually a national record who cares, it's good for us. The rude mechanicals have pulled our chestnuts, only lightly scorched, out of the fire after all. I swear undying gratitude to Sauchiehall (which is true-ish) and promise him a drink at Christmas (which, if I have anything to do with the duty roster, isn't true at all) and bid him, with excruciating unoriginality, lang may his lum reek. His response comes in the form of a cheerful invitation to do something which would require me not only to be invertebrate, but hermaphrodite.

Noting my rising excitement and drawn by curiosity, Sledge and Will close on either side of me until I'm wearing them like headphones. I put down and spin 180 in the chair. 'We're on, boys. Serviceable.'

They take a little convincing, but eventually have to concede that seeing me this animated, it has to be true. We all turn to look at the clock above the ops board.

'What shall we go for?' Will is fidgeting like a greyhound in a starting trap. He needs to start calling crew.

Sledge says: 'They (the passengers) are all checked in, sitting in the Dep Lounge waiting.'

'OK. The cabin's dressed already, so it's just fuel and catering and we're ready. Let's cut us some slack here though, allow for contingencies and make it a 20.00 departure. That'll give us a couple of hours to play with before the crew duty deadline. All agreed say "aye."'

They say it to humour me and we bomb-burst to our respective tasks; Will to call in the crew, Sledge to inform the world of our glad tidings, me to order the catering back aboard and start the flight plans—lots of etceteras like that.

By the 1900 shift change we are in good shape. Everything is ready or approaching readiness and to the oncoming nightshift we must look cheerful and for a change fairly professional. Whilst I am not exactly euphoric, the day has turned out rather well from its earlier unpromising developments. It is only marred by the unjust imposition on me of the day shifts by the Nazi Farter. I even endure the naff high five Sledge offers as we depart for home.

On subsequent investigation, the mystery of the nightshift delinquency I had been blamed for, was solved. It turned out that Tosser Bird had been dialling the wrong number (with more than 20,000 hours logged one can only assume that his flying has been more diligent than his dialling), and he was not ringing Ops at all but the Navigation office, which is unattended at night. That's to say, it would have been, had Flick not nipped in there for a kip. Homeward bound from her latest riotous dissipation, she had come to the fuzzy conclusion that it was too late to go home, and being due on shift at 0700, had decided to doss down there. But despite being moderately hammered, the constant ringing of the phone had kept her awake, until finally she had given in to it and answered. Having no idea what Tosser was babbling about when he upbraided her for the length of time it had taken to answer his call, nevertheless she had taken his message through to Ops to pass to Tony, before trudging back to Nav and blessed oblivion.

Now, in a fair, decent, honest world these findings would have exonerated me. But no, I was left to rot on dayshift until Natural Justice re-asserted itself. Tony, who had been promoted to fill the senior duty officer role when Jed moved to take up the late Bernie's operations manager post, had been pulled off shift. A man of encyclopaedic knowledge, particularly in the flight planning role, he was nevertheless not entirely happy to find himself back in the duty officer's chair, and politely baulked at it. Since Jed was not entirely happy that Tony was back in that chair either, and I wasn't at all happy confined to those stupid nine-to-five days with nothing to do, within a week I was returned to my rightful place on the roster and in two, back on my beloved nights.

On the whole, I thought I had handled the day, if not exactly with aplomb, at least tidily. But no kudos resulted from it, quite the opposite. All anybody remembered about it was that James had been put on days for being a useless git. And people wonder why I'm cynical.

Mind you, there had been worse shifts, infinitely worse; and one in particular, many years previously, bad beyond belief.

India Zulu

I was taking a thrashing as usual, chasing ball after ball as they rocketed across the table in a succession of furious top-spin deliveries. Tim Smith, slight, agile and the best table tennis player in the company, was annihilating me—again. I was lucky to win even one in ten of our games. But he was an affable opponent, the game kept us out of mischief and the exercise did us good.

It was July: the middle of the summer season when charter aviation works flat out to make enough money to see it through its enforced annual winter semi-hibernation, until the following spring. Not that there weren't any hiatuses in the daily programme. These tended to occur between the morning raft of outbound flights and their return in the afternoon. There would usually be another break until the evening flights departed. And the nightshift would be a patchwork of half a dozen passenger flights and one or two cargo flights which would be loaded through the night. Then, in the early hours, the morning's flights would be readied and the whole process would begin all over again.

This evening, we were enjoying one such hiatus and, as the last hours of a long day shift ticked away, the table tennis table had been rigged in the middle of the office. Tim and I were at set point—with me unaccountably leading—when my attention was caught by the great bulk of Percy Bell, the operations duty officer, heaving in from the telex room which separated the Ramp office from Operations.

Percy was a great lumbering creature whose approach was usually announced either by the creak of his odiferous brogues, or the execrable fumes from the shag in his ever-present briar. He was a throwback to an earlier era, both in appearance and character. His customary brown worsted three-piece would not have shamed Bertie Wooster at a Blandings' weekend house party; the brogues were hand-lasted and of canal-barge proportions; a paisley handkerchief adorned the top pocket of his jacket, whilst a heavy watch chain, strung between his waistcoat pockets, bestrode the vastness of his belly. His great head was almost hairless but for some sparse foliage above each ear, and a pair of stout horn-rimmed spectacles scrabbled for purchase on the tip of his nose. Percy, who spoke in deep cultured tones, was ex-RAF with war service, which probably accounted for his rather dour demeanour. On the rare occasions when he did laugh—indicated by a rhythmic rising and falling of his shoulders, to the accompaniment of a series of strange guttural grunts, it was rather disconcerting. Fortunately, this was an uncommon occurrence. Somewhat incongruously for such a big man, Percy's preferred mode of transport was a large BSA motorcycle, like himself, of indeterminate vintage. Thus, he would arrive for work wearing a full-length dustcoat, accessorised with a World War II dispatch-rider-pattern crash helmet, goggles and elbow-length leather gauntlets. The overall effect was that of a man wearing tank-commander fancy dress hired from an unreliable costumier.

But as Tim smashed my distracted return away to a distant corner of the office, I noticed that there was nothing the least comical about Percy demeanour as he stumped by to speak to Jerry the duty officer. Even the pipe was missing. A bad sign.

As he passed by, he muttered: '*India Zulu,* overdue into Barcelona.'

This was not of any immediate significance to Tim and I. *India Zulu* was currently operating from our northern base and did not therefore appear on our daily mayfly. Though her progress was flight-watched in Operations, we in Traffic were not concerned with her movements. We also suspected that as old Percy took things a bit too seriously, he'd blown up a couple of minutes ATC delay into a bit of a drama.

We were quite wrong.

In comparison with today's multiple sources of instantaneous contact, communications in the '70s were still pretty rudimentary, and extracting information from Spain was proving painfully difficult. Just trying to establish a telephone call to another country, via a couple of operators who might not share a common language, was unconscionable. The only alternative to the telephone was to sit before a noisy teleprinter as it chomped laboriously away at responses to your own typed messages—always assuming that there had been somebody at the other end to receive them. But within ten minutes of *India Zulu's* failure to arrive in Barcelona, both methods had been adopted as the anxiety level in the office had begun to soar. The table tennis table was hurriedly stowed away and we were making ever-more frequent visits to the teleprinter room, stopping short at the door of Ops to stare at Percy's broad back as he hunched over the telephone, while beside us Bella the telex operator sat demurely at her machine, rattling off requests for information to our handlers in Barcelona. This was in marked contrast to Bella in her off-duty hours, at least part of which she spent as 'Coral Peach', artfully shaking her booty for the punters in Soho. Nevertheless, despite the decidedly laddish culture of the Ramp, she was treated no differently than any other female colleague, though it was said that one or two of the lads had paid a furtive visit to catch her act. Right now, however, the only thing she was shaking was her head, in frustration at the time Barcelona was taking to respond to her repeated pleas for information.

Soon enough we learned not only that *India Zulu* had failed to make her ETA, but that she was not answering Barcelona ATC's radio calls either. Airliners simply do not fail to appear at or about their ETA, and they never ignore radio calls from ATC unless something serious has intervened to prevent them doing so. There could be little doubt now that some misfortune had befallen the flight.

It was not long before the next message from our handlers confirmed our very worst fears: *India Zulu* had crashed.

Our shift was long since over and the night shift had taken over from us, but we were still in the office, milling around, unable to do much to help, yet too disturbed to knock off and go home. Information was coming to us in snatches from our sources in Barcelona. In the following hours we learned that the aircraft had struck a mountain north east of Barcelona. A huge Spanish rescue operation—consisting of the Guardia Civil, the Red Cross, firemen, soldiers and local volunteers—was on its way. The British Consul and Vice-Consul in Barcelona, British technicians, a pathologist and even an Anglican priest, were also heading into the mountains.

As we learned later, the rescuers were facing difficult terrain. *India Zulu* had come down on a steep, densely-wooded 5,600-ft slope, carving a 125-acre path through a beech wood before exploding. To get to the crash site the team were using bulldozers and diggers to clear a path. When they finally reached the scene, it was immediately apparent that the mission would be one of recovery rather than rescue.

In a very short time following confirmation of the loss, a small Spanavia team, headed by Arthur Fineman the chief pilot, had assembled grim-faced in Ops, preparing to make their way to the crash site. At such moments, the aviation industry draws together and the team would be given seats with whatever airline, on whichever flight they chose to take. A crew bus awaited them outside and before long they were gone, while the office slowly filled with senior management and technical staff.

Gathered once again around Bella at her telex machine, our eyes were glued to the exact point on the roll at which the print was emerging. The odds were incalculably small, the very idea foolish, but we had to make sure. Ops had requested that a copy of the passenger manifest for the flight be sent from Manchester and here it was rattling out. We just wanted to make sure that there was no name on the list that we recognised. The machine faltered frequently as the operator wrestled with some of the more obscure English surnames. But then, suddenly, he/she found a couple of easy ones and banged them out.

Black, James. M

Black, Anne. F

My breath stopped. They were the names of my cousin and his wife, and they lived in Yorkshire, the catchment area for many on the flight. I was at the telephone in three strides. The number rang endlessly. Finally, it was answered and the sleepy voice on the other end—it was the middle of the night—I recognised immediately. But, since news of the crash had not yet been released, I couldn't tell Jimmy why I was calling. Much relieved, I said nothing and rang off. I could explain later.

Telex machines clattered, telephones shrilled constantly, directors and managers arrived, some dressed in whatever had come first to hand. The Air Accident Investigation Branch were on the move. And then the newspapers got wind of the crash and all hell broke loose. This was front page stop-the-press stuff and we were deluged with calls from the city desks of all the national dailies, as desperate night editors strove to get the story in time for the morning editions.

By the early hours, it was clear that we weary day-shifters, still present from yesterday, could be of little further use; the nightshift had it covered, were getting on with the programme—aviation might pause momentarily in such tragic circumstances, but it didn't stop. I recall a horrible accident I'd witnessed at an airshow, when a Stampe biplane performing aerobatics had entered a loop at low altitude and had flown straight into the ground, disintegrating on impact. In the silence that followed, the crowd's gasp of horror was quickly drowned by the sound of another engine behind us and, turning, we saw a rickety Bristol Boxkite taking to the air to distract our attention: the show had to go on. A further glance at the now unrecognisable ball of wreckage and we were amazed to see its pilot emerge from it unscathed. Sadly, on the present occasion, there could be no such miraculous survival. But the show had to go on, regardless.

It was time to go home. I fine summer morning greeted us as we headed for the car park and for some reason a little scene kept running in my memory. It involved another summer morning just like this, and *India Zulu*. Following a long nightshift, I had stood bleary-eyed on the tarmac in company with Gloria, an equally-tired receptionist, waiting to meet the aircraft inbound from a long flight (Las Palmas, I think.) Swinging in to approach the parking stand and drawing to a halt ten feet in front of us, *India Zulu's* nose dipped momentarily to her brakes. In response, on the spur of the moment, Gloria dropped into an answering little curtsy, with me following her lead to give a little bow. This got us brief tired smiles from behind the cockpit windows. That was all it was, a silly trivial thing; there was no reason for me to recall it this morning—except that it was infinitely preferable to allowing my imagination to dwell on the horror scattered across a distant Spanish hillside. The Reaper had been busy tonight, his scythe notched, bloodied and indelibly inscribed with the line's name; a rich, bitter harvest and one that none of us would easily forget.

The Department of Trade and Industry's accident report was published fifteen months after the crash. Though the causes were clear enough, the main question—why it happened at all—was not conclusively established.

Owing to heavy traffic in the Paris area, *IZ* had been diverted from its planned route and directed via Nantes and Toulouse, to join airway UB31 to Barcelona. Though the crew made all the correct reports and responses to ATC, when they reported joining the UB31, the aircraft was in fact thirty kilometres east of that airway, and remained roughly the same distance from its intended track until the crash. Even so, the error might have been spotted but for an untimely twist of fate. As was the common practise at that time, Barcelona ATC requested that *IZ* make a radar identification turn so that the controller watching his radar screen could positively distinguish from the clutter of radar echoes which blip it was. The crew altered course as requested, to 140°. On the controller's screen the target turned as expected and (so he thought), having positively identified it, he instructed the aircraft to resume its course and to continue its decent to land at Barcelona. Two minutes later, *IZ* hit the mountain,

45° nose up, travelling at over 250 mph and disintegrated on impact, with the loss of all 105 passengers and seven crew.

Of all those on board, only Callum the ever-cheerful flight engineer, a local man, was known to us.

The accident report suggested that there may have been a malfunction of the aircraft's navigation equipment. At any rate, the crew's position reports were consistently incorrect. The source of the radar echo identified by the controller was never established, but it was not that of *India Zulu*. "Ghost" radar echoes that mimic real aircraft are not unheard of and there was a nearby aero club from which an aircraft on a visual flight plan might have been operating, giving rise to the misidentification. It will never be known for sure. Nor will it ever be satisfactorily explained how two experienced pilots, with nearly 12,000 flying hours logged between them, should make such a catastrophic navigational error.

The famous pilot and author Ernest K. Gann, summed up aviation succinctly when he quoted his own training captain, the tyrannical Captain Ross's blunt observation after a particularly trying flight through a thunderstorm: 'In this business we play for keeps.' Fifty years later aviation had moved on in leaps and bounds from those pioneering days, yet the statement held true, just as it does to this day.

I left the office at daybreak, thankful that I wouldn't be there when the world woke up to the news. At that time, there was no such thing as specially-trained police officers, let alone bereavement councillors, and disasters such as this were handled in a matter-of-fact, even brutal, way. In this case, a couple of volunteers from the day shift were given copies of *India Zulu's* passenger manifest, each was seated before a telephone and as news of the crash spread through the morning papers and early radio bulletins, the phones began to ring.

Storm

In Ops we'd been concerned about a storm.

'Don't worry,' the TV weatherman—the one who looks so much like the incompetent maths teacher from my school days—tells us confidently, 'because there isn't going to be one.' So that's alright. And that depression down there behind you, to your right, about the size of Wales, every bit as grim and wandering about the Bay of Biscay with its hands in its pockets, looking for somewhere to make landfall, that's nothing to worry about either? Take your word for it, Mickey: you have the moustache, the glasses, the pointing stick and the degree in meteorology and that's good enough for me.

This reassurance doesn't quite explain the sight that greets me on my arrival at Hangar F an hour later. For at the entrance, a recently-arrived bus is disgorging the Banjul crew and the girls are struggling—not always successfully—to stop their skirts blowing over their heads, whilst three stewards appear at first sight to be playing some curious variation on football, employing multiple balls. Closer inspection reveals that they are chasing their hats.

Up in Ops, Fran my assistant tonight, stands at the window staring anxiously out into the roaring twilight as Tony, whom I am relieving at the end of a long and trying shift, flits quickly through the handover. There's nothing much: the fleet is in, with just *Golf Delta,* inbound from Orlando, but with a fifty-knot crosswind already scouring the runway at right angles, not even bothering to look at us and diverting to Luton. It looks like my kind of nightshift: no flying, not much paperwork, tea and a book. No heroics required.

Heroics. There are those among us—a sad, misguided few among us—to whom the AOG, the diversion, the en-route re-routing flight plan, the PAN call, the ops board disfigured with hastily-scribbled notes across the schedule in livid, hysterical red chinagraph, is but grist to their mill. Whereas to me, and surely any right-thinking person, it is but arse pain. I sometimes wonder—as indeed do my superiors, no doubt—if I am entirely suited to the work.

On my way to the little hatch that connects Ops with the pilots' crew room, my eye is caught by the synoptic weather chart Tony—now half way to his car—has been studying. On it, the isobars, with their mix of knobbly and pointy symbols indicating an occluded front, are coiled tighter than Jed's fingers round his wallet when it's his round, and with a barometric pressure reading of 960 millibars sitting in its navel this, even to one who looks on such documents as little short of masonic in their cryptic mystery, is not good. Something must be done.

I turn the chart face down.

The hatch is another of Tony's innovations. It is positioned to the left of the door. Its purpose, to allow cabin crew to communicate with us without actually sullying the sacred carpet tiles of the ops room. In his sometimes-over-active imagination, Tony sees desperate operations staff struggling with critical emergencies, whilst importuning cabin staff lounge in our chairs, sipping post-flight snifters, the while bombarding us with trivial queries and generally distracting us from our duty. Now, most of us (with the exception of the one or two with sticks up their bottoms), quite enjoy this commerce with the flying staff, but Tony will have professionalism in Ops. It's an uncomfortable concept.

By the time I reach the hatch, Cindy Woodham's breasts are resting lightly on it (you have to be at least five eight and quite pert to achieve this), as she proffers the bag containing the Banjul bar takings and smiles—invitingly. No, she doesn't, the "invitation" is unconscious and entirely unintentional, merely the result of a physiological quirk: she suffers from mydriasis, the more-or-less permanent dilation of her pupils. In Cindy's case this affliction is particularly ironic. She is an attractive honey blonde with a friendly manner, but renowned for not being a great socialiser. In fact, if the intelligence is right, she eschews night-stop parties, preferring to keep to her room where, it is said, she likes to knit. There is also a long-term fiancé somewhere, a soldier, for whom she has been waiting for some time. One day no doubt, when the soldier has finished his war, they will be married: there will be a pleasant semi on a tasteful development; the second car will be a Volvo estate; there will be three children and two dogs—possibly matching, possibly pedigree (the dogs not the children, though that is also possible)—and yaddy yaddy yah. There may even be more knitting. What there unquestionably won't be, is any business of the sort her distended pupils seem to invite.

I take the bag of cash, she gives me the eye thing accompanied by a cheerful goodnight, and Fran and I find ourselves alone, listening to the rising note of the wind as it tests the structural integrity of Hangar F. Only a complete fool would go out on a night like this.

I get the van keys.

I'm curious to know what conditions are like on the ramp. The security bloke clearly isn't and with a distracted wave from behind the rain-obscured glass of his post, he lifts the barrier. I could have waved an AK. On a previous occasion, I actually waved a cheese roll at an equally unenthusiastic guard and gained immediate entry.

It's a big airport made to seem even bigger by being uncharacteristically deserted. The rain is horizontal now and, driving out beyond the shelter afforded by the reverse E shape of the buildings with their passenger gates and parking stands, the wind buffets the van like a schoolyard bully, the rain setting up a machinegun-rattle on the metal. Everything that could be tied down, has been. Anything that couldn't is fair game for the savagery of the wind: a set of passenger steps (say, a couple of tons) bowls across the tarmac like a dead leaf, in the direction of the runway, with a couple of industrial-sized waste bins flying loose formation on it; out on the end of the southern finger a big DC-10-30 trembles like a whipped dog in the rising storm; and an engineer, foolish enough to venture outside on foot, is a flash of high-viz orange in his waterproofs as the gale frogmarches him smartly past my bonnet to slam him into a lamp post, which he clings to for support, before legging it to cover.

Over at the General Aviation Terminal, a quite extraordinary sight awaits among the assorted light aircraft parked there. It's a Beech Something-or-Other, or maybe it's a Cessna Thingy (not too hot on the small stuff recognition) and it is flying, all on its own—only a couple of inches off the ground, but it's definitely flying. The only thing stopping it from taking to the night are the cement anchors to which the wings have been tethered. At this point, it becomes clear that the van has similar inclinations, only without the encumbrance of anchors there is every chance that it will succeed. I return briskly to the office, encouraged by a chunk of what looks like hangar roof passing to starboard, heading roughly north west.

By the early hours, it is clear that this is no ordinary storm and, between desultory attempts at paperwork, we are glancing ever more frequently towards the windows. The latest actual (weather observation) for the airport shows the wind gusting 90 knots. I can well believe it, the very air in the office is vibrant with it and nasty ripples have been set up on the surface of my tea.

I'm not be the sharpest knife in the drawer, but if there is one small conceit I am willing to own, it is that I have a finely attuned sixth sense. So, when on occasions the small hairs start to rise on the back of my neck and a vague feeling of anxiety washes over me, I go into a defensive crouch and start checking my six, whilst looking for the emergency exits. Which can be embarrassing when you're in the barber's chair, or half way through a best man's speech. Anyway, finding that my metaphorical fur is now standing on end, I glance first at the streaming black rectangle of the window, then at Fran.

'Let's go next door, shall we?'

She's not arguing. We collect our junk and move out to the other side of the partition, into the pilots' crew room, closing the door behind us—which is when I discover just how finely attuned my sixth sense is. We don't even make it to our chairs before the Ops room explodes in a blizzard of glass shards and rain as one of the windows implodes and a huge, dark, rectangular object fills the shattered frame for a moment before it is gone.

I make it all the way to the floor in a spray of tea and a flurry of paperwork, my previous experience of imploding windows playing vividly in my memory. Fran manages a more dignified reaction, simply stepping back to look aghast at the maelstrom on the other side of the glass. Getting to my feet I come to join her, ignoring the look she's giving me, and we stare open-mouthed at the mess.

It is the work of half an hour to restore a semblance of order in Ops. There is little we can do about the window, that will be a job for Alf tomorrow. (I don't know where we found Alf. He's an old fashioned odd-job man, cum electrician/builder/bodger, with a dodgy ticker and a face the colour of a plum. He's basically a coronary infarction waiting for the right moment. But he's willing to tackle any job we throw at him. We'll be throwing this tomorrow.) Meantime, cardboard and tape at least cuts down the draught from the shattered window. The storm is already moving on, the barometer and thermometer both rising rapidly, and by dawn an air of stunned calm hangs over a scene of devastation. It is not, we find, the only thing that is hanging.

Atop the building, a fifty-foot-long sign proudly advertises the company's name. At least it did until the wind got to work on its fixings and, at the height of the storm, broke the bolts on one end of it, cutting it free to take a Damoclesian plunge downwards, shattering our window at the bottom of its swing. It then spent the rest of the night creaking and batting mournfully against the side of the building, asking to come in like Catherine Earnshaw's ghost.

If any of us had been sensitive to the symbolism of the thing, we might have been better prepared for what was to befall us in the not-too-distant future. But for now, we were too busy sweeping up broken glass.

Auriga

I looked at the board, at the gap where *India Alpha's* actual time of arrival should have been, and felt again that familiar chill in the pit of my stomach: the bloody thing was overdue. Again.

Quite what had attracted me to Auriga International, I can't remember: it may have been the cash, a not inconsiderable increase in what Spanavia was paying me. It may also have been the opportunity it offered—in the operations room—not solely to gain experience there, but also to escape the rigours of the Racebridge tarmac. Having served time in several departments at Spanavia, with varying levels of success, I had fallen repeatedly back into ramp dispatching, at which I was tolerably efficient.

Dispatching is not a difficult job, if it's approached in the right way. All you have to do is chase every department involved in a flight's departures, from the moment the empty aircraft is towed onto stand, to the moment it departs, preferably to schedule—the whole point of the exercise. But getting fuellers, baggage handlers, engineers, cabin crew, flight crew, catering staff, the traffic office (responsible for documentation) and finally passenger-handling staff to function synchronously, requires patience, truckloads of tact, dogged persistence and a smidgeon of low cunning that in other occupations might be considered undesirable. The sometimes-high stress level is just another occupational hazard: either you hacked it or you found another line of work.

Though there was undoubted satisfaction to be had from watching your allocated flight roll on schedule, there were also less attractive aspects to the job. Airports are essentially flat concrete deserts; this means that in summer you could expect to fry in the glare reflected from the ramp, and in winter, in sodden shoes and with semi-permanently-chilled gonads, you wondered what the hell had ever attracted you to aviation in the first place. People—burly people in greasy overalls—often expressed a desire to harm you if you persisted in asking them stupid questions, like when would aircraft be ready? And every department naturally assumed that the dispatcher knew what all the other departments were doing, which in a way was part of our job, but in reality, required a level of omnipotence one could only realistically expect to encounter on Mount Olympus.

It could be dangerous out there too: you needed your wits about you. Traffic roared about the apron in all directions as though some hellish race with an enormous cash first prize was on offer. Thus, a near-Darwinian selection process along the lines of the quick and the dead prevailed, with not that much sympathy for the dead. On one occasion, as I backed clear of an aircraft, a baggage truck t-boned my van, at speed, and hard enough to cave in the roof deeply enough for it to rap me smartly across the side of the head. If I had expected any sympathy, either from the erring baggage truck driver who had crossed a lane marking, or the Spanavia transport department bloke who came to glare at the wreckage of the van, I was to be disappointed. The loader decamped smartly in case I bled on his shoes, and the Transport bloke berated me for the destruction of the van, the tacit implication being that it constituted a greater loss than my own would have been.

I came away from the ramp with nothing more than minor bruising. Others had not been so lucky. Such as the man who was decapitated when he drove his catering truck into the wing on an aircraft; or Tom the engineer, a fine jazz trumpeter, who was working inside an aircraft engine somewhere down the line in Africa, when somebody started it up.

On one occasion, returning post-prandially from the canteen with half the shift, in boisterous form, all crammed into an overloaded ramp van, we were momentarily stunned by the report of an explosion of such force that it physically hurt the ears. Emerging from the underpass into the horseshoe formed by the south and central piers, the source of the bang was horrifically revealed: an aircraft tyre had exploded, with catastrophic results. An engineer had been inflating a mainwheel from a nitrogen cylinder (nitrogen is inert and unlike oxygen less prone to igniting at high temperatures), but he had used a cylinder without a reducing valve to control the gas flow. The tyre had over-inflated and exploded with such force that not only was the massive tyre torn to shreds, but the wheel itself had shattered into lethal flying fragments. The engineer had stood no chance. Flung some distance by the explosion, the rag-doll attitude of his body sprawled on the ground amongst wreckage of the wheel, showed that there was nothing to be done. As the fallen man's mates raced towards the scene, we continued on our way, chastened to silence.

There were lots of sharp things and noisy things and rapidly moving things and blindly-reversing things that you had to watch out for on the ramp, especially when on foot. Though in transport it was hardly much safer; whilst driving it was necessary to emulate the fighter pilot's constant scanning of the sky in search of hostiles. It was also not uncommon to make a routine check of your driving mirror only to discover that it was filled with the advancing physiognomy of a big jet, taxiing briskly up your six.

Jet efflux was another hazard not to be trifled with, though with careful judgement of distance it could be warming on a winter's day. But get too close and reproof was immediate: your hat would depart for the next county in a shrapnel blast of grit and litter, followed by any loose documentation, sunglasses, small people, bits of equipment and the last shred of your dignity. Even closer to the efflux and you'd be joining the exodus yourself, lightly toasted and, Icarus-like, destined for a firm landing.

But there was also fun and excitement. Celebrities were two a penny; famous and infamous, they passed through the airport blazing their ephemeral trails: louche rock bands on tour, actors, actresses, villains handcuffed to escorts, politicians with bright futures behind them, TV personalities with suspicious post-nasal drips, mountaineers, tycoons, sport heroes, the odd despotic ruler heading for Harrods to blow some of his country's misappropriated GNP. We met them all. But did we pass judgement on any of them? You bet we did.

Crooner royalty, in the person of Frank Sinatra, parked his Learjet 23 with us while he went off to some Rat-Packery in London, handing out, as he passed among us, Zippo lighters engraved with the legend "Thanks, Sinatra" to anybody who carried his bag or held a door for him. Hugh Hefner, likewise, parked his all-black DC9 with its Playboy bunny emblem-emblazoned tail on the North Park. But, just in case anybody thought they were going to get a glimpse of the sumptuous interior with its infamous circular bed, it also came with an unsmiling 24-hour guard. The Carpenters UK tour jet was based briefly at Racebridge and we handled the flight. Tellingly, given Karen Carpenter's well-publicised struggle with her health, the catering we loaded on the outbound flight, came back unopened when the aircraft returned. Among the many who came to Racebridge for location shooting, I have the enduring image of Tommy Cooper, clad in enormous shorts and wearing his signature fez, leaning on a first-floor balcony above the concourse, puffing at a cigar the size of a cucumber, between takes for his TV show.

Occasionally, from the windows at the back of our office, we would spot a familiar figure stumping out across the GAT (General Aviation Terminal, where light aircraft were parked) to a twin-engine Miles Gemini, bearing the Shell logo on its tail. We would watch as he made a somewhat unorthodox entry into the aircraft: he'd sit on the port wing root, lift his legs up one at a time with his hands, then shuffle on his backside through the door into the pilot's seat. This was the legendary legless fighter ace of World War II, Douglas Bader: 22 victories, DSO and bar, DFC and bar, and rounded off his war with three years at *Oflag IV-C* (Colditz) after being shot down.

Another notable character who would pass through our handling unit from time to time was the aristocratic Swede, Count Gustaf von Rosen. Resembling somewhat the actor Liam Neeson, he was tall, fair, elegant and refined, an effect heightened by the gold-rimmed pince-nez he wore for reading. These he would perch on the end of his nose to inspect his loadsheet, before drawing out an 18-carat fountain pen in the manner of a dualist selecting a pistol, and signing his name with a flourish. Ever polite, this nerveless adventurer had been flying all his adult life, encouraged to it, it was said, by his uncle, Hermann Göering. Judging by his exploits, Von Rosen could have had little else in common with the Reichsmarschall.

He had started out as a circus stunt pilot, but joined the Red Cross to fly ambulance missions during the Italo-Ethiopian war. After that, he'd flown for KLM until the USSR invaded Finland, prompting him to quit the airline to fly bombing missions against the invaders. Post-war, he returned to Ethiopia as chief flying instructor for the Imperial Ethiopian Airforce. On his return to Sweden, he joined the charter airline Transair, a company we handled, and thus became an occasional visitor to our offices. He also flew for the UN during the Congo crisis.

But one particular visit stands out in the memory, when the Count arrived with three Malmo MFI-9 single-engine light aircraft and the story that he and his two pilot companions were conducting a delivery flight to Africa. Exactly where in Africa was never made clear and he was evasive about the specifics of the trip. We did however notice that the Malmos featured some curious under-wing attachments which, according to Tony Novak our resident aviation geek, were not standard equipment for the type. Whatever the Count was up to, it was really none of our business. He certainly wouldn't be the first airman to pass through Racebridge who's destination and intentions were best not inquired into too closely. So, we supplied our usual services, fuel and catering etc, cleared the flight with Customs for the next leg of the journey to France, and later that day watched the trio of aircraft climb out from Runway 27, turning south-east to dwindle to specks in the afternoon sky.

Only later were we to discover that von Rosen was going to war; that the three aircraft were part of a five-ship batch bound for the rebel African state of Biafra. Ever the champion of the underdog, the Count had been enraged by the cruelty the Nigerian military had meted out to the breakaway state, especially its suppression of relief supplies to the desperate Biafrans. So, with a bit of help from the French secret service, Rosen had obtained the aircraft, fitted hardpoints (that's what they were), under the wings to accommodate Matra 98mm air-to-ground rockets, painted the aircraft in camouflage colours and, with a couple of fellow Swedes and two Biafrans, formed what was to become known as the 'Biafra Babies.'

If the enterprise was Quixotic, it was not without success. Rosen's air force launched offensive operations directed specifically against the Nigerian Air Force which had mounted attacks against civilian Biafrans. These sorties resulted in the destruction, on the ground, of a number of aircraft, including several Mig-17s and Ilyushin IL-28 bombers and various other unspecified aircraft.

When looked at purely strategically, the Biafran war was a lost cause: the little breakaway state stood little chance against the superior force ranged against it. Nevertheless, von Rosen's contribution was invaluable. His relief flights, based on a supply-dropping technique developed by another adventurer, ex-Canadian Airforce pilot Lynn Garrison, saved the lives of countless Biafrans who would otherwise have starved. Seven years later, he was using the same successful technique to drop supplies to desperate famine-stricken refugees during the Ogaden War between Ethiopia and Somalia, when his adventurer's luck finally ran out and he was killed in Gode during a Somalian Army assault.

Coincidentally, while von Rosen was doing his bit for the Biafrans, another rather more raffish adventurer whom we would also see in our office from time to time, was also there; the charming Polish maverick, Marian Kozubski. His adventures were many, varied and not always entirely legitimate. Having fled Poland during the war, he'd made his way to England to fly Lancasters with the RAF. After the war, he had participated in the Indian Partition airlift and the

Berlin Air Lift, raced his own Jaguar at Monte Carlo and had been jailed in Albania over some air space infringement. There was also an allegation of gun-running in Djibouti. Many more such adventures later, found him also in Biafra, flying civilian DC3s and DC4s as makeshift bombers against Nigerian targets. He was seriously wounded, but recovered to run various outfits in England and Europe, which often featured unorthodox operating procedures, over-worked crew, unlicensed engineers and overloaded aircraft. He was one of that dwindling number of airmen who steadfastly refused to be drawn into the comfort and security of an airline. Instead, he sought risk and goaded fate for a living. In another era, such a man would surely have had a cutlass at his belt, a patch over his eye and a hundred guinea on his head.

The ramp then, had been fun. Sometimes. By turns instructive, tedious, frustrating, occasionally exciting and, after a twelve-hour shift, exhausting. It felt like time to move on—and Auriga was where I'd moved on to.

But, sat there at 0200 in the morning, alone in Auriga Ops, with *India Alpha's* ATA glaringly-absent from the board and the teleprinters behind me that would announce its safe arrival stubbornly silent, I was wondering—as I had for some time now—what the hell I was doing in this weird outfit.

And weird it was. For a start it was run, for all we knew, by a vampire. At least, nobody ever saw the short, pinkly-bald stoutish figure of Cameron Angus McGillivray—CAM to all who knew him—in daylight, at least not broad daylight. He lived in the penthouse flat at the top of the three-storey office block that was Auriga's off-airport headquarters and never appeared before 1700. All his business appointments were conducted in the evening, before he Merc-ed off to a favourite local restaurant for dinner. A couple of hours later he'd be back, retreating to his office to work until dawn. At least once during the night he would appear in Ops, for a rundown of the fleet's disposition.

If he popped down tonight, I'd be in the unenviable position, yet again, of having to tell him that, yet again, the Gan flight was overdue. It may have been a regular occurrence, but it was no trivial matter, given the particular circumstances that prevailed for this destination.

The island of Gan, way out in the Indian Ocean on the southernmost tip of Addu Atoll in the Maldives, is a long way from anywhere, if you don't count the necklace of twenty-six coral atolls strung out to the north of it. And for flight planning purposes, you didn't count them, because there was nowhere to land a big Bristol Britannia turboprop airliner on any one of them. Only at the RAF base on Gan.

We had a contract with the RAF to supply their base on the island, mounting a weekly flight there. Owing to Gan's remoteness, it was necessary to adopt the "island hold" protocol when flight planning the trip. The pleasant-sounding title hid a rather uncomfortable fact—that the nearest place to land if not on Gan, was India, hundreds of miles to the north. Which was just a polite way of saying that once the aircraft was committed to the flight, it *had* to land at Gan, there was nowhere else to go. So, two hours' extra fuel was carried, on top of its normal load, as it headed for a scrap of land barely six feet above sea level, measuring just under one square mile, in the vastness of a 27,000 square-mile ocean. If a storm were to hit the island when the flight arrived, or any other contingency prevented a landing, then the aircraft's only recourse was to circle until the runway became available—or till its fuel ran out. The gliding characteristics of a Bristol Britannia were no better than its ability to float. Island hold played for keeps. So, to put it mildly, news of our flight's arrival was eagerly awaited.

It never came, not in timely fashion. The RAF people in Gan were unconscionably dilatory in this respect, never getting around to sending an arrival message until our nails were bitten to the quicks. QUAs ('Where are you?' messages) were simply ignored. Having recently experience the catastrophic loss of the Spanavia aircraft, I found this particularly hard to endure.

The fact was that, beneath our fleet's gleaming paint jobs, the aircraft were decidedly long in the tooth, and on any given day we might expect two out of the five Britannias and Boeings to blow a tyre or cough up a fan blade.

There were other aspects of life at Auriga House, perhaps not of equivalent importance to the Gan thing, but in one particular case nearly as hard to stomach—that was the catering. Marooned as we were for hours on end alone in the ops room, unable to abandon the telephones and telexes, the only way the night duty officer could be sustained was by the delivery of an airline meal from our aircraft catering company.

However, the provender provided was unspeakably dreadful. In time of war, the perpetrators would have been deservedly shot at their stoves. To achieve the consistent level of unpalatability those meals attained, was really quite remarkable—horrible, but remarkable.

Suppose that, as an absolute afterthought, the least qualified, most reluctant operative in the kitchen is given the task of fixing the Auriga DO's dinner. It's around 0200, when the human spirit is guttering like a miser's tallow, the rest of the team have knocked off for their own dinner and Chef No-Mates, far from experiencing any sympathy for the recipient of his food, is concerned more with his acne, or his recalcitrant car or his erring girlfriend, than the task in hand. He finds some unspecified, previously-cooked meat in an unplugged chiller, marries it with withered vegetation that would shame the gulag, covers it with gravy, the consistency and flavour of gearbox oil, and pops it under a salamander just long enough to encourage the campylobacter, but not long enough to allow any trace of warmth to penetrate. He then leaves the lidless foil container on a table, say, beneath the insectocutor, to go to the lavatory, returns with unwashed hands and doles the meal out to the least interested driver with the slowest van to deliver it. The best thing about those meals was the tea I washed the taste of them out of my mouth with: I made that myself.

Food aside, the building itself was pretty soulless and though the staff were decent enough, there was no camaraderie amongst them. When Auriga finally went to the wall—it lasted six years—few lamented its passing. I would not be around for the end.

I had already begun to think that Cam's lunatic asylum of an airline was not for me. It wasn't so much an operation as a daily exercise in crisis management, which in my case had come to a particularly sharp point just two nights previously.

Delays were commonplace, but on this occasion, I had been compelled to flex my duty officer's muscles and get directly involved with delayed passengers. The flight had arrived so late, that the crew were obliged by the duty hour regulations to take rest instead of carrying on to Prestwick, the final destination. This left us with fifty or so travel-weary Glaswegians threatening to sack and burn the concourse if something wasn't done to get them home. There were no other flights but by 0300 hotel accommodation had been found for them. There was however a further problem: our own aircraft would be available to take them home at 0730, but departure could be no later, as it had another full day's programme to complete. The familiar voice of Sandy Hamill the shift supervisor at Spanavia, who handled our flights, spelt it out to me over the phone.

'It's 0300 now, the hotel is twenty-five miles away, and you want me to tell them that they'll have to be back here for an 0730 departure? No. They'll tear us apart.'

I explained that there was nothing else for it. Sandy was of a different mind: 'Oh yes there is,' she said. 'You tell them.'

Fifteen minutes later, I was walking up to the crowd at Spanavia's check-in desk to announce myself. They took one look at my badge and closed around me like I was Sinatra handing out the Zippos—only it looked like they'd be doing it Their Way, not mine. Within seconds, I was surrounded by an angry, bellowing throng. I held my ground, pale and shaken as a sea of angry faces thrust towards me. I was toying with the idea of making a run for it, when the crowd parted to reveal the approach of a big fair-haired bloke, face blistered by the Spanish sun, wearing a loud sports jacket over an open-necked shirt bulging with muscle, and a kilt (the McNasty tartan?) swinging about his hairy legs. He had "self-appointed spokesman" written all over him.

'You're no from Auriga are ye?' (A curious turn of phrase since he meant, the opposite) I said nothing, mainly because he hadn't given me time. 'Right. We're tired and we went a meal and we went et NOW. Yea ken?'

I told him I kenned very well, but when I revealed how far they were going to have to travel to get it, he looked like he was about to draw the sgian dubh from his sock and stick me with it. And I hadn't even mentioned the bit about them having to get back to the airport for an 0730 departure.

'We're going nowhere 'tell we see som'b'dy in authority. I'll see your managing director. You're nae bluidy guid t'us.'

He had about as much chance of seeing Cam as he had of seeing Rob Roy this morning, though I put it more delicately than that. Then, mentally crossing my fingers I threw in the bit about the 0730 departure. The effect was as horrific as it was immediate: a phalanx of screeching women trod down McNasty, launching into some pretty salty Glaswegian.

The redacted version went thus: 'We've wains here wantin' their bed, yea smug bugger. So dae somthin' aboot it afore I come across that coonter to yea.'

'Och, he's nobbut a stupid wee man en a uniforem, Alice. Hey boy, away an' fetch yer boss.'

'Aye, yea bluidy useless sod, getta move on. Ye' went your arses keckin' the lot o' yea.'

I was at a loss. All the diplomacy in the world was not going to prevent them crummocking me if they decided to. It was time to cut my losses and leave. With their shouted threats ringing in my ears, I abandoned the last shreds of my dignity and fled.

0230. The Ops door behind me opened; as there was nobody else in the darkened building but he and I, it had to be CAM. I was pretty fed up with the place, the job, the food, everything; and *India Alpha's* uncertain fate was the toxic icing on a very unpalatable cake.

CAM was his usual direct self: salutation and straight to it, in his broad Gorbals' tones: 'Hello Mike. How're we doing?'

Feeling decidedly peculiar, I launched into a rundown of the disposition of the three aircraft operating that night. It was almost as if someone else were speaking (I just hoped whoever he was he was making sense). *India Alpha,* the elephant in the room, wasn't just there, it was galumphing around the place, trumpeting like Maynard Ferguson soloing on *Birdland.* I noticed that I was sweating.

CAM said: 'And *India Alpha?*'

I felt a tightening in my chest. Just as I opened my mouth to speak, the telex machine, so stubbornly silent all night, rattled into life with a suddenness that made me jump. I turned away to tear off the message, noticing that the lights seemed to have dimmed. They hadn't. I read the message. It was the long-awaited Gan arrival. Why it didn't make me feel any better, I had no idea. Handing the message to CAM, I blundered over to the movements board to put the time up. Returning to stand by the desk, I found I was gripping it for support. When you don't feel that great, you really don't want to see how worriedly somebody else is looking at you. It makes you think you must be in even worse shape than you thought you were. CAM was looking worried, really worried.

My mouth was as dry as blackboard duster, I felt dizzy, sweaty, tight-chested, the works. I should not have been overly surprised if the chorus line of hippos in pink tutus from Disney's Fantasia had pranced *en pointe* through the door and out of the window. It could hardly have been any more surreal than the symptoms I was presently experiencing. And now CAM was gaping at me. I'd had it. I mumbled an apology and stumbled to the door, barely registering his stammered concern as I fled down the stairs and out into the blessed cool of the night.

You don't die of an anxiety attack. You just feel like you are going to. CAM was unexpectedly magnanimous about it and I was given time off. But I was done with Auriga. In fact, I was done with aviation, at least for the time being. There was a park needing its grass cut. I needed fresh air, daylight and nothing more demanding than ensuring the cut was straight. We both benefitted for a summer.

Finals

In Ops, it is spring and in Hangar F, thoughts are lightly turning to redundancy. It is not just the presence of the fat, genial lads with the Dublin accents, the Guinness breath and the unhealthy preoccupation with our office equipment, nor the swarthy men we have seen driving away our MT, but the uncompromising tone of the execution order from Golding. The Third Floor has done its best, in much the same way as Captain Bligh did his best for the crew of the Bounty, only we are not to have the satisfaction of lowering a boat over the side and inviting our captain to climb into it at musket-point. Sledge would have made as good a job of running the outfit as someone I could mention. After all, how much gumption does it take to open the door to the wolf and invite it in for candlelit dinner with granny?

If you really want to know how healthy an airline is, watch what the pilots do. They can spot a career glitch five miles upwind of "maybe." It's uncanny, but they are on the move before any practical sign—no matter how remote—is evident to even the most astute groundling. It must be when they see the small hairs on their first wives beginning to stand on end and they start to call round in person for the maintenance cheques, that the chill wind of unemployment begins to exert its unsettling influence on them. For the only survival instinct sharper than a pilot's, is that of his estranged first wife. And so it is with the company: undoubtedly our final chapter is being written as the spring of 1990 opens and our crews begin to drift steadily away to better opportunities. Even Chan Morgan, who professes to laugh in the face of ambition, has applied to fly joyride bug-smashers in Cornwall, just in case he should end up getting a base check on his P45. Naturally he has no intention of going to Cornwall, but he is in unreasoning high dudgeon to discover that *they* don't want *him,* for exactly the same reason. Meanwhile, the more calculating amongst the pilots have already slid quietly into the few choice jobs available elsewhere, leaving the unwary to go down with the ship, or to apply to the sort of outfits that feature palm leaves on the cabin floor, large terrifying Russian aeroplanes of marginal airworthiness and destinations that look like locations for *Fitzcarraldo*.

In Operations a thick pall of gloom hangs in the air and it's not just Jed's aftershave. But it is oppressive and burdensome to the spirit—so it probably is Jed's aftershave. Despite this, he is his usual gruff and breezy self. I wonder briefly, uncharitably, if this has anything to do with the mysterious recent disappearance of the Ops vans. But it soon transpires that he has worked himself onto a farewell positioning flight to Bournemouth aboard one of the 737s. It is as difficult to figure out just what angle there can be—there has to be one—as it is to guess what excuse he used to wheedle his way on board. But then this is sissy stuff, we are talking about the man who nearly talked his way onto our 737's pre-delivery rejected take-off tests at Roswell, New Mexico back in '89 (as ballast probably.) I believe he actually had the Bisodol and the johnnies packed before Dickie Pullman torpedoed that one below the waterline.

The shift has been handed over to me from the sure, capable hands of Gary Appleby, the night duty officer, who's most surprising and frightening feature is the suddenness of his haircut. Coming upon the unwary, it can be unnerving. However, its owner is affability itself, and as usual his grip on the operation has been sure; it is ticking like a Swiss watch as he signs off duty. Though to be honest, with only *XM* airborne, there is little enough for us to worry about—if you don't count redundancy. Though he's off duty now, Gary is reluctant to go home. I know how he feels. It's a bit like waiting at the bedside of a dying relative—hoping that your name is in the codicils.

In between long periods spent staring moodily at the ops board with its single flight marked up, I cast a fearful eye in the direction of the window, expecting at any moment to see Tony Collins plunge by to the tarmac below. His determination to stop our prized HF aerial, which stands proudly at the apex of hangar F's roof, from falling into the hands of Big Al when finally, we are obliged to hand the building back to them, has a strain of obsessiveness to it that is rather worrying. '*They* aren't going to get it' we've heard him mutter darkly, the perspiration beading on his noble brow. '*They* hate us you know?' he tells anyone who will listen. 'We're only the third airline in the UK to get an HF licence, and they hate us for it. Precedent y'see? (Mostly, we don't.) They could lose business if everybody went in for it.' Tony's paranoia over this is worrying for those of us who care for him.

I move over to the window and pop my head out to squint skywards for the umpteenth time. An elbow appears over the edge of the roof. It is swiftly exchanged for a foot, which is also retracted. Then nothing. I follow the line of Tony's probable descent parabola and note with rising anxiety that the impact point would be in the chief pilot's parking slot. I can just picture Tony and the incomprehensible geometry of the HF aerial, inseparably joined in mutual destruction, scattered gorily across the chief pilot's parking space. This is serious, for Captain Keith Benson Hyphenated Murray does not take kindly to trespassers in his parking space, not even when it's the strawberry-jammed corpse of the senior operations controller, encased in six meters of aluminium tubing. I foresee trouble, once the coroner's wagon leaves. Nobody likes to see those flecks of spittle gather at the sides of KB-M's mouth, let alone be within spraying range when they do. I take another look skyward. Jesus, will you come down Tony before Newton's First Law of Buggeration does it for you?

Tony, whose arrival at Cal Air brought a whiff of professionalism to our advanced bumbling, has consistently tried to get Ops into the top drawer, whilst some of us have clung tenaciously to the bottom sock and knicker drawer, hardly knowing our KOKSY from our ETRAT (flight planning waypoints). Dear Tony has no concept of the impossible, none whatsoever. I once overheard him trying to explain the significance of the saturated adiabatic lapse rate to a rapt Jeep. I believe this was because the latter was labouring under the misapprehension that it was something to do with wet T-shirts. I know I did.

I turn distractedly from the window to see the very same Jeep now learning something about warm fronts as he is crushed to a departing bar girl's bosom. Being crushed against stewardess's bosoms has become a common hazard in Ops in recent weeks (if such a thing can be described as a hazard). Indeed, we have been crushed against many more bosoms than one could possibly have hoped for under normal circumstances. The reason is simple: it's goodbye time and that's how stewardesses say their goodbyes, they crush you to their breasts and "mwah mwah" the air a foot either side of your cheeks. Only, overcome with emotion no doubt, the mwah mwahs have been making contact lately and we are going home not just with lipstick on our collars, but blusher, mascara, lippy, liner, eye shadow, filler, grouting compound, two coats of emulsion and one of gloss. Young Jeff was unfortunate enough to be mwah-mwahed by one of the more overly made-up staff and went home to a major interrogation from his loved one with the girl's physiognomy recognisably imprinted on his shirt like the Turin Shroud.

Phyllis sweeps in from Drab Frocks (Accounts) and—oh, be still my foolish heart—isn't that *another* new cardy, Phil? It is fuchsia and just matches its wearer's complexion this morning. She is not pleased. Who would be with complexion like that?

'Who's had the spare float out without signing for it, Michael?'

Oops, bit thin on the preliminary niceties then. Gary slides out of the door like he's on castors. Nice one. 'Er…'

'Er? What's er?'

'That's me thinking, Phyllis. The more I er the more thinking I'm doing. Remember Alexander Pope's dictum: "To er is human, to forgive, divine." Love the cardigan by the way.' I glance towards the Ops Manager's office. Aston is scratching his stubble, revelling silently in my predicament from behind the glass. Ratbag.

'There is a spare float in the drawer.' I offer helpfully.

Phyllis's expression modulates from barely suppressed annoyance, through contempt, to one of patient forbearance in the face of obdurate stupidity. "There are *two* spare floats, aren't there?"

'Y-e-e-e-s.' I play it thick, like I don't know where this going, because— because I don't know where this is going.

'There is only one there now.'

'What? Float's been nicked, has it?' chirrups Jeep unhelpfully, dabbing absently at a livid streak of lippy on his tie.

'Well, I can't say that, can I?' Returns Phyllis loftily, so obviously wanting to that she might just as well have biroed it on her forehead.

And then Jeff comes up with one of those strokes of genius that proves that my nickname, Stupid Boy, is grossly unfair to him.

'Mike, don't forget you have to see that bloke over at the cargo sheds.'

Brilliant, and more or less true. No need to tell Phyllis that the bloke in question runs Gut Buster's burger van.

'Christ! Sorry Phyllis, have to go. I'll put a man onto the lost float.' (For one blissful moment my words summon up a mental picture of the MD tossing— appropriately enough—on a raft in mid-Atlantic). Call you later.' This over my shoulder as I dash for the door. Now I think I've got it straight; it's a bacon roll for Jed and a jumbo hotdog with extra onions for Jeep. Phyllis's face is a picture. I bet she's having bloody Ryvita with Marmite. No butter.

I arrive back in time to see somebody I've never seen before wheeling a filing cabinet out to a hire van. It looks suspiciously like our safety pilot Bob Campbell's "office" to me. This asset-stripping is getting out of hand, we still have aircraft in the sky—okay *an* aircraft in the sky—and they are dismantling the place round us. At this rate, by the time *X-Ray Mike* gets on chocks, we'll be running the outfit from the back of the Astra—always assuming we can find the Astra. HCA is a wounded antelope and, scenting it, the wolves are gathering to strip the carcass. I just wish they'd wait until we roll over with our hooves in the air before they start noshing. It's a most uncomfortable feeling.

Climbing the stairs, I pass other items of office equipment going south. Marching into Jed's office in an indignant lather, I slap his bacon roll on the desk and vent my spleen. Jed is in lazy conference with Tony. I get lifted eyebrows in query.

'It's an outrage, the bastards are stripping us clean. Thieving sods can't even wait until we close down.'

'What are you snivelling about now, James?'

'Hi Mike.'

'Hi Tony. No luck with the aerial then? Looting, Jed, that's what I'm snivelling about. The place is being scoured. I've just seen a Big Al bloke walking out with a computer…'

'Ah…'

'What do you mean "Ah"?'

'I take it that Upstairs has refused your bid for one of the computers then.'

'That has *nothing* to do with it!'

'Nooo, course not.'

'Some things are above mere trade, Jed.'

'Well, everything is up for grabs. You'd better get your bids in quick. Jeep just put a deposit on the MD's sofa…'

'Yes, I know that, Tony. I expect it will come off with a wet cloth. What I want to know is, when is it all going to stop?'

'At a rough guess I'd say when Trotsky goes home with the nav bags. I reckon that would be about ground zero.' Jed takes a huge bite out of his roll.

'When Big Al get its hands on that HF aerial, more like.'

206

We both shoot Tony a worried glance. Bless him. Christ knows what they are cooking upstairs, (it smells like the books), and even the executive shagpile (how appropriate, if rumours are true) is being "relocated," yet Tony's only trophy is the Ops log. Sweet.

'Well, it's an outrage.'

'Noov med mat...' Jed swallows and tries again: 'Yes, you've said that already. You're getting repetitious. Out cur and get some fookin' tea in here.'

'You're a barbarian, Aston. I only hope that in your next job they let you wear that feldwebel's uniform that Julia says you have in the wardrobe at home.'

'Out cretin! And it's a sturmbannfhürer; Death's Head Legion, Knight's Cross with Oak Leaves and the Eastern Front clasp, you ignorant git.'

'Ooh Jed, really. Ha ha ha.'

'Nah, he means it, Tony. The man's a raging Nazi.'

'Out fool! Isn't there some work you should be bollocksing up? How about one of your Bermuda Triangle flight plans?'

That was a low blow. 'I...I...I shall go and make some tea.'

Okay, it's not one of my best retorts. That was a foul. I am big enough to admit that my flight planning is not quite up to par, but there has never been any major problem with them (except that maybe one or two didn't go to the right place). Admittedly this is largely because I phone up Phoenix for all the difficult ones and got them to do it for me. But hey, doesn't everybody? Ok, maybe not Tony—the only bloke who actually knows where the Sandetty Light Vessel is. But nobody understands his flight plans anyway. Well, maybe Sam Ford does, but then nobody understands Sam.

I recall the course somebody fixed up for us before the 737s were delivered. They found a classroom for us and Turk "Psycho Chicken" Ripslinger from Boeing to take us through "hot and high" ops with the 737 400s. The bright young things (Greg, Sam, Robin, etc) were all up front, note pads at the present arms, brains clanking audibly through their ears, whilst I gave into my narcolepsy behind the water dispenser. At the end of it, the lads came out with a pretty good grasp of the important stuff, and I came out with a Boeing tie-pin, a biro and the revelation that Amanzimtoti is in Natal. (Needed to know that, Turk baby). Strangely enough, when a few years later Greg Porter visited Boeing in Seattle, he was quite unable to trace Psycho. Nobody in the company could recall him. Spooky.

But as I absently stir Jed's tea with the centre tube of a telex roll, these are merely wistful reminiscences on a closing chapter of my life. Coming to work has always been a pain for me—just as it has for my employers if I'm honest—but *leaving* this job is proving, somewhat to my surprise, even more painful.

At that very moment, my reverie is disturbed by Tony who pipes up from the ops room: '*X-Ray Mike* on chocks.' And that's it, HCA has just ceased operations.

A short time later, outside the hanger, I find myself atop a cherry-picker, having hitched a lift with the photographer engaged to immortalise our death throes. We hover over *XM*, crew and staff gathering beneath us for the line-up, and I grab a few snaps for myself. Twirling the focus on my old Olympus, the diffused image in the viewfinder resolves itself into a sea of familiar faces, including Harry Tailor (looking like a cross between a bingo caller and a surgical appliance salesman), Len Borer with one of his interminable letters in his hand (I make a mental note to stay out of range or he'll be wanting to know why the bloody Palma was forty minutes late, last year), the MD's delightful secretary Trish; Gary "Slick" Silver, looking sharper than a rack of Sabatiers as usual; and lots of pretty faces, well-filled uniforms, exquisitely quaffed hair—in fact I never realised we had so many stewards. And there, standing on the right, at the very end of the line, smiling like the President of the Guild of Assassins, stands our leader, celebrating our demise with forty-six teeth. I think about our respective pay-offs—mine probably wouldn't pay for his bridgework. His would probably buy *X-Ray Mike.*

My film runs out just as the cherry-picker lurches, emits a noise reminiscent of a sack-full of tea trays falling down a lift shaft, and starts earthwards. I gaze down. There as some pretty cool people down there, and it suddenly dawns on me that I might miss some of them. On the other hand, given the behaviour of the cherry-picker, it might not be that many. There are also quite a few I won't miss a bit, and just a couple I wouldn't use to rod a lavatory. The sinking feeling isn't entirely the cherry-picker's fault.

A few days later a small band of us stand in the forlorn vacancy of Ops, wondering what the hell to do next. The room is now completely empty but for a single grey telephone standing on the floor, its grubby umbilical snaking away across the carpet tiles. On the wall of the crewing office, a row of vacant hooks marks the spot where the aircrafts' clipboards hung, before even they were removed by the ransacking Paddies. And a pale circle high on the wall betrays the theft of the clock. It's finally over then; it has been a long slow decline, but this is it: finish. We troop out onto the landing and Jed (where did you get those jeans, Buster Keaton's trashcan?), fumbles with the key to lock the doors. I take a last look in over his shoulder and this time I'm absolutely right, unquestionably right—it is all as per the board—wherever the hell the board is.

Valedictory

I've discovered that by moving my chair close to the desk I can hunch over to plant an elbow on it for support. This enables me to rest my head almost face down on the palm of my hand, whilst pretending to write with the other. That way I can catnap without the rest of the office rumbling me. It's a blessed—albeit brief—release from the purgatory that is Haxair's operations room. The drool on the flight plan request form I pretend to be working on is easily dabbed away; the fuzzy ink stains it leaves behind are not. A little enigma to tweak some filing clerk's curiosity.

With a mortgage to pay and the three-month's redundancy from HCA running out faster than my enthusiasm for the whole business of aviation, I needed a job. Big Bro next door might have given me one, but for some reason I chose Haxair. Bad move (I specialise in them.)

The outfit is big, its fleet many times that of HCA's, yet the ops room isn't even on the airport; it's in an office development on the industrial estate. The movements board extends across one entire wall of the room, the aircraft scattered across it like buckshot. Behind me at an elevated desk sits the Duty Operations Manager, to my left is the Operations Duty Officer; I am the equally grandly-titled Assistant Duty Operations Officer and to my right sits the Flight Planning Assistant. There are various other roles present, whose exact duties are not always immediately apparent to me, and they all have smashing job titles. After careful thought, I have come to the conclusion that at HCA the duty officer did most of them, including out-of-hours crewing, with the help of one assistant—though to be fair, that wouldn't work here with this huge operation.

Many of the staff are half my age and twice as clever. The rest are half my age. They are predominately male and the place runs on testosterone and locker-room banter. Example: Nick, the D.O. next to me, has his Cuban-heeled, pointy-toed boots on the desk and his hands clasped behind his head, as he swings restlessly from side to side on his swivel chair, eyeing the board like Wellington planning the defence of Hougoumont. He drums his fingers on the arms of his chair as he hatches a decision. Then he barks what could be an order but, as he defers to the Duty Ops Manager, is in fact a suggestion he'd like permission to implement:

'Charlie Mike's thirty late. Put *Victor Mike* on the Brussels?'

'Do it!' And they do it like it's Blue Section breaking right to engage the enemy. It's really no fun being the Ops womble in the midst of all this testicular enthusiasm. The plain fact is, I'm about as much use here as a carpet-fitter's ladder.

If they have lockers (and if they do, I don't have one) Nick will have a Top Gun poster stuck inside his. Maverick or Iceman, most likely. Not Kelly McGillis, that's just skirt. Maybe the F14 Tomcat. Well, they can have it: the glory, the kudos. I hanker for the little outfit down at other end of the room. It's from here that Haxair's domestic arm runs its fleet of 40-seat commuter aircraft, mainly to UK destinations. There is one duty officer, who does everything from flight watch to nipping out to the aircraft on whatever pretext he chooses. Best of all, he is required to answer to nobody—mostly because nothing ever happens there. Nothing. Ever. Period. I've dubbed it "Carlsberg Complaints" after a popular TV ad which features a dusty, unused office nobody ever visits. But my repeated requests to transfer over to Carlsberg Complaints are denied.

So, it's basically a taxi rank here, with wings, and all I do, despite the fancy title, is obtain ATC departure slots all day. This entails hanging on to the end of a telephone line to a martinet known the Flow Controller, listening to it ringing out endlessly until a hurried voice at the other end gives you rather less than two seconds to respond to its peremptory "Flow," before it's gone again and you are back at the end of the queue. We see neither aircraft nor crew: it's basically just an office; there is no camaraderie, no excitement and worst of all, no joy. To make matters worse, my job entails constant early shifts, the very opposite of the near-permanent nights I managed to wangle at HCA. This place is doing nothing for either my latent depression or my narcolepsy.

Yet, one year on from my joining, this morning's shift is quite different—and rather uplifting. I smell a rat—and, if it's the rodent I think it is, a very welcome one at that. It starts as I turn into the car park in the pre-dawn chill. At this hour it should be deserted, except for the cars of the Ops shift. It's not. It's full of expensive well-waxed motors of the sort favoured by suits: Beemers, Jags, Audis. Something is afoot, I only hope it's what I think it is.

It is.

We're broke. Busted. Bankrupt. Out of business and, to prove it, freshly-shaved men in dark suits are bustling round Ops, delivering Haxair's valedictory orations in the form of peremptory instructions to us to stop doing things. The aircraft markers on the board have been swept to one side, except for those presently airborne. I hope my face is registering the appropriate expression. I hope so, because it's lying through its teeth. Everybody else looks like they've just lost a near relative and discovered, not only that they weren't mentioned in the will, but that said relative didn't even have a funeral plan. I maintain this cosmetically gloomy countenance for a couple of hours more, before we are finally dismissed and I can leg it for the car park with a perfectly cretinous grin on my face.

Haxair has folded owing millions, at least some of which, it is eventually revealed, has gone up the nose of senior management at some memorable parties. At least, I have that in common with them: Haxair got up my nose too, only with nothing like the euphoric result. So, that's it; not only is Haxair in the bin but so, I have decided, is my career in aviation. Either I have outgrown it—after all, it really is a young person's game—or it has outgrown me. It doesn't matter which, but as I leave the building, my mind is already made up: It's time to find another line of work.

A perceptive man once wrote: "Yesterday is a foreign country; they do things differently there." They certainly do. Did. And that, I have finally realised, was just how I liked it.

Epilogue

The canteen was busy but I was back within half an hour, replete, ready to go, looking around for the crew as I breezed into the Ramp. They weren't there. Even as I asked after them, I noticed how uncharacteristically quiet the place had become.

Somebody said: 'You haven't heard?'

I hadn't. They told me. Jimmy, spotting a sudden break in the weather, had called the canteen. But the noise up there had been so great that I hadn't heard the telephone. They had taken off without me and, less than five minutes later, *Hotel Alpha* had ploughed into trees just below the summit of a 600-foot hill south-west of the airport and plunged to the ground, where it exploded and burnt out. They never stood a chance.

A few years ago, I visited the crash site—still quite a remote place—to gaze up the pleasant green hillside to the summit where the trees snagged cloud in their tops, just as they had so lethally on that day over forty years ago. I thought of the two pilots and all the years they had missed. I thought about the largely unremarkable but utterly precious life I had enjoyed since then. And I thanked fate, my still-sharp appetite, and the feebleness of the canteen telephone bell for allowing me to live it.

With me on that visit was a little boy who had come with me to hear the story: my son. And such are the fortunes and the coincidences of life that, without the least encouragement from me, today he is an airline pilot.

Ω